John P. Mackintosh on Scotland

Edited and introduced by *H. M. Drucker*

Longman
London and New York

Longman Group Limited
Longman House
Burnt Mill, Harlow, Essex, UK

*Published in the United States of America
by Longman Inc., New York*

First published 1982

British Library Cataloguing in Publication Data

Mackintosh, John P.
John P. Mackintosh on Scotland.
1. Scotland – Politics and government – 20th century
I. Title II. Drucker, H. M.
320.9411 JN1211

ISBN 0-582-29574-2

Library of Congress Cataloguing in Publication Data

Mackintosh, John Pitcairn, 1929–1978
John P. Mackintosh on Scotland.

Includes index.
1. Scotland – Politics and government – 20th century. 2. Scotland – Economic conditions – 1918–1978. 3. Decentralization in government – Great Britain. 4. Regionalism–Great Britain.
I. Drucker, H. M. (Henry Matthew) II. Title.
JN1213 1982.M32 941.1082 81–13749
ISBN 0-582-29574-2 (pbk.) AACR2

Printed in Great Britain at The Pitman Press, Bath

Contents

Preface

This book is an edited selection of John P. Mackintosh's most important and representative writings on Scotland. A companion volume of his other writings is edited by Professor David Marquand. Professor Bernard Crick has acted as general editor for both these books in his dual capacity as adviser on Politics books to Longman and as literary adviser to Dr Una MacLean in relation to her late husband's publications and papers. I am grateful to them both for having asked me to undertake this task and must make clear that the opinions expressed in the introduction and the selection are entirely my own responsibility.

When Dr MacLean asked me to edit this volume, Bernard Crick assumed that I would find more than enough meat amongst Mackintosh's published works. As there are more than a million words about Scotland to be found in his published works, his assumption was hardly surprising. John Mackintosh was, in the best sense, a publicist. He had a truth to convey and he wanted to convey it to different audiences and to apply it again and again to each new relevant situation. For this reason we both thought my main task would be to find the best presentation of each of his important ideas from already published work.

We were wrong. When I examined Mackintosh's unpublished work I was delighted to discover some powerful and characteristic essays which deserved publication alongside the printed material. When choosing between works I have tried to keep a balance between academic writings, newspaper articles and speeches.

It should be noted that David Marquand's book also contains a full bibliography of John Mackintosh's writings and that his papers have recently been deposited with the National Library of Scotland.

H. M. Drucker

Introduction

John Mackintosh (1929–78) stood in a venerable Scottish tradition of radical intellectual publicists and activists. At the end of his life he was Professor of Politics at the University of Edinburgh, Labour MP for Berwick and East Lothian and a regular columnist for *The Scotsman*.

The subject Mackintosh professed, within the University, in Parliament and in Scotland, was democracy. No respecter of the existing machinery of government, he strove constantly to make it more responsive and responsible to its citizens. If, compared to some Scottish radicals of this century, like MacDiarmid and John Wheatley, he was close to the Establishment, he was always committed to making it more alert to the demands of the people. He saw himself as one of their tribunes against the administrators and the policy makers. If he consorted with the Behemoths of Westminster and the universities, they never swallowed him. Mackintosh knew how to accept and to give hospitality, enjoying it vastly, but could not be bought.

In his battles with the administrators, Mackintosh was armed with formidable weapons. He was clear-sighted, a lucid writer and unremittingly hard working. This did not always make him easy or pleasant to work with. David Steel put this well:

> He would have made an infinitely more imaginative Minister than many of the dull men who succeed in Government. He would have made a superb Vice-Chancellor, but in both the political and academic worlds he was too much the loner, the unorthodox, and openly impatient at other people's slowness and stupidity as he saw it, which scarcely endeared him to less robust colleagues in either field.[1]

But his gifts gave him the power to rip platitudes apart and construct alternatives in a forceful way which none could fail to understand and few could resist. He gave some of the best lectures I ever heard.

Much of John Mackintosh's writing concerned Scotland. He had powerful convictions about the reform of Scottish government. But there was much more to his Scottishness than this: in many ways his style and his approach were a product of the Scottish education system and the Scottish intellectual tradition. Englishmen, Americans and others have approached his subjects, but none have approached them in his way and related them to one another as he did.

One touchingly unfashionable feature of Mackintosh's Scottishness was his flair for lecturing. There was something paradoxical about a man so critical of established institutions and practices, expressing himself so successfully in formal lectures as well as political speeches. For not only did he favour this traditional Scottish form of instruction – itself, let it be said, part of the authoritarian tradition of Scottish teaching – but he often lectured, to his last days, from complete hand-written texts. He was a brilliant extempore speaker and debater, but his lectures were something different.

Every new lecturer is warned against writing out his lectures word for word. Normally this is a sound warning for few of us can make our written work conform satisfactorily to the needs of public speaking. But Mackintosh could. It is not surprising that he wrote his first lectures out word for word. Most of us do that. But he still wrote out some lectures word for word, often on House of Commons stationery, even towards the end of his life. Several of the lectures in this book owe their survival to this habit.

John Mackintosh inherited his energy and zest for life from his mother, Mary Pitcairn, a Londoner. Through her he might well have claimed the right to consider himself English and to follow the many talented Scots who sought careers in 'the big smoke'. This he never did. London friends who knew that his attendances on Parliamentary committees were sometimes, so much did he take on, irregular, were astonished to learn of his absolute regularity and attentiveness in Scotland. Gerald O'Brien, his constituency agent in Berwick and East Lothian, provoked a gasp of surprise at the Memorial Service in the House of Commons when he said: 'In the fifteen years that he was with Berwick and East Lothian, he missed only one General Management Committee meeting, a fault which was entirely mine and was the only time that John lost his temper with me.'[2]

*****

John Pitcairn Mackintosh was born on 24 August 1929, in Simla, where his father was in business.[3] At the outbreak of the Second World War the family sailed for Edinburgh where, in 1940, John went to Melville College. When in 1946 he entered University at the age of 16, his friends recall that he had little of the robust self-confidence so characteristic of his later life. In his first year at university he was taught British History by Professor Richard Pares, a man he came to idolize, and by the time he graduated with a First Class degree in History he had lost much of his earlier self-doubt.

During his first year at university Mackintosh went through a period of religious crisis but it was not long before he was converted to socialism. '. . . when I entered Edinburgh University . . . the post-war Labour government was in its most constructive period . . .'[4] He read R. H. Tawney's *Religion and the Rise of Capitalism* (1926) '. . . and felt that it explained . . . why the early industrial nations had turned to doctrines of self-help, individual initiative and the sort of Protestantism I had known since my childhood.'[5] James Burnham's *The Managerial Revolution* (1942) '. . . argued that the new system of production produced new classes. This seemed eminently sensible to me.'[6] In 1948 he joined the Labour Party and helped found the National Association of Labour Student Organizations in opposition to the Communist Front Student Labour Federation.

Some of his early ideas can be glimpsed in a paper he wrote in May 1951, when he was reading PPE at Oxford.

> The Calvinist tradition whereby the minister was no better than his flock and preached that all might understand, the comparatively good system of primary education and the low fees charged by the four Scottish Universities all combined to produce what the Scots call their sturdy independence and self-assurance and what foreigners might call the self-confident obstinacy of the petit-bourgeois mind. Whatever we call it, the social background which produced such a great identity of sympathy and outlook between the farmers, the artisans and the lower ranks of the clergy and professions was of vital importance in Scottish politics in the 19th century. It was this tradition of one son staying as the ploughman, one becoming a stone-mason, one joining the army and one going to Edinburgh to study theology that gave Scottish radicalism its power and, with the additional attraction of London society for the wealthy, gave Scottish Conservatism its unreality . . .[7]

Mackintosh had benefited by this tradition whatever one calls it. While at Oxford, which he found snobbish, remote and uncongenial, John became a Bevanite. When Bevan resigned from the Government, he sent him a telegram congratulating him on his stand.[8] Mackintosh then read for a Master's degree at Princeton, took his first teaching job as an Assistant Lecturer in Glasgow University and soon moved to Edinburgh to rejoin Pares as a Lecturer. Shortly after returning to Edinburgh in 1953 he spoke to a Conference of Freshers on the topic 'Teaching if nothing better offers' – a lecture published here for the first time which shows both his dedication to teaching and his fluency. He said:

> As a lecturer in history I have always considered that I am a member of the teaching profession. . . . It is interesting and perhaps rather sad that some of the University staff have remonstrated with me for describing myself as a teacher. I remember that in my first visit to the University as a freshman, even before the start of the term, the Director of Studies asked me to fill in a blank on my matriculation form entitled 'intended occupation'. When I said I had no fixed intention, he put down 'teaching if nothing better offers'. [7.1]*

Mackintosh had asked his own history students if they wanted to teach – and for their reason. Of the 18 he asked, 3 wished to teach, 11 did not and 4 would if 'forced into it'. He deplored this state of affairs.

> In my own case, I have always thought that teaching has tremendous attractions. There can be little more satisfying than bringing on a good sixth form – or winning the confidence and exciting the imagination of a junior secondary class.'

'And', Mackintosh added revealingly 'in the holidays one can write, travel, start a Ph.D or stand for Parliament'.

John Mackintosh's comments on teaching and education rarely failed to focus on status: the status of the profession, the elitist pretentions of the graduates of English public schools and Oxford; the petit bourgeois status of Scottish University entrants and the status-consciousness of the teachers and graduates. Of his students, for example, Mackintosh reported:

* Numerals in square brackets refer to the writings included in this book.

Their chief reason for turning elsewhere was a feeling, expressed in different ways, that the profession lacked confidence, lacked pride in itself, was unexciting, contained too many discontented or dull people, produced small-minded men and women who stood on their dignity. . . . [7.1]

And then a remark which gives a clue to the nature of his socialism:

In a year in America I travelled in every sort of conveyance over most of the continent, but whether the person giving me a lift was a dirt-farmer, long-distance lorry driver, oil tycoon or fellow under-graduate, when I said I intended to teach, the response was the same – 'But you look as though you're fit to do a proper job.' Indeed, in any society where status and earnings are as important as in Britain and America . . . teaching is likely to suffer. [7.1]

His feelings did not entirely escape his students of the time, if some of them did not pursue them as rigorously as they might:

I remember a student of mine who came up to visit me while he was at Moray House College of Education and complained that 'they treat you like children'. I asked for some instances and he said 'You know at the Union here, there is no distinction between staff and students – you can sit anywhere in the dining room. On my first day at Moray House, I sat down at a table and was shoo'd away –'Reserved for staff only'. 'Very poor', I agreed, 'And what made it so much worse, I had to sit with some non-graduates.' [7.1]

He saw education as a very important social force. It could provide a 'Jacob's ladder' for a 'lad o' pairts' (such as John Mackintosh himself) into a skilled or learned profession. But more often it was misused – particularly in England – to deepen and strengthen class differences and status:

. . . There lingers on, even among left-wingers, the idea that the University also provides a certain social grace, a critical appreciation of cultural forms, which cannot be obtained elsewhere, or, if obtained elsewhere, is not worth having. . . . This social pattern often produces a type of academic left-wing who thinks there is an intellectual case for Socialism, that it is less wasteful of resources, and would produce a more civilised society – always, of course, organised by the elite to which he himself belongs.

And yet, surely, one of the basic principles of Socialism (unless it is simply about efficiency, about the relative merits of physical and monetary controls over the economy) is that no section of the community is inherently more valuable than any other.[9]

During this period he moved away from the Bevanites. Crosland's *The Future of Socialism* impressed him deeply. He began to take an active interest in politics, being adopted Labour candidate by Edinburgh Pentlands in 1956. He started writing occasionally for *The Scotsman*.

In 1957 Sir David Milne published his authoritative history of the Scottish Office. Mackintosh wrote a review, apparently never published, on what was to become the most important concern of his political and intellectual life, the government of Scotland and the devolution of power. The Scottish Office in 1957 was (as it is still in the 1980s) the main administrative arm of British government in Scotland, solely responsible to the Westminster government. The review contained the germs of his mature critique of this form of 'administrative devolution'.

Will it pacify the average Scotsman to know that his pet project was turned down not by some ignorant Englishman but by a Scots civil servant living in the same street? I doubt it.

The great weakness of our current government is just this:

the public is not informed of the reasons for preferring one policy to another. The matter is settled behind closed doors. It is curious when one reflects on this country's great capacity for facing the facts, for accepting (as often in wartime) hard truths, that there is such tremendous official reluctance to let the electorate hear the debate that goes on before a decision is reached.[10]

The following year the Scottish Council of the Labour Party abandoned the one vague commitment to a principle – devolution – which it had previously held and which offered hope of producing open government for Scotland. He put his first public argument for devolution at the Annual Conference of the Scottish Labour Party in 1958. Only a year after his first criticism of the existing system he had a positive proposal for improvement: a directly elected all-Scottish Council, a County Council for Scotland as devolution was then understood. Often improved and elaborated upon, this is the idea for which he fought for the rest of his life. Few political writers can so quickly have come up with proposals to remedy ills: few Scots were so consistent in their views on this question. The arguments first advanced in 1958 were developed in his evidence to the Royal Commission on Local Government in Scotland (1967), his book *The Devolution of Power* (1968), his evidence to The Royal Commission on the Constitution (1970) and the debates on The Scotland and Wales Bill and finally the Scotland Act. But in following the logic of Mackintosh's mind we skip 20 years of his life.

In 1959 and 1960 the Labour Party was riven by a fight between the Bevanites and the Gaitskellites: 'I found myself agreeing with the Crosland–Gaitskell point of view.'[11] Like many in the Labour Party he experienced the Conservatives' third successive electoral victory – with an increased majority – in 1959 as a shattering blow: 'After . . . the most immoral, cynical government . . . nine months of prosperity had blotted out the record of Suez, of Conservative colonial policy, and of years of domestic inactivity.'[12]

It was not only in national politics that things failed to go Mackintosh's way. Edinburgh University tired of him too.

> Just as the Conservative establishment at Westminster clung to the vestiges of Empire, in the University the older professors clung to their largely despotic powers. I was told, after a speech in the Senate, that the non-professorial staff were present to listen and learn, not speak; and at one meeting of the Faculty the first item on the agenda was a resolution 'to instruct Mr Mackintosh's professor to find sufficient teaching and research to keep his mind off the affairs of the University'.[13]

'In a mood of deep depression I cast around and decided to go to Africa.' For two years, from 1961–63, he was a Senior Lecturer at Ibadan, Nigeria. In 1962 his most substantial contribution to political science, *Cabinet Government*, was published.

Cabinet Government was a turning point in Mackintosh's intellectual development. He had been preparing notes on it for years before its publication. It was his major work of scholarly research – his other books depend more on the polemical force of a logical and remorselessly pursued argument. In his other books (with the exception of *Nigerian Politics and Government*) facts are adduced and anecdotes are advanced more to illustrate points than to prove them. In *Cabinet Government*, he allowed the weight of his material to dictate the shape of the argument. *Cabinet Government* is a fine piece of historical writing which has had an enormous impact on academic political science and on many politicians' views of their world. It set a standard for cross-disciplinary studies of British politics. R. H. S. Crossman, for example, drew heavily on it in his Introduction to Bagehot's *English Constitution*. Mackintosh's theme was that gradually the Cabinet, like the House of Commons before it, had lost the power to check the executive. Now the Prime Minister was more than *primus inter pares*. Democrat as he was, Mackintosh disliked this development. The theme of this book is of a piece with Mackintosh's worries about the 'secret' and undemocratic government of Scotland by the Scottish Office.

Disenchanted by African politics and frustrated by the role of academic observer, Mackintosh returned after two years to take up a Senior Lectureship in the University of Glasgow. At about this time Harold Wilson '. . . for whom I certainly would have voted'[14] was elected Leader of the Labour Party. Mackintosh was adopted as parliamentary candidate by the Labour Party in the apparently safe Conservative seat of Berwick and East Lothian. But safeness became a relative term in the mid-1960s. His old friend from Edinburgh University, David Steel, was little over a year away from pulling off a sensational feat by winning the neighbouring seat – Roxburgh, Selkirk and Peebles – from the Tories. Berwick and East Lothian, however, remained loyal to its true blue traditions in the 1964 General Election, albeit with a greatly reduced majority. So when the University of Strathclyde established a Chair in Politics in 1965 Mackintosh was free and was appointed to fill it.

Not for long. In 1966 he won Berwick and East Lothian for Labour. He was particularly pleased to sit for a seat which partly overlapped the area (Midlothian) once held for the Liberals by one of his boyhood heroes – William Ewart Gladstone. Soon after his election (in May 1966) he gave his Maiden Speech. As is traditional with Maiden Speeches, he spoke about a constituency interest: in his case, agriculture. Mackintosh quickly developed an expert interest in agriculture and agricultural economics, subjects about which he previously had been totally ignorant (he once joked to me that before entering Parliament he hardly knew one end of a sheep from another). As one of the very few Labour MPs who sat for a seat with a large farming vote, he immediately became a Member and Vice Chairman of the newly established Select Committee on Agriculture. In line with his earlier writings he disliked the secrecy by which agricultural policy was decided between the Government and farming pressure groups. Speaking to a seminar of agriculturists in the 1970s he subtly suggested that this system was not necessarily in their interest:

> The leaders (of the NFU) got used to the system, they like its known routine, they like the sensation of living 'on the inside', they learn to respect the officials and want, in their turn, to be regarded as 'sound' and 'responsible'. Thus it is quite possible for a serious gap to arise between the leadership and the members, the sort of gap that recently led to a breakaway movement under Mr Wallace Day and the defeat of the then President of the NFU who was replaced by a more militant figure. It is at least arguable that the privileges of constant consultation and confidentiality can draw the teeth of a pressure group and that it might mount more actual pressure by operating entirely from outside the governmental machine.' [5.1]

None of these doubts and arguments ever dampened Mackintosh's immense pride at holding down a partly agricultural seat for Labour and he often came to use the entrepreneurial success of agriculture as a model for all of British industry.

John Mackintosh also served for seven years on the Select Committee on Procedure, where he was one of the most active members and acquired a reputation as a 'maximalist'. He favoured creating strong Select Committees which could rigorously examine civil servants and Ministers and hold them accountable to the public through Parliament. This change to stronger Select Committees (which R. H. S. Crossman promised to advance) has moved forward fitfully – advancing more under Conservative governments than Labour. When a Scottish Assembly looked a possibility in the late 1970s he hoped that it would set an example in this – and other – respects to Westminster.

Shortly after he entered Westminster, Mackintosh's ideas on devolution were acquiring their final form. In time, while the Royal Commission on the Constitution was deliberating, he published *The Devolution of Power*. He envisaged the creation of devolved assemblies for England. By granting similar powers to each assembly Mackintosh hoped to avoid demands from each for additional powers. The neat quasi-federal framework envisaged in *The Devolution of Power* points again to the logical character of his political thinking. At times this could be over logical. He tended to worry and ponder about basic principles which, when once established, were to be applied systematically, even (very much the style of the man) when they went against partisan advantage. But if *The De-*

volution of Power was over-schematic, he knew quite well, and often said, that clear principles were precisely what the whole debate lacked, especially the Government's thinking.

This approach distinguished John Mackintosh clearly from other figures in the devolution debate. Specifically, it distinguished him from the mass of pro-devolution Scottish Labour Party members who acquired their commitment to devolution only in blind panic at the rise of the SNP. John Mackintosh's beliefs about devolution were formed, as we have seen, when in the late 1950s his party was moving away from devolution and towards centralist solutions to Scotland's problems. Moreover, his convictions were not specifically nationalist. He favoured devolution as a solution to the weakness of democratic accountability in the whole UK – not simply Scotland. Later he came to see that Scotland had an historic case for more devolution than the English regions. But this was because the wide range of Scottish Office powers needed democratic control, not because Scots were any different from anyone else.

Some of John Mackintosh's best writing on the constitution came when he was temporarily out of Parliament – between the two 1974 General Elections. It was then that he wrote the three unpublished lectures: 'Setting up a Scottish Parliament' [3.1]. The difficulties in the path of a Scottish Assembly which he foresaw in these lectures have an even greater permanent value than his later criticisms of the Labour Government's precise recommendations. For the problems he foresaw will confront us again whatever schemes are proposed, whereas the Scotland Act (1978) is dead. One such problem was the cynical obstructionism of civil servants.

> Recently I was invited to lunch by a Minister at the Civil Service Department in London to meet his staff. Before any introductions, I asked a senior official what he did. 'Oh', said he with a grimace, 'I'm on the devolution caper.' 'Do I take it, you would define the word "caper" as an essentially silly and meaningless performance conducted simply for the effect it has on those watching?' 'That sums it up perfectly,' he replied. [3.2]

Another was the attitude of the Scottish Bench. Speaking on the Committee Stage of the Divorce (Scotland) (No. 2) Bill, Mackintosh rose after Nicholas Fairbairn had commented on the major repercussions which the transfer of divorce cases to the Sheriff Courts would have for the Court of Session:

> . . . I am surprised to hear the argument on a Bill dealing with the public and the public's interest in divorce being turned into a question of the security and financial remuneration of a small and select profession. I also find it very interesting and entertaining to hear people saying – and I respect the point of view of the hon. and learned gentlemen – what a specially Scottish institution the Bench and the Bar are and how specially they have kept Scottish traditions going. Yet as soon as one says let us therefore devolve them to Edinburgh – my God, then we are British; we are under the Crown; let us have nothing so limited. We have universal application. This cannot be restricted to Scotland. But there they are – the pride of the damned place. They have kept it going, so far as we can see. Without them there would be no Scottish national feeling, no Scottish National Party. But do not devolve us to that dreadful thing, a Scottish Assembly. It was certainly a jolly joke to listen to all that.[15]

Even more strongly than the Kilbrandon Commission he saw that all Scots had dual-nationality. They were both Scottish and British and the separation of Scotland from England would do their national aspirations as much injustice as the status quo. The point was to create dual parliaments to reflect the dual-nationalism.

Mackintosh felt himself to be a dual-national: British and Scottish. And he could get quite angry at Englishmen who patronised Scots as well as nationalistic Scots who denied their Britishness. In 1974, when the SNP was on the rise and threatening to destroy Labour's base in Scotland, he wrote in the *New Statesman*: 'I recall being told by a former editor of the *New Statesman* that all Welsh were thieves and feeling a little annoyed but then positively angry when he gave it as a serious opinion that there could be no talent in Scotland, for anyone of ability was bound to have left to take a job in London.'[16]

Three years later when SNP Vice-Chairman Stephen Maxwell accused him of thus denying Scots the right to a genuine nationalism, he shot back:

> For Stephen Maxwell this description (dual-nationality) of Scottish history and current experience is, in the first place, some kind of slight on the Scots. It is to deny them 'the status of a genuine nationalism'. Secondly, he seems to think he must find a personal or psychological aberration underlying my motives for reporting in this way. It must be due to a 'sense of isolation' derived from living in London or a lack of cultural values or, in other places, a desire to please English readers, or to be accepted among 'the new self-regarding European elite'.

On these personal points I have only one comment. In my experience, there are two ways in which one can feel Scottish and I think I have experienced both. One (which seems to predominate with Stephen Maxwell) is to feel a resentment against the assumptions of superiority, of absolute standards, so evident in the older English universities, in London media circles, among Whitehall civil servants and so on. The other, when one has been in and through all these groups and their activities, is to be reasonably confident that the best of what is done in Scotland and by Scots is as good as anything that these custodians of proper standards can produce. The latter is, I believe, a happier and healthier stage to be at but it inevitably exposes me to charges of having 'sold out', of having joined the enemy . . . [4.3.2]

In this respect Mackintosh commended Margo MacDonald, then SNP Senior Vice-Chairman and a forceful and dynamic nationalist. Elsewhere he commended the SNP for being led by people like MacDonald and George Reid. This commendation, personally deserved as it was, is particularly interesting because MacDonald and Reid were on the left wing of the SNP. Like many Scots Socialists of his generation, Mackintosh found some difficulty in taking Conservatism seriously. The Tories were absentee landlords who patronised their own people while feigning to represent them. When the SNP could credibly be painted as 'Tartan-Tory' Mackintosh fought it. When it was more 'Tartan-Socialist' – as it was at its most vigorous – he made common cause.

Typically Mackintosh had not wanted the Royal Commission on the Constitution set up – it was 'a stalling device' – but as time went on he came to appreciate that the force it was meant to stall – the SNP – was the one power which could provoke the Westminster parties into granting devolution. He thus allied himself with a party whose aim he distrusted. When the SNP first broke through to electoral success, John Mackintosh argued that their victory was solely due to Labour ineptitude and that in any case the Nationalists' arguments didn't add up. In those pre-North Sea oil days, the SNP argued that a poor Scotland deserved bigger handouts from Westminster. Once, to be sure, on 28 February 1977, after the failure (since the Liberals voted with the Tories) of the Government's attempt to obtain a guillotine on its Scotland and Wales Bill, Mackintosh openly flirted with the National Party. Speaking to a meeting of the Andrew Fletcher Society a week later, he desperately noted:

The terrible problem of the defeat of the Home Rule Bill last Tuesday night was that it cut the ground from under the feet of those like himself who had

> wanted expression for the dual nationality of the Scots. The anti-devolvers, with the adamant insistence that one could only be in a unitary country or opt for total independence, had won the day. In fact, the message from the House of Commons was that if the Scots wanted devolution the only hope of getting it was to vote SNP. . . . The only solution now was for all . . . who favoured devolution to join with the SNP and insist . . . that there must be a federal solution and they must trade their votes at Westminster for some solution of this kind with whichever Government was prepared to cooperate. [4.2]

His frustration with the compromises which would soon make the devolution package an indefensible mess were to grow as the Labour Government pressed on with its plans. John Mackintosh was a product, here as much as anywhere, of the Presbyterian tradition which knew the difference between right and wrong and did not trust compromise between them.

In the middle of 1975, at the height of the devolution enthusiasm, Mackintosh acquired one of his happiest roles, that of a regular political columnist for *The Scotsman*. From November 1975 until his death in August 1978 – with a break only in each summer – he wrote a column which appeared every other Monday. The column was a success from the start. It was often the best thing in *The Scotsman* – then a strongly pro-devolution paper. It led to some of the liveliest correspondences in the paper in the intervening fortnight. Mackintosh varied his pace, sometimes he did a speculative piece, sometimes he wrote of current doings in Westminster; and he varied his subject. Devolution was his favourite subject but he also wrote of party politics, the EEC, Africa, agriculture, abortion, teaching methods, local government and industrial development. The freshness and vitality of the column is evident even when they are read through now at one sitting. This achievement, which more than anything he did, gave him a place in Scottish society, caused him to be universally spoken of as a first Prime Minister of the hoped-for Assembly. Characteristically, he wrote these pieces on Sunday mornings, straight out of his head, taking only an hour and a half, rarely if ever needing to revise. He had the talents and skills of a first-class journalist as well as politician and scholar.

Still, success at *The Scotsman* and his backbench seat at the House of Commons did not consume all his energy. He applied in 1977 for the Chair of Politics at Edinburgh which had been vacated by James Cornford. In October 1977, he took up a half-time appointment and began to turn his mind back to the underlying principles from which he had originally derived his reformist proposals.

In *The Devolution of Power* he had observed:

It is typically British to imagine that it is possible to reform local government – or any institution – without first being clear about its purpose, without first settling the value judgements and marking out the objectives of the reformed institutions. It is assumed that by looking at the particular machinery, by taking evidence about how the present arrangements work, inconsistencies will emerge, obvious changes will suggest themselves and the problem will be solved.[17]

Toward the end of his life, he reproached himself for falling into this trap. The many reforms he had worked for, reform of parliament, and of local government, entry into the Common Market, and most of all devolution, either failed to be realised at all or were so compromised as to defeat their own ends.

In the hitherto unpublished Earl Grey Lecture, delivered at the University of Newcastle in 1977, he observed:

All through the 1960s we in Britain tried to reform our institutions without . . . a philosophy and the results were confused, inadequate or just trivial. For instance, I served for seven years on the Select Committee on Procedure of the House of Commons and we produced report after report but got nowhere because there was no agreement about how the House of Commons as an entity should be able to scrutinise, check or reject the work of the government. The reform of local government has been unfortunate for the same reasons: no-one was clear about the degree of local autonomy that was desirable. How far should local government have a free hand and over what subjects with what degree of financial independence. One could multiply these examples by looking at Civil Service reform, the reorganisation of the health service, or the current debate on devolution.

This is why I think that the adoption of certain devices or reforms – for which there may be powerful arguments – such as direct primaries, fixed term parliaments or proportional representation, will only lead to further frustration if the basic principles are not worked out first. [9.3]

But he was not granted the time to work out these principles. Even before he could take up the Edinburgh Chair, in the summer of 1977, he was struck by a growth on the heart which nearly killed him. But he appeared to recover and bounce back with extraordinary speed. Thus it was that in the last year of his life John Mackintosh poured his apparently limitless energy into his three great roles: professor, MP and columnist. The radical spirit of Calvinist capitalism can have produced few truer sons than this Scottish Socialist.

There had always been two different arguments for devolution: a nationalist argument and a democratic argument. The SNP put the nationalist argument and were willing to back devolution, but not for its own sake, rather as a step toward what they really wanted – independence. No-one was fooled by the Nationalists; they never tried to fool anyone. They were willing to settle for devolution for the time being. But their instrumental advocacy of the government's plans made them dangerous allies. Any proposal backed by them could be tarred as separatist.

This made it particularly important that the other argument, the democratic argument, be heard. John Mackintosh had the best credentials to put the democratic argument. He could have made the need for democratic accountability understood and he alone could have discredited the fatuous disingenuity of those who claimed that a vote against the Scotland Act would lead to the emergence of a better devolution Act later on.

When the moment came, however, to make this democratic argument there were two problems. The Government's devolution proposals were a mishmash of ideas impossible to defend in their own right. John Mackintosh could indeed be accused of carrying his passion for logical solutions to extremes. His proposal to divide England into regions, each with an Assembly, was logical, but hardly sensible given that few Englishmen had wanted it. But for all that, the proposals, if John Mackintosh had had a hand in formulating them, would have been more coherent, comprehensible and popular. The recognition that, like the reforms of the Lords and of the committee system of the House of Commons, the proposal for devolution was an unprincipled mess enraged him.

But his death in July 1978 prevented Mackintosh from having an influence on the closing stages of the debate and the referendum. It is no romantic desire to undo what is done which makes many think the Referendum result on 1 March 1979 might have been different had he lived and dominated the campaign. Few other Scottish Labour leaders believed in it sincerely; most of those who did were tainted with the other failures of the by then thoroughly bedraggled government. In the Labour Movement his voice would have an authority others lacked. Outside it, his great advantage was that almost alone amongst devolutionists no-one could accuse him of being a secret separatist. He had the will, the zeal, the ability and the platform to put the case for a democratically accountable Scottish government, which is condensed and ordered in this book: the case that the anti-devolutionists never answered. It is the case which needs to be put when devolution rises again.

Towards the end John Mackintosh was true to his upbringing. In the Earl Grey Lecture – quoted earlier – he concluded:

> At the moment we have a partial, confused and sometimes unsatisfactory democracy in Britain and as an old believer in the value of rational thought about problems, I only hope I have not made matter's worse. [9.3]

He hadn't.

References

All works are by John Mackintosh unless otherwise specified

1. Steel, D. 'A Personal Reminiscence', originally in *The Scotsman*, 31.7.1978. Quoted here from '*In Memory of John P. Mackintosh 1929–78*' a memorial brochure published by Political Quarterly
2. O'Brien, G. 'Tribute at Memorial Meeting at the House of Commons, 2.8.1978, in *In Memory of John P. Mackintosh*, p. 8.
3. See Appendix for chronology of John P. Mackintosh's life.
4. 'Forty Years On', *The Political Quarterly*, Jan.–March 1970, reprinted in *In Memory of John P. Mackintosh*, p. 41.
5. 'Forty Years On', p. 42.
6. *Ibid.*, p. 42.
7. 'The Chartist Movement in Scotland', unpublished essay, p. 11.
8. 'Forty Years On', p. 44.
9. 'The Scottish Universities', *Universities & Left Review*, Spring 1957, Vol. 1, No. 1, p. 60.
10. 'The Scottish Office – Sir David Milne. Government Behind Closed Doors'. Unpublished review 1957.
11. 'Forty Years On', p. 44.
12. *Ibid.*, p. 46.
13. *Ibid.*, p. 46.
14. *Ibid.*, p. 48.
15. HC *Debates*, 31.iii.76, col. 172.
16. 'The New Appeal of Nationalism', *New Statesman*, 27.9.1974.
17. *The Devolution of Power: Local democracy, regionalism and nationalism*. Penguin Books (in association with Chatto & Windus and Charles Knight), 1968, p. 39.

Part 1

Regional government and the reform of local government

Compared to other Western democracies, the United Kingdom has a highly centralised government. Its focus is in Westminster and Whitehall. In theory it is responsive to the British people as represented by their democratically chosen MPs. In some parts of the United Kingdom there are regional outposts of central government. Scotland has the most elaborate such outpost in the Scottish Office. Yet there is no mechanism, even in theory, by which this outpost can be directly responsive to the wishes of the Scottish people. As an outpost of Whitehall it is responsible to the Westminster parliament. However, Scotland, like the rest of the country, has a system of local authorities, each of which is responsible to its local citizens.

During the late 1950s and throughout the 1960s many people, both inside government and out, began to puzzle over this position. They were worried that central government – already very powerful – was becoming even more powerful. There were no elected regional governments (as there are in most other Western democracies). Local government was ever more effectively undermined by central government.

Few things enraged John Mackintosh more than the failure of planners, policy makers and public officials to think these problems through as a whole. On the contrary, the official line was to draw, to Mackintosh's mind, quite artificial distinctions between local, regional and central governments and to reform each without reference to the others.

1.1 'Local government by region' (*The Scotsman*, 2.11.1963)

Five years after Mackintosh had first called for a single elected all-Scottish council, he returned to put a similar proposal when the Government published a White Paper on local government reform (*The Modernisation of Local Government in Scotland*, Command 2067). As Mackintosh's 1958 proposals on devolution are lost, this 1963 article is his first extant contribution to the debate.

For local government to work satisfactorily it is necessary to have units with a sense of community where some of the citizens will be sufficiently interested to stand for election and to carry out the work of the council, while many will be moved enough to cast their votes. At the same time the units must be sufficiently large to perform the necessary functions efficiently and rich enough to raise adequate sums to pay for these services.

Of the two levels of authorities proposed by the recent White Paper, the lower tier enclaves of about 40,000 people which would combine towns with the adjoining countryside have been most severely criticised. A recent article on this page pointed out that these units would have no sense of community and that there was no justification for depriving the existing burghs of their identity. It made the excellent suggestion that the lower tier should consist of the burghs with the surrounding areas that naturally depended on them and that no particular size limit should be imposed. About 145 of these authorities would cover Scotland.

A second article went on to accept the idea of some 13 enlarged counties as the upper tier, but added that these would be inadequate for planning purposes and proposed three regional planning commissions – for the Highlands, the Midland Belt and the Borders.

Surely these 13 counties fall on both the criteria outlined above for successful local government units. This is proved by the simultaneous admission that they could not perform the vital tasks of planning, overspill, higher education, economic development and reclamation of derelict areas, all of which have to be passed to the planning commissions.

In the matter of arousing interest and a desire to take part in local self-government, there is no evidence that these enlarged counties will be more effective than the existing counties and there will be the problem of longer travelling times for councillors, which may further reduce the numbers willing to take office. On the administrative level the most that can be said for the proposals is that they are a step in the right direction. Thirteen counties would make it possible to do away with the joint committees running fire services and to cut down the number of police forces so that each county could look after its own needs in these respects.

But the Glasgow conurbation which should be treated as a unit would still fall under four authorities (it is under 14 at present) and its overspill and redevelopment would still cross many local authority boundaries.

The great objection to the existing units is that they cannot manage traffic control, river pollution, higher education and many other functions which have either to go by the board or be passed to joint committees or to the officials in St Andrew's House. The last is unsatisfactory, as there is no proper control by an elected body and the result is usually a very timid series of actions. Joint committees are undesirable because they may accept far-reaching schemes without having financial responsibility since they requisition the member authorities for their funds. The whole purpose of a larger local government unit is to stop the drift of functions and powers into St Andrew's House and to do away with joint committees.

The task of a genuine and effective reform is to find an area which will be large enough for this purpose and which has a sense of community, a real public interest in the affairs of the unit as such. The only satisfactory answer is an elective council for the whole of Scotland.

This solution is eminently practical. All the functions of the proposed three planning commissions would fall to the Council for Scotland. It could manage Highland development, drawing on the greater financial resources from the industrial areas and on the interest felt by most Scots in this question. The problems of the central belt could be dealt with as a whole, new towns planned, factories and people moved out of Glasgow with the one authority controlling both the sending and receiving ends.

To fill in the details of the proposal, Scotland would still obtain a two-tier system of local government. The top tier would be a single council elected every three years of perhaps 142 members (two for each Parliamentary constituency). This council would receive a block grant from the Treasury equivalent to the total grants now awarded to Scottish authorities and would raise a uniform rate for Scotland. (More or new sources of local revenue might be provided but this scheme can be carried through quite apart from any review of local authority finances.)

The Council for Scotland would control planning, development, overspill, river purification, main roads, fire and police services and valuation, and would supervise education, health, child care, water and sewage. Below it as second-tier authorities would come the existing four cities and then the local 'natural' units – a town and the surrounding countryside, a group of villages, a single valley or an island.

Second tier authorities of varying sizes are perfectly possible once it is accepted that all authorities need not exercise the same powers. Many local government systems developed from the British pattern overseas have adopted this method of granting only those functions appropriate to the size and wealth of the council in question. The powers would be determined and granted by the Council for Scotland, the cities clearly retaining most of their present functions but care being taken not to overburden the smaller, poorer councils.

This system would also permit a reform of the local government service which could be turned into a unified profession with an established training and common method of entry, grading, salary scales and superannuation. Small authorities could hope to attract able young men who, having proved themselves, would move up the scale to a larger authority or to the staff of the Council for Scotland.

This plan would bring local government here on to the size of unit that has worked best in Canada, the United States and Australia. These countries have federal systems but the powers of the central government have grown so much that the states are now in effect providing the more important local government services while a second tier of cities, townships, or counties look after the immediate neighbourhood.

One great merit of this scheme is that it would draw upon the great interest in Scottish affairs. There is a real concern about our educational system, the Highlands, the need for new industry, preserving the countryside and so on which is not felt for the same questions when split between four cities and 13 enlarged counties.

Nor can it be said that Scotland is an inappropriate area for administration. The existence of St Andrew's House is adequate proof that most services can be (and usually are in fact) organised at this level! The Report of the Royal Commission on London Government has just recommended a Greater London Council covering almost 9 million people in the Metropolitan area with 52 second level authorities beneath it . . .

The case for the regional authority in Scotland is infinitely stronger in that there is a common history and current problems, long-standing Scottish institutions, a genuine sentiment and an already established regional administration.

The Civil Servants who prepared the present White Paper did consider this solution, but their reasons for rejecting it were all political. They argued that the White Paper asks for as much as they are likely to get, but this is surely up to the public to determine. Then they say that a Council for Scotland must rapidly drift towards Scottish Nationalism. There is no evidence for such a view.

Scottish Nationalism has been hopelessly beaten at the polls, and the public are only too well aware that the major questions of economic development, defence, foreign affairs and taxation must be settled on a British basis. In Northern Ireland demands for more independence or full Dominion status have always been flatly rejected.

Under this proposal there would be three elected authorities. The first at the local level would deal with matters concerning the neighbourhood, its streets, amenities, housing and schools. The next, at the Scottish level, would settle broader issues in education, health, main roads, and plan town and country development. National questions would always attract most attention and be debated and decided at Westminster. This is a natural and readily understood division and there is no reason why it should lead to a total change in the political attitudes of Scotsmen and a quite new demand for separation.

The final argument of the officials is that they do not want to be controlled by a council composed of the mediocrities they say they encounter on Scottish local authorities and on the Scottish Grand Committee. It would be hoped that a Council for Scotland would attract the best and ablest members of the community. It would be a triumph rather than a disaster if the major decisions on Scottish affairs were, at long last, taken in the open by an elected authority rather than by innumerable boards, departments and officials unknown to the public.

1.2 'Devolution, regionalism, and the reform of local government: the Scottish case.' (*Public Law*, Sweet and Maxwell Ltd., spring 1964, pp. 19–32)

The following spring Mackintosh set out his position in full, and showed the futility of distinguishing between local, regional and devolved government. Mackintosh cut through the 'guddle' and proposed a single all-Scottish tier of government and a lower tier of small authorities which could reflect local conditions.

It is understandable that politicians who specialise in persuasion should on occasion react to the emotive connotation of words rather than examine their actual content. But political scientists also fall into this habit in some cases. For British students of politics, local government has always been regarded with approval and its decline in recent years has produced general cries of alarm. Professor W. A. Robson has led the way in arguing that local government should be revitalised, reorganised in larger units, and given more powers, more financial freedom and be less supervised from the centre.[1] The criteria by which local government is judged and found praiseworthy are also

[1] See especially his Introduction to the 3rd edition of *The Development of Local Government*.

generally agreed. Local government fosters self-reliance and civic virtue, it reduces the dependence on officials who are the agents of the central government and it allows services to be administered in a way which meets the needs of the locality by men who are known to and can be approached by the citizens.[2] There have been very few suggestions that local government is desirable because different areas could then pursue different policies. Indeed stress is usually placed on the need for uniform standards in such services as housing, education, and child care throughout the country. In Scotland the one marked variation was in the rent policies of some councils and the Secretary of State ultimately used his statutory powers to investigate the conduct of certain of these authorities, later ordering them to modify their approach.

On the other hand, when political scientists turn to the idea of devolution, both their reactions and their criteria usually change. The word conjures up Gladstonian talk of 'home rule all round' with a musty nineteenth century smell. Devolution is usually advocated by uncivilised men from the remoter areas who have little idea of the real problems of government and it is usually enough to mention Northern Ireand to show that the whole notion is absurd. In 1956 an article in *Political Studies* by Mr R. J. Lawrence examined the position in Northern Ireland and concluded that 'enthusiasm for parliamentary devolution is misplaced because it raises hopes that in the nature of things cannot be fulfilled.'[3] The reasons he adduced were that an authority of this kind could not raise any extra or special type of taxation and that no great variations of internal social or economic policy were possible. The normal criteria applied to local government – do the inhabitants like it? do they turn out to vote? are services run in a manner that fit the needs of the area? are the elected representatives and officials easily accessible? – were totally ignored.[4] Indeed the prejudice against devolution is so strong that some writers have insisted on excluding it from the category of local government. G. D. H. Cole considered that it was 'of the essence of local government that its institutions shall be, in the last resort, under local elective control; and, on the other hand, we exclude from it institutions which are primarily

[2] See C. H. Wilson, 'The Foundations of Local Government,' in *Essays in Local Government* edited by himself.

[3] R. J. Lawrence, 'Devolution Reconsidered,' *Political Studies*, February 1956, p. 1.

[4] He passes over as barely worthy of consideration the general acceptance of devolution in Northern Ireland and the defeat in April 1955 at the Northern Ireland Labour Party Conference of a motion calling for a return to direct government from Westminster by 16,800 votes to 1100 votes, *ibid*. p. 16.

legislative or parliamentary in form, even if their jurisdiction is limited to a fairly small area.'[5]

There is no reason for this distinction. The Stormont Parliament has its powers conferred on it by Act of Parliament. These powers are very precisely limited and the question of whether an enactment is *ultra vires* or not has to be kept constantly in mind. Ministries in the Northern Ireland Government carry out functions on behalf of both the local and the Westminster Parliament. It is estimated that the Ministry of Agriculture, for instance, spends five-eighths of its time administering Imperial services on behalf of the Whitehall Ministry of Agriculture; mainly the guaranteed prices and market clauses of the 1947 Agriculture Act.[6] The Northern Ireland situation is essentially a form of local government in that permission to handle certain problems for a given area is granted by the central parliament, but the prejudice against considering it as one possible form of local government continues. When the Scottish Grand Committee was considering the recent White Paper, *The Modernisation of Local Government in Scotland* (Cmnd. 2067, June 1963), Mr William Baxter, MP for East Stirlingshire, tried to advocate a two-tier system, the upper tier being Scotland as a single unit, and was ruled out of order. The Chairman, Dr Horace King, held that a single council for Scotland could not be considered under the heading of local government in Scotland.[7] The most extreme example of this attitude was revealed in the conduct of the *Royal Commission on Scottish Affairs, 1952–54* (Cmd. 9212, July 1954) which was asked 'to review, with reference to the financial, economic, administrative and other considerations involved, the arrangements for exercising the functions of Our Government in relation to Scotland.'[8] The Commission took this to mean that it should consider ministerial responsibility, administrative devolution, financial arrangements, the problems of the Highlands, the structure of local government, indeed every topic except the possibility of an elected local government council for Scotland.[9]

However in the cases alike of England, Scotland and Northern Ireland, contemporary problems and a more realistic approach are break-

[5] G. D. H. Cole, *Local and Regional Government*, p. 21.
[6] F. H. Newark, ed., *Devolution of Government*, p. 55.
[7] *Parliamentary Debates*, Scottish Grand Committee, Third Sitting, Tuesday, July 23, 1963, cols. 144–145.
[8] *Royal Commission on Scottish Affairs, 1952–1954* (sometimes called the Balfour Commission), Cmd. 9212, p. 7.
[9] This was quite deliberate and was explicitly stated by government spokesmen in response to questions in the House. See *Hansard*, July 24, 1952, Vol. 504, col. 770.

ing through these prejudices and distinctions. Recent work on Northern Ireland has taken a more balanced view expecting less and adopting some of the criteria normally applied to local government. Professor F. H. Newark in a recent essay held that devolution must be judged on two grounds: relieving Westminster of some of its congestion and giving local region 'the chance of pursuing policies appropriate to the peculiarities of local conditions.' On this second point, 'the industry, commerce and, in particular, the agriculture of Northern Ireland have received attention such as they never knew in the old days.'[10]

It is well known that Ulster Unionists have deliberately sought to follow Westminister 'step-by-step,' as the policy is called, but even then, after examining education, the social services and health, Professor T. Wilson has concluded that 'a number of important differences have been made on a scale which, in my view, justifies the existence of a separate Parliament.'[11] There have been efforts to persuade the inhabitants of the Six Counties to return to direct rule from London and, on the other hand, to move in the direction of dominion status. Both have failed and it seems clear that the citizens have three levels of interest. These are the immediate local matters settled by the local borough and county councils, questions affecting the agriculture, health, and industrial problems of Northern Ireland for which its citizens look to Stormont, while on broader national questions of defence, foreign affairs and the general direction of social change, attention focuses on Westminster. This division of interest corresponds to the nature of the issue and area which is affected. It is quite stable because no one expects the Stormont Parliament to produce easy solutions or totally new cures for perennial problems but most Ulstermen consider that devolution has definite though limited advantages.

In England the weaknesses of local government, chiefly small and inappropriate areas and inadequate resources, have led to a general review by the Local Government Boundary Commission and by a Royal Commission on Local Government in Greater London. The instructions of the Boundary Commission and the White Paper on *Areas and Status of Local Authorities in England and Wales* (Cmd. 9831) both assumed that the broad existing structure of local government would be retained and the Commissioners declared that 'it is outside our powers to propose a completely new structure (as has been urged upon us by some people) either on a regional basis or by joining town

[10] T. Wilson ed., *Ulster under Home Rule*, p. 51.
[11] *Ibid*. p. 210.

and country in new all-purpose authorities.'[12] As a result such suggestions were put aside, but the facts in certain areas forced the Commissioners in the direction of a regional solution. In the Tyneside Special Review Area they recommended a new continuous county of 916,033 people which would control aerodromes, ambulances, fire, police and traffic, and supervise civil defence, highways, housing, sewage and town and country planning.[13] But a larger North-Eastern area which includes Tyneside had its economic problems examined by Lord Hailsham as he then was. Public reactions to the Tyneside Review showed that some were ready to go beyond the restrictions placed on the Commissioners and consider a local government unit which would cover the entire North-East. Councillor T. D. Smith, the leader of the Labour Group in Newcastle City Council, pointed out that with the North-Eastern Development Council, the North-Eastern Association for the Arts, and regional control of the airport, the Commission's plans were out of date. 'To match this we need a new regional local government unit.'[14] *The Guardian* proposed a two-tier system for South-East Lancashire, the upper unit being a regional authority covering 2.4 million people, and submitted its scheme to the Commissioners.[15] *The Economist* came down in favour of 16 regional authorities as the upper tier for local government in England, Scotland and Wales.[16] The Royal Commission on Local Government in Greater London also had the regional solution deliberately excluded from its terms of reference but its conclusions went as far as possible in this direction. Again the recommendation was in favour of a two-tier system with a single Greater London Council (covering 8.7 million people) in control of education, planning, traffic, main roads, refuse, fire and ambulance services while other powers were to be shared with the lower tier of boroughs.[17]

In Scotland the case for a reform of local government has been even more striking. The present system is both old-fashioned and complex. The four main cities of Edinburgh, Glasgow, Dundee and Aberdeen

[12] Local Government Commission for England, Report No. 1. *Report and Proposals for the West Midlands Special Review Area*, May 1961, p. i.
[13] Local Government Commission for England. Report No. 5. *Report and Proposals for the Tyneside Special Review Area*, July 1963, p. 57.
[14] *The Times*, July 17, 1963.
[15] *The Guardian*, February 20, 1963.
[16] *The Economist*, May 18, 1963. *The Daily Telegraph* has carried articles in favour of a regional authority (by Ivor Gowan, August 7, 1963) but it is not clear whether this is the declared policy of the paper.
[17] *Report of the Royal Commission on Local Government in Greater London, 1957–60*, Cmnd. 1164.

have councils responsible for all local government functions. Then there are 33 counties (two pairs – Perth and Kinross and Moray and Nairn – are united for all administration) which include 20 large burghs, 175 small burghs and 199 district councils. Large burghs are independent of the counties for all functions except education and valuation for rating. The small burghs look after housing, unclassified roads, sanitation, clean air, parks and other amenities and enforce regulations connected with factories, shop hours, cinemas and taxis. District councils are only responsible for public ways and footpaths and a few amenities. Rates are levied by the cities, large and small burghs, and by the counties in the landward areas.[18]

All weaknesses evident in English local government are found in a magnified form in Scotland. In particular the authorities are small and the areas do not fit modern administrative requirements. The counties vary from Peebles with 13,352 inhabitants to Lanark with 577,672, thirteen being below the 30,000 mark. The category of large burghs, with all the major duties of local government except education, includes towns like Arbroath with a population of 19,679, and there are four other large burghs containing under 30,000. Counties and burghs of this size cannot employ a properly trained staff for such functions as town and country planning. Child care is now a specialised service requiring trained personnel but such persons naturally prefer to join authorities with a proper department and promotion ladder rather than become the one overworked employee which is all these councils can afford. Of the 175 small burghs 56 have under 2000 inhabitants and yet each of these constitutes a housing authority several of which have an annual programme of one house, while many are in the 5–10 house bracket.[19]

As might be expected many functions have had to be removed from these councils or handed to joint committees and *ad hoc* boards. Police forces are controlled by 32 councils or joint committees while Scotland has been divided into eleven areas for fire services. An Act of 1951 created nine River Purification Boards on which local authorities are represented. There have been various combinations to set up remand homes and operate the probation service while from 1956 several counties have worked together in the task of valuation. These joint boards are never very satisfactory in that their responsibility is not

[18] The only recent account of the system is *Local Government in Scotland* published by HMSO in 1958.
[19] These figures are all taken from *Rates and Rateable Values in Scotland, 1962–63, Population and Area, 1962*. HMSO Edinburgh 1963.

clear. They are often persuaded to adopt impressive schemes (which may be highly desirable) but without any consideration as to cost since the task of raising the money falls to the individual councils.

Even with these amalgamations some of the most important local problems cannot be accommodated. The Clyde Valley conurbation, which has some of the most acute urban and industrial difficulties in Western Europe, comes under fourteen planning authorities. The management of Glasgow's overspill programme is made much harder by the poverty of the small burghs which would benefit most by the influx of workers and factories. Depopulation, unemployment and all the problems of poor soil and long distances affect the whole of the Western Highlands. In the seven Crofters' Counties, as they are often termed, assistance and development are required on a scale far beyond the county councils' capacities and they have had to be supplemented by the Advisory Panel on the Highlands and Islands, the Red Deer Commission, Advisory Committees on Health and on Technical Education, Agricultural Executive Committees, the Crofters' Commission, and the Highland Transport Board.

Despite a considerable interest in the broader questions of Scottish development, local councils have suffered from public apathy. At city and burgh elections in the last three years only some 500 out of 900 seats were contested and the average poll in the contested seats was around 44 per cent, Glasgow falling as low as 28 per cent. The standard of councillors is poor, most of the work being done by ten or a dozen members. Even in a major city like Edinburgh which has prestige and carries an automatic knighthood for the Lord Provost none of the upper ranks of business or the professions and few of the major industrial trade unions are represented. Membership tends to be confined to builders, contractors, lawyers whose companies are closely involved in property matters, the unions concerned with shops, municipal or transport workers, and a sprinkling of housewives.[20] There are regular complaints about the activity or inactivity of local councils but few citizens are willing to do the work, stand for office, or even vote at election times.

Yet none of these weaknesses has produced a public reaction or a demand for reform. The pressure for a change has come from the senior civil servants in the Scottish Office often referred to collectively as 'St Andrew's House.' Most of the officials in the larger town and

[20] An analysis of the occupations and connections of the city councillors in 1961 is contained in my 'Politics in Edinburgh', contributed to the *Third Statistical Account of Scotland* volume on Edinburgh due to be published in 1964.

county councils have also become convinced that action is now essential. The question has been brought to a head and ministers induced to open up public discussion by one specific aspect of the problem. Scotland's persistent tendency to double the English level of unemployment has been a constant source of weakness to the government and three seats were won by Labour on this issue in the 1959 general election. When the Toothill Committee investigated the Scottish economy, they emphasised the value of proper services in attracting industrialists and the importance of the Glasgow overspill programme.[21] Both these fell largely to the local authorities and proved their inadequacy. Two cases arose to emphasise the point. The British Motor Corporation built a factory near Bathgate and needed houses for its workers, water, sewage facilities and road links. Most of the planning was carried out by the Scottish Office but some tasks, chiefly housing, had to be shared by West Lothian County Council, Bathgate and Whitburn Burgh Councils. They did not all show the same enthusiasm and the Scottish Office had to set up an unofficial co-ordinating committee to start the processes. More recently Rootes offered to set up a factory at Linwood in Lanarkshire and the Burgh of Johnstone was willing to build the necessary houses. The County Council feared that this might ultimately give Johnstone grounds for claiming the status of a large burgh and used its planning powers to suggest an alternative (and less convenient) site for the houses in the county. The result was considerable delay both in building the houses and in bringing the factory into production.

This evidence finally turned the scales and the Secretary of State for Scotland, Mr Noble, agreed to let the new Development Department (set up on the recommendation of the Toothill Committee)[22] frame some proposals for a reform of local government. The result was a White Paper entitled *The Modernisation of Local Government in Scotland* (Cmnd. 2067, June 1963). After a review of the situation and its difficulties, the White Paper proposed to leave the four counties of cities as they are. The 33 counties would be more manageable if they were amalgamated into larger units. The precise number and boundaries were not set out but 'reliable sources' indicated that the Department had some eleven units in mind. These would then constitute the top tier of a general two-tier system. The lower level would consist of

[21] *Report on the Scottish Economy* by a Committee of Inquiry under the Chairmanship of J. N. Toothill, CBE, published by the Scottish Council (Development and Industry) pp. 195–196.
[22] *Ibid*. p. 178.

new units combining towns with the surrounding countryside and running at an average of about 40,000 people. Most of the major services would fall to the enlarged counties – education, child care, fire services, police, health and welfare, planning, roads, valuation, water and sewage. The new borough and rural councils would have local amenities and many regulations to enforce but their chief task would be housing.

These proposals have had a mixed reception. The officials of the counties and large burghs are reported to be in favour of them provided there are proper safeguards for existing staff, but reactions among the general public and from the more vocal elected councillors have been hostile. Most of the public criticism as revealed by the press and at meetings of such bodies as the Saltire Society assumed that the proposals are an attack on local government and evidence of a desire for more control on the part of officials.[23]

Labour Party spokesmen in the Scottish Grand Committee considered that the White Paper was out of date but made no counter-suggestions except that the first priority should be local government finance.[24]

Despite these criticisms, the White Paper was a definite step forward and the officials and ministers are to be congratulated for resisting any temptation to hide behind a Royal Commission or independent inquiry. There is no reason for this method of procedure given a definite desire for action. The local authority associations in Scotland are not high-powered bodies with many positive ideas to contribute. The Counties of Cities Association does not have an independent existence and any request for its opinion simply means that the four cities are circularised by the Edinburgh Town Clerk. The Convention of Royal Burghs has an Edinburgh lawyer as part-time secretary and he likewise usually consults a few of the town clerks who are particularly interested in the broader issues. The Association of County Councils in Scotland is more effective but again its views are those of half a dozen county clerks all of whom are well known to the officials in St Andrew's House. The latter have all the facts and have heard the few constructive points that can be made over and over again and were right that what was needed was a positive proposal. The critics among the general public have, however, fastened on two valid objec-

[23] Comments were reported in *The Glasgow Herald* for July 30, August 8, September 6, 9, 10, 11, 13, 1963 and in *The Scotsman* for September 6, 9 and 16, 1963 and in *The Evening Times* for September 11, 1963.
[24] *Parliamentary Debates*, Scottish Grand Committee, Third Sitting, Tuesday, July 23, 1963, cols. 110–118 and 147–152.

tions. The first is concerned with the choice of areas. On what basis were the eleven amalgamated counties constructed and is there any evidence that they will be more satisfactory units than the existing counties? The new counties will have an average population of 300,264 or 346,426 if the four counties of cities are included. The average rateable value will be £5,362,803. (There is no point in including the four cities which have much higher rateable values at an average of £10,278,889.) This is quite a reasonable size and it would allow two services to be restored directly to the counties, namely fire and police. There are at present eleven fire areas which could easily be adapted to fit the new structure. The Royal Commission on the Police recommended a reduction in the 32 independent forces which could well come down to 15 forces, one for each city or county.[25] Only River Purification would still require representatives to sit on boards covering rather different areas. But there remain unsolved problems. The Highlands would still be divided between several relatively impoverished counties and the various *ad hoc* boards and commissions could not be absorbed. Worse still, these new units would leave the Clyde Valley conurbation split between at least three authorities. It is hard to escape the conclusion that the planners plumped for these units not because of their intrinsic merit but because it seemed the most that they would be likely to get at this juncture.

But there is one further point to be made to explain these proposals. Suppose there was a strong Secretary of State ready to fight for a complete and far-reaching reform who simply asked for the ideal units, what areas would be chosen? Several writers have suggested that Scotland would be better organised on a basis of five or six regions.[26] They can point to the fact that there are five regional hospital boards. The civil servants concerned almost certainly considered this possibility but rejected it. The reasons are that a viable region has to have considerable population and wealth and Scotland cannot be divided in this way as all the towns and industry are concentrated in the narrow central belt. The major problems of this central belt – planning, overspill, clean air, traffic, and redevelopment – should come under one authority but to accept this would leave the West Highlands, Borders, and North-East as the other regions, all predominantly agricultural

[25] *Royal Commission on the Police*, Cmnd. 1728, pp. 84–86.

[26] A Conservative Political Centre pamphlet called '*Change and Challenge: Next Steps in Town and Country Planning*' suggested (in 1962) six regional planning authorities for Scotland. *The Economist* for May 18, 1963 carried an article entitled 'Federal Britain's New Frontiers' which outlined four regions for Scotland but observed that two of them, Solway and Caledonia (the North), would be very thinly populated.

and relatively poor. The fact that there is no easy division into a few large regions each composed of urban as well as agricultural areas is likely to have been a strong reason for adhering to the more modest proposal of eleven enlarged counties.

A second point made by the critics is that these counties will be largely artificial creations without any sense of community. It will be harder to excite interest among the voters and the numbers willing to stand for election will be reduced even further by the greater travelling time that will be required. This objection has a great deal of force.

Is there any other solution? There is one rather obvious course of action which would achieve all the objectives of the White Paper and to a large extent avoid its weaknesses. The notion of a uniform two-tier system is admirable but there is no reason why the upper tier should not be a single regional council for the whole of Scotland. This would have many advantages. As an area for administration, it combines an industrial belt with poorer agricultural land. Police, fire, river pollution, overspill, aspects of economic development, trunk roads and higher education, could all be handled by such an authority. The existence of St Andrew's House, a civil service department running a whole series of functions for Scotland as a unit, shows how suitable the unit is from an administrative point of view. Also such a council could take over the duties of the consumers' councils in the nationalised industries and appoint the popular representatives on the hospital boards. Many supervisory functions which have been assumed by the civil service would not be necessary once there was a local authority of this size. Highland development could be rationalised under a single department and subjected to control by elected representatives for the first time.

As regards popular interest and participation, this is by far the most likely to awaken a response. Scottish Nationalism has never had any widespread support but there is a great deal of concern about Scottish problems. The quasi-nationhood of the Scots has been preserved by a separate Church and legal system and by different methods and traditions in education and local government. There are bonds of sentiment uniting city dwellers with the Highlands from which many of them came and where they often return for their holidays. Much of the rather querulous criticism of Whitehall and bureaucracy springs from a feeling that while parish pump matters are left to local decision many important issues affecting Scottish interests are never openly discussed and people do not know how or where they are settled.

The Royal Commission on Scottish Affairs lamented that critics in Scotland did not know how many of these decisions were taken by officials in Edinburgh rather than in London.[27] But this misses the point, for the geographical location can be of no significance if matters are settled *in camera*. What is wanted is that the questions should be settled in public after an open debate by elected representatives in Scotland.

For the second tier of more specifically local authorities, the White Paper sets up enclaves of some 40,000 people combining burghs with the neighbouring rural areas. But such an artificial device is only necessary if it is assumed that the same powers have to be given to each unit. It would be better to preserve genuine local connections and the traditions of burghs or rural districts as they stand by creating as second-tier authorities whatever is the natural local community. These could vary from cities like Edinburgh to self-contained fishing villages or a single valley including a town. Each unit could be given the powers (by the Scottish council) appropriate to its needs and resources. Such a reform could be combined with a review of local government finance and the creation of a unified local government service or it could stand quite well on its own.

A solution of this kind has been considered by the senior civil servants in St Andrew's House and rejected for a number of reasons. The first goes back to a fixed notion of what comes under the heading of 'local government reform' and what does not, and is therefore by definition excluded. It is argued that the former must mean a reshuffling of existing local government areas and the reallocation of functions currently thought suitable for local authorities. To suggest an area that would be large enough to undertake some of the tasks at present allocated to St Andrew's House would be to trespass on the functions of the central government and would raise totally different questions that should not be considered at this stage and under this heading.

Such an objection is, however, just a matter of fixed patterns of thought. Though some functions, such as street lighting and refuse collection, are clearly local while foreign and defence policies are always national, there is a considerable overlap between duties that are sometimes suitable for local authorities and sometimes for the central administration. There are tasks (such as the maintenance of certain classes of roads) that have been taken away from local authorities because they are too complex or too costly but which would have remained had the local units been larger. Also many services are administered locally but supervised by the central departments. The close watch kept by St Andrew's House (or the equivalent English Minis-

[27] *Royal Commission on Scottish Affairs, 1952–54*, Cmd. 9212, p. 15.

try) over many aspects of education, housing and health is usually deplored. It seems strange to argue that units which would not require such supervision would be trespassing on what were essentially functions of the central government. But if the delegation of extra powers causes any difficulty, the case for a single upper tier council for the whole of Scotland can rest on the greater ability of such an authority to discharge what are, or have been till recently, purely local authority functions.

A second and powerful objection is that Scotland has had the unique advantage of a Minister in the Cabinet to argue the case for extra or special consideration from the Treasury.[28] Civil servants are fond of pointing out that subsidies for slum clearance are larger in Scotland than in England. A strong local government unit on a regional basis would mean far less for the Secretary of State to do and the office might not retain Cabinet rank if its main task was to lobby for an increase in the annual block grant for Scotland.

On the other hand, the growing alarm about industrial and social malaise in certain regions of England has led to the designation of Mr Heath as Minister of Trade and Industry and Regional Development (as well as President of the Board of Trade) and it is not evident that he is going to be less successful in demanding aid for the North-East or for parts of Lancashire than the Secretary of State is in pressing Scotland's case. The latter's capacity to win extra subsidies for certain services may not have been due to his special position but because there is more slum housing, more sickness and a higher death rate in Scotland than anywhere else in the UK. While these circumstances may have allowed Secretaries of State to press for additional assistance in tackling certain problems, it is also possible that policies which might have been desirable in Scotland were prevented by the rest of the Cabinet for fear that these solutions would create awkward precedents for the English Ministries. From the point of view of the country as a whole, a Minister whose task is to administer and lobby for a single region is an anomaly and it would be fairer to include Scotland with the other regions when the distribution of moneys is being considered. There is a more general and sentimental argument that the loss of the Secretary of State would mean the end of Scotland's voice in the Cabinet. This would imply that there is a special Scottish view on defence, foreign and economic questions, a suggestion which has never been substantiated and which overlooks the fact that this kind of representation is the task of the Scottish MPs.

[28] *Ibid*. The Commissioners press this point repeatedly throughout their Report.

The further objections are largely personal and political. The civil servants in St Andrew's House are for ever lamenting the very low standard of representative they say they encounter on even the larger local authorities and in Parliament. Pointing to the poverty and tedium of the debates in the Scottish Grand Committee, they clearly shrink from any notion of control by a similar body in Edinburgh and ask whether a different set of elections is likely to produce anything better. It is certainly true that the standard of members in Stormont is very poor. But there would probably be considerable enthusiasm at least at first for an all-Scotland elective authority, and those selected would not have to give up their professions or business – a factor which discourages many from standing for Parliament. How far the standard could be kept up would probably depend on the opportunities for decision and action open to the council.

A deeper worry comes out in the allegation that such an authority would be essentially unstable as a council for Scotland would rapidly move towards the nationalist standpoint demanding more and more power and ultimately total separation. A small but symptomatic part of this fear is the accusation that such a body would probably be conducted on parliamentary lines rather than in the fashion of a county council. To take this last point first, it reveals a further fixed mental assumption that only one form of procedure is proper for a local council. Yet apart from any question of areas and powers, one of the great handicaps of the existing local authorities is the prevalence of the committee system. This means that every trivial routine point has to go before the relevant committee and a conscientious town councillor in Edinburgh or Glasgow has to spend more time at his duties than many Members of Parliament. This procedure frustrates the officials who cannot get on with their work, obscures in a mass of detail the few issues of principle which should be settled by the councillors, and discourages busy men from standing for councils. A ministerial system whereby the major issues were debated in the council chamber leaving the 'ministers' in charge of the various departments to apply the agreed policies would help to revive local authorities.

If a regional authority adopted this form of procedure, it would probably be most suitable but would not necessarily be a challenge to Westminster. Scotland's 71 constituencies could each be halved producing an elected council of 142 members which might meet for some two months of each year. A month in April for the estimates followed by a fortnight in the late summer and a fortnight around New Year would permit thorough discussion of all the main issues. Adequately paid, such a body might well attract some of the ablest men in business, the professions, trade unions and from the country areas who could thrash out the problems, present local and sectional points of view and then leave the task of administration to selected members or 'ministers' and the civil service.

The idea that such a body would inevitably demand more and more powers till it adopted an entirely separatist position is curious as there is no evidence to support it. Scottish nationalism has been steadily advocated by a small party and as consistently defeated at the polls. In Northern Ireland demands for a greater degree of independence and even dominion status have been rejected by overwhelming majorities. The individuals elected to such a council would, like the vast majority of Scotsmen, appreciate that the general pattern of financial, social and economic policy must be settled for the whole country in London. But there are matters of application, particular issues and interests which are best determined at the regional or Scottish level while purely local matters are left to town, village or area councils. This is a natural and comprehensible division of responsibility and no reasons have been adduced to show why the existence of an elective council at the regional level should suddenly lead to a total change in the long-established political views of a majority of Scotsmen.

If this scheme were adopted there would be difficulties and certain losses but the reward would be an elected body clearly responsible for each of the three major levels of decision instead of a complex and declining local government system and a regional administration operating largely on its own. The normal criteria used in choosing local government areas, that is a unit which can perform the necessary services, where there is a common interest, tradition, and sense of community, all point to a Scottish regional authority. It would be ironical if the pressure for a regional unit is more readily conceded in the case of the North-East of England just because that area has less obvious unity, no existing regional institutions or administration, and far less common sentiment than Scotland.

1.3 Debate on the Local Government (Scotland) Bill, 1973

(Hansard, *H C Debates*, 19 June 1973, cols. 599–602)

Nine years later a Bill to reform local government was nearing the end of its parliamentary process. In June 1973 John Mackintosh was the MP for Berwick and East Lothian. He was in a better position than most to view the long road to reform as a whole and he was in a better position than most to deplore the hotch-potch the government had made. His speech on the Third Reading of the Local Government (Scotland) Bill reflects his frustrations. The words he used would be heard in the mouths of others, many times over, later on.

I am sure that we all pay tribute to the work done by the hon. Member for Inverness (Mr Russell Johnston) in his three hard years on the Wheatley Commission.

Viewing the situation now, I feel closer to the position than my hon. Friend the Member for Midlothian (Mr Eadie). I remember when this long, weary trek for the reform of local government started with the White Paper produced by the Conservative Government and the right hon. Member for Argyll (Mr Noble), who was in the Chamber a moment ago. It started 10 years ago. Then the Wheatley Commission began work.

I was honoured to be the first to give evidence before that commission. I remember the excitement that I felt when I gave evidence and realised that here was a commission which was dedicated to the idea of a major constructive reform of local government which was to combine greater efficiency in handling services with greater democracy – a new system of local government for Scotland which would have a degree of independence from central Government, a degree of initiative and of power to do things for the people in its area. It was exciting.

When the Wheatley Commission reported I could not help feeling what a better system it advocated for Scotland than Maud advocated for England: a two-tier system adapted to Scottish needs. Admittedly, Scotland is a difficult country to fit into a single pattern, but the pattern evolved was the best that could be produced for Scotland, based, as it was, on the regional concept of government with difficulties in rural areas.

I admired what the Wheatley Commission did. I hoped that, as a result of the Bill that we would put through the House under one Government or another subsequently, we would get this great step forward in local democracy and efficiency that I wanted.

Looking at the Bill that we are passing through this House for Third Reading, my feeling of disappointment is almost overwhelming. What we have now is a bodge, a mess up – something that I fear will get rid of the good features of the present system without rising to the levels and the achievements that Wheatley hoped we would get with the new system. I am very frightened that we shall have produced something in the end which will be worse on the major criteria than the old system which we are now abolishing.

I should like briefly to point to the major things which worry me. First, the regional system, which had a certain logic and coherence, has been destroyed due to political weakness and wetness on the part of the Government, who have allowed the regional concept to be broken in the east of Scotland by the retention of one county, Fife, as a region, thus spoiling the regions that Wheatley set out to the north and to the south. Unfortunately, the island authorities, which were entitled to a greater measure of self-control, should not have been taken out of the strategic planning area of the Highlands. These were weaknesses, and they have broken, basically, the Wheatley structure as it was set out.

Secondly, a major problem, and one much more serious, is that the relationship between central Government and local government shows no fundamental sign of changing. Although there is a schedule of relaxations, the whole approach of the central Government at St Andrew's House has not taken that leap of greater confidence in local government which Wheatley said was absolutely essential to the system working. There is every sign that there will be the same degree of centralised control. As my hon. Friend the Member for Midlothian said, instead of having to control a large number of authorities, there are now nine regions that can be got together in one room in St Andrew's House to have their heads knocked together regularly.

This is not only a matter of central Government controls. There is no real system of finance, which Wheatley said was essential to setting up the independence of these new authorities. There is no clear reduction in central Government control. Not only that, but in terms of functions, some functions have actually been taken away from authorities. The health functions that local authorities used to have have been taken away and given to area health boards. The Government's lack of confidence in the new local authority system is so great that, although the new area health boards are identical in area to the regions, they are not being given to the democratic control of the regions to administer because the central Government do not trust these bodies with the amount of money involved.

In effect, it is clear from the start that this system is starting without confidence in this new relationship. Part of the evidence of this we see throughout the Bill. One piece of evidence is that the Government have not removed the disqualifications of important sections of the community which would want to serve. We had a second piece of evidence yesterday when we asked for salaries, which Wheatley said were essential for councillors at both levels. The right hon. Member for Argyll told his own Front Bench that this system would not work unless they had the proper new form of councillor paid an adequate salary for an adequate job. What were we told by the Conservative Front Bench, as a great joke? They said 'We cannot tell you the attendance allowances; but do not blame us because if they did get salaries we could not tell you about them either.' That was a bit of a laugh.

The Government have shown no confidence in the new system that they are erecting. In neither the structure nor the functions, nor the kind of people, is it showing any great change of the kind that the whole Wheatley concept set up. What are we doing? We are sweeping away the liveliest section of Scottish local government today, the small burgh system, and setting up new large regions which have no intrinsic existing loyalty or enthusiasm.

We wanted to get that by conferring a much wider degree of power on local government and by trying to get new groups in the community to take part in local government. There is no evidence that this is happening. There is no evidence that the people coming forward are anything but the people in the existing pattern of local government with the existing attitudes and ideas. They are coming forward into a system with the same degree of central Government control and domination. All the hope that we put into the Wheatley system seems, I fear – I say this with regret – to be already disappearing.

As I look ahead I have only one overwhelming feeling, and that is of sorrow that this great opportunity that we had of recasting a greater, more democratic system of local government for the rest of the century has been seriously lost due just to a lack of imagination, confidence and courage on the part of the Government. I for one feel a great sense of disappointment at what has happened in this House.

1.4 'What's to be done about local government?'
(*The Scotsman*, 1.9.1975)

When the newly legislated system was only six months old, Mackintosh used his *Scotsman* column to point the lessons for devolution of local government failure.

Whatever the future of the new local government structure, it is a great pity it has got off to such a bad start. The reasons for the public's present disenchantment are reasonably clear but they are not altogether fair. The new councils, especially the regions, seem remote and something was lost when the small burghs ceased to exist as local government units.

Then there is the massive increase in rates with virtually no improvement in the services being provided. Finally there are specific issues which have tended to discredit the system; examples of cheap house loans, car loans, high salary increases and other perks and conflicts over Press access to meetings.

It is important to try to assess what has gone wrong and to think about improvements. This winter, the Government has to produce its Bill for a Scottish Assembly and though the Assembly will legislate in its allocated area of competence, it will also execute these policies or laws and, in this sense, it will be a form of local government. So it is essential that any mistakes that have been made in setting up the new system of local government are not repeated over the Assembly and the relationship between the Assembly and the present pattern of local government will have to be carefully thought out.

What then has gone wrong? The reform of the old system of local government was undertaken with high hopes and great care. Nothing could have been more thorough than the work of the Wheatley Commission.

It is only fair to record that what emerged in the Local Government Scotland Act was profoundly different from the recommendations of the commission. Perhaps the commission was too optimistic but it hoped to recast not just the boundaries and redistribute the functions of local government but to alter the atmosphere and context in which the councils would operate.

It is not often appreciated that the commission emphasised that if all that happened in the reform was the creation of fewer, larger councils with the same personnel, the same restrictions and controls from the centre and the same sources of revenue, the whole operation would be a failure.

Yet this is precisely what has happened and a large part of the blame lies with Parliament and with the then Conservative Government, the then Labour Opposition and with the civil servants advising the Government. The Wheatley Commission had stressed that a new form of taxation was necessary other than rates, that the new councils should be given far more freedom from central government control and that councillors should be paid a proper salary. The idea was to give genuine policy-making scope to the authorities and then to attract candidates from far wider sections of the community.

As the Bill went through Parliament, it became clear that for many MPs on both sides of the House, local government's task was to execute policies decided on in Westminster; not to make policies of its own. As far as the civil servants were concerned, they also feared that the new councils would not be able to operate without guidance and control from St Andrew's House. As a result, as the Bill went through the House, one by one the Wheatley ideas of transforming the atmosphere and style of local government were discarded.

No new forms of revenue which would be less regressive and less burdensome than rates were devised. No salaries were to be paid to councillors. No basic changes were made in the dependence on central government. No wider powers – particularly control over health boards – were restored to the councils.

Slowly it became clear that what Wheatley had feared most would happen. The old councils with their centuries of tradition and their customs and loyalties would be abolished but all the existing practices of local government with the same councillors, the same officials and the same approach would be transferred to fewer, larger, less accessible councils. As someone who had been an enthusiastic supporter of the original concepts underlying local government reform, I personally felt so unhappy about what finally emerged that I seriously contemplated voting against the Third Reading of the Bill.

This then was the extent of the change. There were to be fewer, larger councils but everything else was to stay the same. And one of the features that has contributed to the public's sense of dismay has been that practices that went on unobserved in some of the old councils (such as car or house loan schemes) have come out into the open with the transfer to the new authorities.

Then the understandable desire to make the reorganisation acceptable to the staff has led to sharp increases in salary for a number of officials and this too has taken place in a blaze of publicity and has been followed by a general salary increase for the whole service.

But perhaps the most unfortunate aspect has been the impact of this year's record rate of inflation. This can be seen most clearly if one looks at a regional council that has not been in the news, that has pared its expenditure to the bone and has avoided any of the forms of expenditure that have attracted adverse publicity – the Borders. Despite all this, the rates in the landward section of Berwickshire have gone up, with the transfer to the new regional authority, by anything from 215 to 246 per cent. Where rate payers were paying 26p in the pound, they are now paying 90p, and this for no improvement whatsoever in the services they receive.

If the reasons are analysed, 15p of the rise was due to Berwickshire's specially low rates dependent on underspending before 1975,

8p was due to the change in the rate support grant formula in favour of the cities, 6p to the cost of running their own water board, 1p to the extra cost of a joint police force with the Lothians and the rest to inflation.

There are, in fact, no more staff employed on local government now than there were before reorganisation and some forms of expenditure, particularly on roads, have been severely cut. It is scarcely surprising that the public are either disenchanted or up in arms about what appears to be the huge extra cost of the new system of local government.

So what can be done to improve matters and what should be the relations between the present councils and the Scottish Assembly? One thing is clear. There is no need for district and regional councils as well as an all-Scotland unit of government. The Wheatley two-tier pattern was devised as an alternative to an Assembly, not as a supplement to it. If the Assembly is to do a worth-while job, it must take over policy-making and the execution of these policies in the more important functions such as roads, land use or strategic planning, recreation and education.

Some will object that such functions, for example education, could not be administered from Edinburgh for the whole of Scotland. But this misunderstands the proposal.

At present the Scottish Education Department does, for some purposes, run all Scottish education and this would be taken over by the Assembly. So would some of the minor policy-making functions currently in the hands of the regions. (It is curious to argue that Strathclyde Regional Council can perform these functions for places as far apart as Coll and South Lanarkshire, but an Assembly could not do the same for Scotland as a whole.) Detailed local administration of schools would then be devolved to the one tier of local councils below the Assembly.

For some, these proposals have been summarised by the slogan 'abolish the regions,' but this is too simple. What is essential is that the structure of local government below the Assembly be left to that body to decide. One of the virtues of an Assembly is that it can devise different systems to meet the needs of such different communities as Clydeside, the Border burghs and the Outer Isles. In some cases, the regional council or island authority may be best, in others the districts may be more suitable or new areas altogether might be needed.

But the major lesson of this whole sorry episode relates to the Assembly itself. If it is to be a success, if good candidates are to be attracted and high standards established, then it must not be so short of powers that it looks and behaves like one of the old county councils or one of the new regional councils. This would be a total disaster. There is only one way to avoid this and that is a generous grant of powers and of revenue-raising capacity so that the Assembly rises totally above the unfortunate atmosphere that has now come to be associated with local government.

1.5 'A cure for corruption?' (*The Scotsman*, 16.8.1976)

One of the most frequently whispered criticisms of local government is that it is corrupt. Astonishingly, there is almost no serious study of local government corruption in Scotland. Mackintosh had the courage to tackle this subject. This newspaper column remains therefore one of the best available analyses of the problem in print.

In the aftermath of the Poulson affair, the Labour Government in late 1974 appointed a Royal Commission on 'Standards of Conduct in Public Life'. The worries underlying this act were strengthened by a trickle of councillors being accused of bribery, a few going to prison, by the accusations of Eddy Milne, the former MP for Blyth, and then by the conduct of Mr John Stonehouse.

The first question is whether these cases (there were 179 convictions between 1966 and 1974 and by 1975 a further 53 were awaiting prosecution) represent merely the tip of an iceberg. No-one can tell. If Poulson had not gone bankrupt and if he had not kept such meticulous notes of all his expenditure, his network of connections would never have been discovered. And it is possible that if John Stonehouse had not done his disappearing act, he might have been able to cover up the other frauds of which he was then accused.

It is more useful to move on and look at the next problem. Why did these men offer and accept gifts, free entertainments or direct bribes? Lord Houghton, in his addendum to the report of the Royal Commission, claims to have put his finger on the main reason. 'The substance of over a year's inquiry boils down to the temptations arising from the commercial relationships between the construction and civil engineering industries and public bodies. . . . During the 1960s the coming together of planners, developers (and even architects), property-owners, contractors and local authorities provided all the basic ingredients of corruption.'

The finger of accusation is pointed much more at local government than at central government for one simple reason. Local government is executive in the sense that councillors actually decide who will get planning permission, who will be awarded a contract to build or, in another guise, who will get a licence to open a pub. MPs are no better people but they are not executive in this sense. They do not take this kind of decision and are simply not worth bribing.

In the case of MPs, there are other, rather different forms of corruption and much turns on the precise meaning of the word. The bulk of issues in Parliament are settled along party lines and no form of inducement makes it worth an MP voting against his own party thus endangering his renomination. But there are other kinds of corruption. First, there is John Stonehouse's type where an MP may use his position in politics (or as a past Minister) to get an entrée to firms, banks or foreign governments which might have been more difficult if he were an ordinary businessman.

Secondly, some concerns and organisations like to keep MPs well disposed by giving them talks over a free lunch, trips to see what is happening in their overseas factories and a few may pay one or two MPs a small fee for looking after their interests. Some of this has always been accepted as legitimate and just at what point a fee paid to an MP becomes a corrupting influence is a very difficult matter to determine.

If it is held that hope of money or position which can on occasion lead an MP to act contrary to his basic views constitutes corruption, then by far the most important source of such influence is the desire for one of the 85 ministerial offices which the Prime Minister can bestow on suitable members of his own party in the House of Commons.

These types of influence are important but they do stretch the concept of corruption. In the more normal sense of money changing hands so that the giver of the bribe is placed in a position to make larger profits, the bulk of cases occur in local government for the reasons that have been set out. Even then, the explanation given by Lord Houghton is not entirely satisfactory.

No-one has suggested that Mr Poulson with his huge firm of 750 employees built bad houses. He might well have got these contracts on the merit of his work and the prices he was quoting. Mr Dan Smith, a leading accomplice, was also one of the most dynamic and public-spirited figures in local government and could have been highly successful without becoming involved in such dubious practices. It is still by no means clear whether Mr Pottinger would not have pressed for Poulson to receive certain contracts irrespective of any holidays or help with his house which he may have received from Mr Poulson.

Anyone running a large concern dependent on contracts from public bodies is likely to get to know the councillors on the relevant committees. It is only common sense and decent behaviour to extend some hospitality to these men and women and to try and get to know what they want; what ideas they have about future policy. And if party A is committed to a big building programme and party B is opposed and if a contractor also believes that a big building programme is desirable (not just for him but for the people who are going to live in the houses), is he to be stopped from dipping into his pocket to help party A to win the local elections?

It is easy to draw a line and say that if money is given to a councillor or an official to swing a contract to a firm which would not otherwise have been given the job on grounds of quality or of price, then this is corruption. But many small contractors with two men and a boy in their firms have gone into local government and emerged ten years later as managing directors of large enterprises without any evidence of direct acts of corruption of this kind. And there is no reason why such men may not have succeeded by their ability and why their council work may not have been motivated by the same constructive drives that made them successful businessmen.

Nevertheless, there is a problem, or rather a series of problems. The British view of public service on elected bodies or in Parliament derives from a period when landowners, successful businessmen or those with private means went to council meetings in the evenings (or into the Commons). On the local authorities, they dealt mainly with regulatory matters and their officials were a small group of clerks or part-time lawyers.

All these have changed. The councillors have a real problem about attending three or four meetings a week, often in the daytime, and the £10 allowance per meeting brings odium on them without in any way compensating for the disruption of their work or the loss of their earning power.

Secondly, they are dealing with full-time officials who are earning twice or four times as much as they are and they are giving out work worth thousands of pounds to businessmen who are often equipped with expense accounts and company cars as well as large salaries. In the rather different case of MPs there is the similarity that virtually every civil servant (and most of the clerks of the Commons) whom MPs meet are paid more than they are and the MP who returns the hospitality of businessmen or journalists has to do it out of his own pocket. Finally, councillors (and MPs) have seldom managed large enterprises and are not trained for the job or warned of the pitfalls of high-level financial dealings.

So what can be done? The Royal Commission recommended more penalties and powers for the police but what would be more useful would be a rethink of the old concept of democratic control through part-time, unpaid or underpaid amateurs. There are alternatives. In the United States, in some cities the voters choose a highly trained and well-paid expert as 'city manager' while the elected council simply debates his decisions but has no executive powers.

If it is preferable to keep councillors who are the kind of persons thrown up by the political and electoral system, then it would seem to be desirable to extend the net as widely as possible. It seems stupid nowadays to exclude all local government (and central government) employees from standing. The Germans insist that any elected representative who wants to serve fulltime has his or her job kept available with promotion and pension rights secured and anyone can stand, thus ensuring a wider range of candidates.

If this is not done, if local government continues to be the target of so much abuse, if the allowances remain both inadequate and resented, then the only people willing to stand may be those who have some special interest in local affairs, the kind of interest that may easily slip into a relationship which is prone to corrupt influences.

As far as MPs are concerned, so long as they are paid less than the average professional man and civil servant, and their position is also insecure, they will be tempted to take any lunches, trips and 'consultancy fees' that are going. Much more would need to be done in the way of parliamentary reform before that special kind of corruption, the lure of office, receded and before MPs found being a backbencher a satisfying job in its own right.

The Royal Commission proposed a useful series of measures designed to make it easier to catch and punish those guilty of corruption (thus, it is hoped, deterring others). But so long as the gross disparities between elected members on the one hand and officials and contractors on the other hand remain, the temptations will persist and some will succumb.

What is needed is a reconsideration of the best means of democratic control in an age of huge public sector spending and a real solution must produce a system where those elected are sufficiently competent, well-off and confident not to feel attracted by the range of inducements which large companies can and do lay out before those with whom they hope to do business.

Part 2

Westminster stalls devolution

John Mackintosh was quick to detect the rising tide of nationalism and to see how it might sweep devolution home to port. Like so many Scots, he was also impatient with Westminster's delay. The Queen's Speech of 1968 promised not reform but a Royal Commission to consider reform. The profferred Royal Commission was 'a committee to kill devolution' in the words of the then Secretary of State for Scotland.

In the event the Report of the Commission proved a big step forward for devolution because it gave its *imprimatur* to a devolution scheme. But that result could not be anticipated at the outset. Indeed, had the deaths or resignations of some anti-devolutionists on the Committee not occurred, the Report would probably have been quite different.

2.1 Debate in the Scottish Grand Committee (Hansard, *H C Debates*, 1 Nov. 1967, cols 303–10).

Mackintosh's impatience for reform can be detected in this speech delivered the day before the SNP's first by-election victory at Hamilton on 2 November 1967. His words recapture the tension among Scottish MPs as they felt the first tremors of the earthquake to come.

Mr John P. Mackintosh (Berwick and East Lothian). Every Scottish Member who worked in the constituencies this summer and has been around the country would agree that there is a very serious problem of worry and alarm among sections of the community about the satisfactory or unsatisfactory nature of the Scottish system of Government. I know that this subject has been raised time and again on the Floor of the House and many have, no doubt, like myself, given evidence to the Royal Commission on Local Government in Scotland. This is a very important body, and we shall have to think very carefully when it reports, but, in the interim, there is still this worry about whether our methods of Government in Scotland are, even at the moment, entirely adequate.

This has been raised before. Looking up the precedents for the proposals I intend to make, I noticed that I have the very proper antecedents of my right hon. Friend the Member for Edinburgh, East

(Mr Willis) and my hon. Friend the Member for South Ayrshire (Mr Emrys Hughes), who put down an identical Motion in 1948. Nevertheless, it is worth bringing it up again.

Some of my hon. Friends feel that this tide of worry about remote Government rises and falls inevitably and regularly, and that if we wait it will disappear again. In discussing this, they cite the most significant example, in 1948–49, when the Scottish Covenant Movement obtained 2 million signatures on a proposal for a kind of devolution. That movement then had a good deal of strength. It then died away and it is argued that, presumably, this will happen again.

This time, the situation is much more serious, for a number of reasons. The first is simply the passage of time and the fact that we have not been able to meet these criticisms. When the Conservative Government came to power on the last occasion, they appointed the Balfour Commission to investigate Scottish Government, and it reported in 1954, saying this:

> 'We find that an important source of discontent arises from ignorance of the existing machinery of government in Scotland . . . popular opinion should be better informed about the wide powers which the Secretary of State already possesses for dealing with the affairs of Scotland'

Since that was said in 1954, there has been even more administrative devolution. Not only do we have, as in 1954, health, education, housing and home affairs under the Secretary of State, but there was the extra devolution of trunk roads and the rise of economic planning under the control of the Scottish Development Department.

This is a mass of devolved administration. Indeed, I can think of only one area which could reasonably, within a United Kingdom framework, be further devolved, and that is the Board of Trade's powers to stimulate local industrial development, although it would be very difficult. Apart from this, I can see no further administrative function which we could safely, in a United Kingdom framework, devolve to the Secretary of State in St Andrew's House.

This has been the case for 20 years, yet it can still be said, on Scottish Nationalist platforms, that we are ruled in a remote fashion from London. After all the work of those of us who have taught Scottish administration, of the journalists who have expounded and the hon. Members of both sides who have explained it at meeting after meeting, the fact that this is still the case suggests that it is not a failure of ours but a failure of machinery and communication at a much more serious level.

The second reason why I think that this matter is now more serious is that this is a particularly unfortunate juncture for Scottish energies to be turned aside from our own development to carping about what is, largely, a non-existent quarrel.

I was talking the other day to officials of the Scottish Council for Development and Industry about their work and they said that the really heartening thing was that for the first time the gap in investment which had existed for a long time between England and Scotland seemed to be disappearing, and that we now have development similar to that in the rest of the United Kingdom. I was delighted to see that the Confederation of British Industry survey struck a similarly optimistic note in saying that private investment was holding up under the squeeze better in Scotland than in any other part of the United Kingdom. We also have now heard from the Secretary of State that there is a chance of a real halt in the emigration figures.

Mr Ian MacArthur (Perth and East Perthshire): A halt?

Mr Mackintosh: That is what we have been told. I think there is some evidence of a new spirit in Scotland in industrial activity.

I think it would be very sad if the energies of our people were developed in raising political complaints instead of doing the things we want to do and which we can do when they are put into our own hands, and the machinery is available.

The third reason why I think this is particularly serious at the moment is that I think that in a sense there is truth in the complaint, some reality in the feeling, that however devolved our administration, Government nevertheless is in a sense remote, even if it is not remote geographically, and the reason for this is fairly clear, and that is that the Government, in response to popular demand, have been doing more and more. We have been creating bodies to carry out things desired by the electorate and often supported by both sides of the House, but many of those bodies are not under the control of elected representatives. I shall not weary the House by enumerating them all, but we have set up the Highlands and Islands Development Board, there is to be a Countryside Commission, we have amalgamated police forces and water authorities. I will not go through them all. I remember the last time I ran through them I listed 49 *ad hoc* bodies of one kind and another in Scotland, all doing a good job, and yet there is a feeling that they are remote and hard to control. The average citizen does not understand them.

I do not think that this feeling is peculiar to Scotland. I think it exists in Wales, too, and in all parts of England. It is the functioning of large-scale government. Because we in Scotland are a nation our objections take the form of nationalism. Whereas in England identical forms of complaint, such as that of control over the siting of Stansted Airport, for instance, are only an anti-Government argument, anti-bureaucratic, the argument in Scotland about such a thing, had it happened there, would have contributed to Scottish nationalist feeling.

For these reasons I think we must take note of this. What then should we do? What proposals can we make in this House to meet the situation? I know that the traditional answer, the one we have always been given, time and time again, is that we have here a Scottish Grand Committee, a Parliament within Parliament, where, as well as on the Floor of the House, we can consider matters concerning Scotland. This argument fails to satisfy. I do not know how many hon. Members have used it, but I do not think any would have found that it produced a ready response, an enthusiastic acceptance from their audiences. I do not think it meets the case myself.

I think there are two reasons for this. One is that the Scottish Grand Committee, with all its merits, does not have enough time, and the second is that what we do is not sufficiently known and appreciated in Scotland.

On the first of those two points, the difficulty about the Scottish Grand Committee, I feel, is that though we take Second Readings of Bills, and though we have our six Estimate days debates, and although we have our subject days debates, all these are not very much when we consider the amount of authority the Secretary of State has, and when we have to discuss such various subjects as health, housing, education, agriculture, roads, fisheries, economic development – all these matters; and yet we have to cover them in this very limited time. This last summer I recall we had a debate on Scottish education for two and a half hours of which the Front Bench spokesmen took one hour and 35 minutes, and this meant that of the 40 back benchers present only four could contribute. That was all we had on the subject of Scottish education, and on Scottish agriculture we did not have a debate at all.

I know the stock answer to this is to say that the subjects are chosen by the Opposition and that if hon. Members would not speak for such a long time a few more back benchers could get in, but I do not regard that as satisfactory, because whatever the subjects we choose, and however short our speeches, we would still only have six periods of two and a half hours with which to cope with a matter.

Mr MacArthur: I do not want to interrupt the hon. Member in the very interesting argument he is advancing, but in order to avoid worsening the process of communication, will he call attention to the fact that these are not the only times when these vital matters are considered by Parliament?

Mr Mackintosh: I quite appreciate that. I appreciate that we have Adjournment debates and full-scale debates on some of these matters. Hon. Members opposite can choose a Supply Day, if they care, to discuss the Scottish economy and things of that kind. Nevertheless in the Scottish Grand Committee as a Parliament within a Parliament we do not have so long as I should like to have and an established and guaranteed time to discuss these topics. This is the weakness of the situation.

As to the difficulty of people understanding what we do, hon. Members will have seen various articles in the newspapers, especially a feature article last Monday in *The Scotsman*. It is a little tedious when one finds reasonably informed people writing articles referring to our sitting here as 'inactive, dumb, spineless Members'. I have heard many criticisms of English and Welsh hon. Members, but I have not heard them described as dumb or spineless. It seems that people do not know about the long morning sittings in Committee upstairs.

What is possible as an interim measure? I say 'interim measure' because I reiterate that we must wait for the Royal Commission Report for a final solution. I am not proposing a final solution to the problem but an interim measure to add to understanding and to help to solve the problem. I suggest that we should take the Scottish Grand Committee to sit in Edinburgh for a week in each of the Recesses, the last week of January, a week in the Easter Recess and a week in the Whitsun Recess. If we did this it would be entirely possible for us to open with a Scottish Question Time. We could then have a debate, for example in January, on a Second Reading. I appreciate that some Second Reading debates would have to come on early in the autumn, but others could take place in January, and we could have debates on the principle of Scottish Bills.

During the Easter Recess I should like us to have debates on some subjects we do not consider adequately in Scottish Grand Committee. I am thinking particularly of the Planning Council in Scotland, which is no doubt a very worthy body but people do not know what it is doing. Important decisions are being taken about the siting of new towns, roads, and the whole pattern of future development. Yet people have very little chance of finding what is happening and debating it so that intelligent public opinion may be created.

In the Whitsun Recess sittings of the Scottish Grand Committee we could have a fuller discussion of the Estimates which now we discuss in morning sittings of 2½ hours. It is important that this should be done in a Recess. I would be the last to want hon. Members from Scottish constituencies not to play their full part in this House in Scottish Questions. In a Recess we would get a tremendous amount of publicity. It would be very evident what we were doing and what the devolved powers of St Andrews' House were.

I find it amazing that my argument does not appeal more to my right hon. Friend the Secretary of State for Scotland because I have so often witnessed his batting the ball back at Question Time and making mincemeat of hon. Members opposite. I am surprised that he is not happy to do this before the full gaze or blaze of Scottish publicity in Edinburgh.

What are the arguments against this solution? I heard one – I will mention no names – that if we had good administration, it does not matter about democratic control. This is the old colonial argument: 'The natives are grumbling in the bazaars, but while the district officer is competent we need not bother.' I do not agree with that kind of argument, and I think that we can dismiss it, although I have heard it advanced.

A much more important and serious argument, which I accept as genuine, is that this would be the slippery slope, the first step of a cataclysmic slide towards utter nationalism and total separation. In fact, I think that the reverse is true, and that is why I am particularly concerned to refute that argument. I believe that if we refuse to meet this demand to make Government less remote, if we say that everything is perfect and wag our fingers at the objectors, telling them that they are foolish and that they do not know the true situation, then we drive into the arms of the very small number of genuine nationalists the very large number of people who want to remain part of the United Kingdom but who are not entirely happy that everything is well with the present system of Government in Scotland.

We have evidence of that in the result of the Gallup polls in Scotland. We see that 70 per cent of those who responded said that they wanted an elected body in Scotland to control purely Scottish matters. Only 18 per cent said that they wanted the solution of total independence. I say quite frankly that I wish to drive a wedge between these two groups and to reassure the majority that our existing machinery of

Government can be adapted to meet their needs so that, with the growth of a complex and elaborate Government machine, we can also foster the growth of an adequate system of democratic control to match it.

I regard the argument of total nationalism as utterly disastrous. The vast majority of nationalist speakers never try to make that argument. They go on complaints and moans, which we could answer if we had the time and if they could see us at work in the Grand Committee. They do not normally argue for total independence. I do not want to say anything which might be calculated as insulting to our friends the Southern Irish Nationalists. I supported their demands up to 1922, as will be seen, in a retrospective sort of way, but the facts show that the objectives which they had have not been adequately met. Capital development in Southern Ireland has been very poor, the standard of living is far below that in this country, the heavy emigration has not been solved and 800,000 Irish citizens have poured out of Ireland to live in this country. None of the problems which the Scottish Nationalists are pointing out was solved by self-government in Southern Ireland. We want to separate the people who basically are United Kingdom in outlook, who represent the vast majority of Scots, by saying that we have a positive, clear-cut answer to their problems and by inviting them to come away from the very small number of people who are separatists.

When canvassing recently I encountered a lady who told me that in future she would vote for the Scottish Nationalists. When I asked her why, she said that it was because her council house rent had risen. I pointed out delicately to her that the Scottish subsidy per head was £28 13s. 5d. and that the English subsidy was £15 6s. 4d. I asked whether she realised that not only was she subsidised by other people in her own community but she was subsidised by the English taxpayer, and this was news to her. Yet, as hon. Members know, we have bandied it about continually in our own debates. She is the kind of curious person who is voting nationalist for a negative, backward-looking solution because she is not adequately informed about what we are doing.

I appreciate that this is not a perfect solution and that it would cause great inconvenience. It is, however, a serious problem, if we wish to adapt our democratic machinery so as to convince our electors that what we are doing has a point, that they can participate, that they know whom they can tackle and that within the framework of the United Kingdom we are meeting our needs.

2.2 Debate on the Queen's Speech 1968 (Hansard, *H C Debates*, 4 Nov. 1968, cols 554–57).

This speech came almost exactly a year later and registers John Mackintosh's opposition to the proposed Commission.

Mr John P. Mackintosh (Berwick and East Lothian): I should like to continue the discussion of the last point raised by the hon. Member for Perth and East Perthshire (Mr MacArthur) on the question of the Constitutional Commission. Unlike most hon. Members who have spoken, I am a little unhappy about its appointment. I was particularly unhappy about the arguments of the Leader of the Liberal Party, when he seemed to think that the whole future development of our constitution, its internal relationships and the role of this House should be handed over to a body of appointed people for their mature deliberation. It seems to me that to do this would be to suggest that neither the Ministers, the Shadow Cabinet, nor the collective wisdom of this House is equal to the task, and that would be the greatest condemnation of Parliament and of its present position that anyone could make.

I was aghast at the thought of sitting here for three or four years waiting for a group of people to produce some proposals which we would then have to accept or reject. After all, as the hon. Member for Carmarthen (Mr Gwynfor Evans) pointed out, such a body would be composed of people who would be in no way less political than we are. They would simply have different views or prejudices. It is a fundamental matter for the Government to decide and propose and then for Parliament to debate and accept or reject.

I cannot see why the Government have produced this unfortunate proposal of a Constitutional Commission. One possible argument put forward by my right hon. Friend the Home Secretary at the Labour Party conference at Blackpool was that the facts are not fully known and need to be investigated. With respect, I doubt that.

On financial questions, the facts are as well known as it is possible for accountants to extract them. In 1952, we had the detailed Report of the Catto Committee, set up by right hon. and hon. Gentlemen opposite. That went into the matter and produced a return. Those items which it could not allocate are unallocatable. I have asked the Treasury to produce an up-to-date return, but more detail cannot be produced, given the present financial structure of the country.

Even if one could produce the facts, they would not have much effect on the people arguing the case. After all, it is not a 'hard cash' case. We know that Britain could exist as separate parts, which might be better or worse off. But, basically, that does not affect the argument.

On administrative facts, also, the matters are well known. The House is obliged to the hon. Member for Perth and East Perthshire, who read the list of functions of the Secretary of State. They are well known to most people, certainly to most students of the subject, and we do not need to research them to establish the position. I cannot accept that we need a Commission to establish the facts.

The value judgments cannot be established by a Commission. They are not open to judgment. I was interested in the argument advanced by the hon. Member for Carmarthen that, if Wales was a separate nation, there would be an upsurge of cultural activity, vitality, enthusiasm and confidence. I hope that that would be so, but no one can establish it. We can look at countries where it exists and at countries which have achieved independence where, if anything, art, literature and letters have declined. They have become inward-looking, narrow and parochial.

If we in Scotland became independent, standards would decline. Most of the art, literature and letters which have stimulated a Scottish response have come from outside. There is a great deal of narrowness in my country, and I am not confident that a separate Scottish Assembly would be more liberal or progressive in cultural matters and encourage and stimulate people more than is the case at present. It might, but that is no reason for appointing a Commission to pronounce on the matter.

I can only assume that the reason the Government have chosen to set up the Commission is because of a fundamental difficulty in their ranks in deciding on the matter. Indeed, there is not only a disagreement amongst the Government about what should happen. It exists among right hon. and hon. Gentlemen opposite as well. The Leader of the Opposition has pronounced in favour of an elected assembly and has set up a Committee to investigate it. I shall not be surprised if the Committee turns down his proposal. I know that there are tremendous tensions among hon. Gentlemen opposite who represent Scottish constituencies. The same is true of these benches, and I respect people's view on these matters. But, ultimately, it is a matter for the Government to determine, to reach a conclusion and to put forward their views.

I would press my right hon. Friends to realise the dangers of delay. Politically, they are serious. But, by that, I do not mean in terms of the prospects of either of the major parties defeating nationalist candidates. That is not such a serious matter. I think that the wisdom of the Scottish electorate will accept the general arguments in favour of unity and reject separatism. The evidence is that the vast bulk of people voting nationalist do not accept nationalist policy on this point. Most people reject it, and what we must consider is why they vote in this way.

The chief political danger in delay is that it suggests to the public that the Government, the Opposition and this House have not grappled with one of the central questions of our community. In a sense, we are rudderless on the matter, and this contributes to people's disillusionment with politicians and the machinery of government.

There are administrative dangers in delay in that the way in which we run our country, in its highly centralised form in England, at any rate, has produced a great slowing down in the whole machinery of government. I am much impressed by the rate at which some countries, for example, can put up advance factories when the two in my constituency took long negotiations and, in one case, 13 months and, in the other, 17 months to construct. I was discussing this with a senior civil servant in the Scottish Office who is an old friend and associate of mine. He told me that one of the big problems in negotiating any Scottish economic development is the number and wide variety of bodies which have to be consulted, all with their own *amour propre*. The result is that our pace of economic activity in regional terms, despite the tremendous energy of Ministers, has been slowed.

There is also a weakness on the consultation side. Having gone through this long process, we spring plans on people, and there is then a failure of consultation and contact. There is then delay, as we have seen in the Central Borders plan, where, misguidedly, one county council turned it down, the whole matter ground to a halt, and now has to be got going again. The chief danger is that delay will turn the political atmosphere sour.

I will not go into the merits of the interesting and moving clash to which we listened earlier between two hon. Members representing Northern Ireland constituencies. In my view, that deep and bitter clash was the product of the greatest error of our statesmanship in the 19th century. Sensible devolution for Ireland was delayed for 30 years, when it was demanded by Protestants and Catholics alike and when it could have been brought in without separation and maintained the unity of the country.

This is not a matter of separation at all. It is a more complex matter of what is to be decided centrally and what locally. I have had the good fortune recently to be touring Europe, and this problem deeply exercises the Governments of France, Germany and Italy, to take only three examples. General de Gaulle thought that he could decentralise administration to the prefects, by building them up more powerfully, without popular participation. The days of May last year, with their frustration and bitterness, were part of a revolution against the over-centralisation of France. He has had to make concessions. In Italy, there is an autonomous council in Sicily and Sardinia handling matters of development in the context of the national framework. In Germany, they have the division between the Länder and, a highly prosperous united country.

The problem of what is to be put out to the regions and what is to be kept central is a subtle, interesting and intricate one which is only soluble on political lines by the Members of the Government bringing forward proposals and putting them to the House so that they can be tackled.

I would urge upon my right hon. Friends that the most fruitful part of the Queen's speech is that which says that they will not hesitate to go on with this work, despite the setting up of the Commission. I hope that they will let the Commission alone, make up their own minds and give us something to consider before the expiry of this Parliament.

2.3 Written evidence to the Royal Commission on the Constitution (Submitted January 1970. Commission on the Constitution, *Written Evidence* Vol. 9, pp. 116–35, HMSO Crown Copyright 1972.)

Mackintosh's unease at the Commission's appointment did not prevent him from doing his best to steer it on to the right lines. In his written evidence to the Commission he succinctly summarized the arguments of his book *The Devolution of Power*.

Task before the commission

The first problem in placing evidence before the Commission is that of the time-scale. Any discussion of 'the present functions of the central legislature and government in relation to the several countries, nations and regions of the UK' has to start, as these terms of reference suggest, from the *present* situation, yet it is by no means clear what this situation will be when this paper reaches the Commission, because by that time the Government White Papers on the future of local government in England and Scotland may have been published. By the time the Commission has assembled all its evidence on 'developments in local government organisation and in administrative and other relationships between the various parts of the UK', Bills passed possibly not on the White Papers but on the views of new ministers who may be appointed after the General Election may be going through Parliament, while by the time the Commission comes to report, a new system of local government may be in the course of construction.

If the work of the Redcliffe-Maud and Wheatley Commissions had been exhaustive, if they had covered the entire problem of what local – as opposed to central – government should consist of and if they had proposed the most satisfactory system on the basis of such an investigation, there would be no function for the Crowther Commission. But the Government deliberately limited the former two Commissions to a study of the 'existing functions' of local government, and though each glanced at the more fundamental question of what local or devolved government should consist of, they carefully avoided going beyond their terms of reference; indeed they interpreted these terms rather narrowly.

The Redcliffe-Maud Commission never seriously considered the problem of what to do about functions withdrawn from local government in recent years or how democratic control could be exercised over the *ad hoc* boards and commissions that have often been described as 'intermediate government', being neither central nor local. The Wheatley Commission did glance at these topics under the heading of 'the all-Scotland solution' and dismissed them in four paragraphs saying simply that 'the whole scheme seemed to us as much an expedient to effect of a constitutional change as to effect a reform of local government. Our terms of reference exclude constitutional change' . . . (p. 166). With no written constitution in Britain, there is no distinction between constitutional changes and alterations in any of the arrangements for government and this quotation simply means that the members of the Wheatley Commission were not looking at this aspect of the problem because they had decided to interpret their terms of reference (probably correctly) as an indication that the Government did not wish them to consider these matters.

But these decisions meant that the Commission could not give proper weight to the arguments in favour of the kind of areas or structure needed if local government is to take over, for instance, the work of the hospital boards, the river pollution boards, the countryside commissions, the tourist boards, major roadways or higher education and so the Commissions' findings were seriously biased in favour of smaller units than might otherwise have been found desirable. Nor did the

Commissions go into the question of precisely how much real power and discretion was given to local authorities at present when they were nominally awarded the functions of education, housing, planning and so on, though the Wheatley Report did say that 'in almost every field of local government activity the present statutory code will have to be rewritten if full effect is to be given to our recommendations' and 'all arrangements for inspection, technical scrutiny of designs and plans and advice or instruction by circular should be rigorously reviewed, to see how many of them could be modified or withdrawn altogether' (pp. 224–5). The Redcliffe-Maud Report barely looked at this question, which in many ways is central to the whole question of devolution and to the reality of local government.

Finally the Commissions failed to look at sentiments which are a major part of political life, regarding these in some sense as 'political' and therefore illegitimate, when the lifeblood of any viable democratic system comes from its capacity to attract public interest and loyalty. For instance, although the Wheatley Commission took little evidence on this point and gave it little weight, their Report amounts, in one sense, to the argument that people north of the Border are Highlanders, Greater Glaswegians, North Easterners and so on before they are Scotsmen – that the latter sentiment is only relevant at international football matches. One would have thought that recent political events in Scotland would have demonstrated the inadequacy of this view. Similarly, Redcliffe-Maud laid most weight on efficiency in the conduct of existing functions and spent almost no time on political sentiments nor did they consider whether, if no sentiment for a larger unit existed, it was easier to create a sense of identification with a provincial unit or with an enlarged 'unitary authority'.

The seriousness of the present position is that if a reform of local government based on these two Reports is carried through, because of the limitations in their examination of areas, functions and sentiments, the result will not last. Reform will involve a tremendous and often, for individuals, painful shakeup of the entire system of local administration without any proper solution of the problems that have clogged central departments, produced a widespread sense of alienation among the voters and made the execution of many projects and plans desired by the community desperately complex and slow.

Nor can it be maintained, as some have tried to argue, that a more satisfactory system of local or devolved government can later be slipped in between the 58 proposed unitary authorities in England and the seven proposed regions in Scotland and the central government. If an all-Scottish or all-Welsh authority and English provincial authorities are to make any sense, they must exercise many of the powers at present earmarked for allocation, in name at least, to the unitary councils or to the Scottish regions. And to take those functions which would be better dealt with at a regional level away from the new local government units would make it unnecessary to have so few and such large units. If an effective provincial unit of government was established, the councils below the provinces or regions would then become a second tier and could be much smaller, meeting the sentiments of a different, more intimate level of community. In short, if the Crowther Commission is to have anything of value to say, it will be treading on quite new ground as compared with the material on which the Government is basing its White Papers. If the Crowther Commission is to make any new proposals, the White Papers or Bills will have to be substantially modified and should therefore be held up till the views of this Commission are known.

This urgency applies only to the devolution question in Great Britain. Northern Ireland is a separate case where a system of devolution has worked well in administrative terms but has broken down seriously at the political level. It might well be best in this case, contrary to the situation in Britain, to delay recommendations till the later stages of the Commission's work when it may be possible to see whether the recent reforms introduced in Northern Ireland are having an effect on political and social conditions or not. For much more satisfactory reasons of quiescence and order there is also no urgency about the Channel Islands or the Isle of Man and therefore this evidence concentrates on what it submits is the main and very urgent task of the Commission, to pronounce on the shape and form of relations between central and local government in Britain before the field is pre-empted by inadequate reform Bills based on partial examinations of the problems by the recent Local Government Commissions.

Objections to devolution not yet properly considered

As has been argued, the basic question of the degree of decentralisation the public (electors and governors) actually want has never been faced, much less resolved. Thus it is possible for the present Government both to proclaim their intention of reviving local democracy and at the same time announce a Bill to force all local authorities to adopt the comprehensive pattern of education and berate certain local authorities for not achieving the housing targets set by the central government. The same mixed intentions are revealed in the reactions to the Redcliffe-Maud and Wheatley proposals, devolvers regarding them as a real step forward while senior civil servants in Whitehall and St Andrews House see them as simply creating more effective agencies for implementing central government instructions. This is because the purpose of local government reform – more efficiency in carrying out the same national policies or more regional autonomy and variation – has never been established; the reforms that have been proposed do not clearly come down on one side or the other and so the protagonists of each approach can imagine they have gained their point.

Moreover, if it is decided that more devolution is desirable, the consequences in administrative and political terms have to be thought through and settled. For instance, at present the Treasury works out the five-year rolling programme of public expenditure on a functional basis. Headings such as housing, law and order, education, health and welfare cover the whole country and the rate of increase to be permitted is fixed for each category at a certain percentage. This has several effects. The procedure requires careful control of local authority capital and current expenditure by the central government in order to prevent the functional totals exceeding the allotted figures. It means that a council which wishes to spend more on roads and less on education cannot do so; such a transfer between programmes is not permitted. It makes it very hard (see 'A Scottish Budget' produced by H M Treasury in October 1969) to set out the total government expenditure for Scotland, Wales and even harder for an English region. It would require a major change in British administrative and financial thinking if the allocation and authorisation of public expenditure was to be altered from a functional to a regional basis, at least for those services to be administered by local government.

In administrative terms, political responsibility to a single cabinet and the career structure of the civil service place the maximum possible emphasis on uniformity and central control. For example, though it seems obvious that agriculture is different in the different areas of England (and it was for this reason that the Ministry of Agriculture created a regional administration), the first circular sent out by the Ministry to its regional controllers pointed out that they were to avoid any local policy variations which might give rise to embarrassing questions in the House of Commons. This responsibility to the same cabinet and legislature is the chief force preventing the Scottish Office in Edinburgh from developing any distinctive policies. In evidence to the Select Committee on Agriculture, officials explained that it was an accepted convention that the Scottish Departments would undertake nothing of significance without first consulting the relevant official in the English Department to ensure that no awkward precedent was being created. And the pressure for this uniformity does not originate from civil servants but from politicians and the public. If MPs flip the pages of a joint Bill or a Scottish Bill closely following upon an English Bill, their eye first lights on any differences and their immediate reaction is not 'how admirable; conditions in England are in fact different and, no doubt, merit different treatment'. The immediate response is to guess which method or proposal or payment appears to be most satisfactory and then to ask why the other country has not been equally favoured. This reaction among MPs occurs even more strongly if it is found that policies are being administered differently in the different administrative regions in England. And the public react in the same way. Even in the case of the few duties largely left to local authorities (such as devising and operating house allocation schemes), the constant cry is for uniformity of treatment and MPs are always receiving letters asking why a house can be obtained with certain qualifications in one area but not in another, the suggestion being that the central government should intervene to impose uniformity.

The same pressures apply to the civil service structure in the regions, civil servants regarding posts there as temporary sojourns in an administrative Siberia, promotion being back to Whitehall where there are not only the senior posts but where a degree of initiative is permitted or even encouraged, while it is not looked on with the same favour when emanating from provincial controllers. Similarly local authority officials, though possessing their own career structure and often well paid compared even with Whitehall, clearly feel subordinate to 'the man from the Ministry' who is in the superior position in terms both of power and prestige. It is interesting that this is an example of the effect of status. Because the Government of Northern Ireland is regarded, having its own political masters at Stormont, as a proper government organised on ministerial lines, its officials are treated as proper civil servants, recruited in the same way as the British civil service and they can be encountered at the Civil Service Administrative Centre courses showing no signs of inferiority. Yet GLC officials or those of Glasgow or Birmingham Corporations who, for some purposes, administer as many or more people than the Northern Irish Government are regarded as 'local' officials to be recruited and trained and treated in a totally different manner.

Finally, in political terms, local elected positions carry little weight simply because their occupants wield negligible powers. In the eyes of the electorate, voting in local elections has little to do with the record of local councils, the swings being much more methods of indicating reactions to Conservative or Labour policies as revealed at Westminster. Few Labour authorities, however good their record, were able, for instance, to withstand the reaction against the Labour Government between 1967 and 1969. Also service on local authorities is, with a few exceptions, not regarded as a training ground for Westminster, those seeking parliamentary and those seeking local candidates being usually in non-competing groups. Thus there are virtually no figures in local government who have achieved a national political standing, who are capable of giving a lead in any way different to that of the party leaders at Westminster. The one possible exception, Mr Dan Smith, when he became Chairman of the North-East Planning Council, found that if his priorities on the closure of mines differed from that of the Ministry, he was put right on his next trip to London by an Assistant Under-Secretary, the Minister being too busy to see him.

The point of outlining these problems is to show that the pious words about a widespread belief in local democracy, which occur in so many speeches and documents, are largely empty. Britain is, in fact, one of the most centralised and united of the major industrial countries and there is a deep suspicion of local political and administrative initiative. Those interested in the arts and cultural activities suspect that local councils will be more censorious than the central government, the national party leaders suspect that stronger local councils will make it harder to pursue their own policies throughout the country. Medical men, academics, planners and all professional leaders dislike being under lay control but would, if it has to come, far prefer the central government or an *ad hoc* body, to a locally elected council. The civil service suspects local government of being inefficient, of wanting to engage in expenditures which it would be difficult to contain in a coherent national programme and of lack of balance in selecting priorities. The public may not place great confidence in its national politicians or award great prestige to MPs but it has considerably less faith in local councillors.

All this has to be faced because, if there is to be a measure of devolution of any significance, it must cut across these deeply ingrained practices and attitudes in British political culture and such a reform can only be carried if the critics appreciate the extent of the revolution that will be involved and the forces that will have to be countered. Moreover, the arguments in favour of devolution will have to have the greatest cogency.

The case for devolution

If these are the forces against any change in the central/local balance of power, it will be asked; why proceed?

1. The first reason derives from traditional British political theory, the democratic doctrine which is still accepted, though it has become increasingly empty of real content. It was assumed in the late Victorian period, when Britain was becoming a democracy, that all public decisions of importance should be put before the elected representatives of the community. For this reason the many boards and agencies created in previous centuries were gathered into a single departmental system and the heads of the major departments were included in the cabinet which had to explain its policies to the House of Commons. The few decisions which could not be taken for the whole of Britain, because they had to meet local conditions, were collected into groups and allocated to elected county or borough councils. Since this system reached its apogee in the period between the 1880s and 1914, there has been a slow departure from it in practice though the principles are still nominally accepted. In fact, more and more weight is being placed on experts in administration and the complex of groups governing the country have come to have increasing doubts about the value of popular elections and of the democratic element in decision-making. However, for those who still accept the democratic doctrine that the government derives its legitimacy from the consent of the governed and much of its capacity to govern from the degree to which it can carry public confidence and even enthusiasm with it, the democratic element is essential. Thus, for democrats, the most important aspect of the contemporary drive for governmental reform is once again to do what was done in the late nineteenth century, that is to draw together the bodies involved in policy-making, to group the boards, commissions and departments in such a way that it becomes possible to submit all the important decisions affecting the lives of citizens to a small number of democratic assemblies, thus producing a measure of public understanding and influence. Any study of current governmental practice shows that, leaving aside the efficacy of Parliament at the centre, if the next elected element in the governmental system is at Redcliffe-Maud's 'unitary authority' or metropolitan level, there will be many intermediate decisions which will escape any reference to elected representatives. Examples vary from any regional element in central departmental activity to making the plans of the regional councils, running hospitals, preserving the countryside, planting forests, determining the shape of major roadways and of public transport, siting and managing new towns and local airports and organising tourism. Given this area of intermediate government, it seems clear that if the democratic principle is to be adhered to, there are three basic levels at which governmental decisions will have to be grouped in order

to bring in the element of popular scrutiny and suggestion. One is the national level, the second is some sort of administrative region or sub-state and the third is the local level. Naturally different services and different geographical conditions may indicate different optimum units but, with reasonable compromises and adjustments, all important decisions affecting citizens' lives could be attached to one or other of these three levels and the democratic share in government could be re-established.

2. A second argument for devolution is that with the government intervening so much more often in the task of creating and preserving a suitable environment for individuals and communities, a powerful and relatively independent unit for local decision-taking is necessary and it should, in certain instances, be capable of altering the local impact of central government policies. For instance, it may make sense to pursue a series of national policies including closing uneconomic mines and railways, creating large comprehensive schools and building new motorways. But the pursuit of these individually admirable policies can destroy a particular community which may find itself off the new road, with no railway, its only source of employment gone and no secondary school. Similarly, the priorities for a region may differ from those of the nation as a whole. For instance, the North-West Council at one stage decided that a north-south motorway would do more for the area than extra educational expenditure but were unable to get the overall priorities for the region altered. Again, most passenger transport authorities may want a certain balance between bus and railway services but in certain areas, where there are special conditions, a different balance may be more desirable. Unless such decisions can be taken at a regional level, the desired effect of sensible, well-devised national policies will not occur in a minority of cases.

3. The attempt, as at present, to try and meet this situation by a combination of regional divisions of national ministries, *ad hoc* bodies and joint committees of the local authorities, is unsatisfactory for several reasons. In the first place, no one body has the task of co-ordination or the right to claim that it represents the popular will, so progress requires a high degree of agreement. Thus one or two authorities being difficult can halt the whole process, one of the heart-breaking features about modern British administration being the time taken to get any action. This is made worse (*a*) by the distrust central government feels for local administration so that again and again projects have to be referred back to Whitehall for approval and (*b*) by the fact that the voice of the general public who will benefit by better roads or a new housing scheme is scarcely heard while individual objectors

have not only rights but extensive delaying powers and (*c*) by the resultant preference for moving only if there is considerable degree of consensus.

4. A further result of this suspicion of local government and of the insistence on constant reference of all sorts of issues and stages in the administrative process to Whitehall is that central government is choked with detail and its senior officials find it hard to stand aside and consider the more fundamental issues of policy. This was evident when all appeals under the Town and Country Planning Acts had to go to the Ministry of Housing and Local Government so that there was a queue of over 10,000 appeals and a four-year delay. There is far too much detail in British central government so that planning ahead is inadequate and far too much of the time of senior officials is spent clearing their desks of such detailed points.

5. A combination of these factors, of the sense that many wise national policies do not entirely fit particular situations, of the lack of consultation of the electorate so that the government's reasons are not known, of delays and disappointments, have together helped create the sense of alienation which has been so evident in British politics in the 1960s. The most obvious manifestation of this alienation has been the rise of the Scottish and Welsh Nationalist Parties. This has happened despite the fact that Scotland and Wales have benefited greatly from the present government's policy of pushing industry into the development areas and from the redistributive effect of combining equal levels of taxation with social expenditure according to need. The result, as 'A Scottish Budget' produced by HM Treasury in October, 1969, shows, is to subsidise Scotland at the rate of about £400 million a year. It is also significant that Scotland and Wales are the two areas enjoying the greatest administrative autonomy and yet neither of these facts has reduced political discontent. The reason is not the rise of a special nationalist sentiment (never more than 20 per cent of nationalist voters accepted separatist policies) so much as the lack of the legitimacy conferred by democracy, by a sense of involvement. It makes no difference if an irritating decision is taken by the man in London or by the man next door (in Cardiff or Edinburgh) if the decision was arrived at in secret, if the reasons were never explained and if there is no-one representing the citizen, no-one who could have put the citizen's case at the appropriate time and to whom, even afterwards, complaints can be made. This same feeling has appeared in England, though lack of a nationalist party has led it to take the form simply of abstentions or anti-government voting and of such resistance as was evoked by the attempt to put an airport at Stansted or to build a

motorway box in London. Some party leaders have thought that because apathy, abstention or nationalist voting has died down with the approach of a general election, the phenomenon can be safely ignored. Nothing could be more dangerous and it is a sign that something is seriously wrong with a political and governmental system if large masses of people desert their normal party allegiances and assume and 'opt-out' political creed or relapse into inarticulate hostility to the system.

6. A final consequence of the refusal to concede any effective political power to elected bodies outside London has been to make sure that the groups accustomed to governing, the 'political classes', are London-based. Outside the south-east of England, there are no families or sectors of the community accustomed to public life. So true is this that even those who enter politics from a regional background find that it is far easier to operate from London and even men as versatile and energetic as Ramsay MacDonald and Lloyd George moved to London. Thus there is no such element moulding the life and thought of the North-East, Scotland, Wales or East Anglia – there is no place for them to concentrate, no powers for them to exercise, no area of decision which appeals to men of action or catches the attention of the public. It is for this reason that the accusation of immaturity and inexperience can be levied at Welsh and Scottish Nationalists – these parties have had to draw entirely new men and women for their political leadership. The loss to Britain can be seen in two ways. One is to consider the contribution the men trained in the states or regions have made to the political life of decentralised states such as Germany or the United States – men such as Brandt, Adenauer, Helmut Schmidt, Keisinger, Stevenson, Rockefeller and Lindsay. The other is to consider the weakness in terms of trained talent of either major party in Britain if it has lost two or three sucessive general elections when there is no other training ground except Westminster-Whitehall.

The form of devolution

A. The case for provinces in England If it is accepted that these six arguments make a case for a genuine element of devolution, how is this to be achieved? It is often argued that something should be done in Scotland and Wales because they have a history, a common sentiment and an existing measure of regional administration. But, it is said, there is no point in moving in the same direction in England. If there is a local patriotism, it may extend to counties such as Yorkshire or Lancashire, it may identify with accents or characters (such as being a

Cockney or a Geordie), but there is no sentiment attaching to the Standard Treasury Regions. Thus many admit that the present counties and boroughs are too small and while moving to an extended local authority area such as the Redcliffe-Maud unitary authorities is feasible and has some meaning for the inhabitants, there is no such understanding of an East Midlands or Yorkshire and Humberside unit. On the administrative side, this case is supported by the contention that the regional planning councils have done nothing effective (with the possible exception of the North-East) and so there has been no sense that this is the natural planning and therefore executive unit.

While these points have some force, there is not much in the lack of regional sentiment. Britain is highly centralised, there are no regional *foci* of loyalty and the issue is whether to try and create an interest and loyalty around certain new units of government rather than others. The key question is which set of units is most likely to be able to exercise real powers – because it is these that invite participation – and which can be built on for a generation. While local councillors and MPs may be able to raise their eyes as far as an extended county, the present units plus a bit more, if the power wielded by such a unit is no greater than that of one of the present county councils, there will be no more interest shown than there is in the affairs of Northamptonshire or Berkshire today.

Moreover, the vital powers in the local government of the future are land use and economic planning together with the attendant powers to plan and run transport systems and to determine the location of industry, holiday areas, housing estates and new towns. Redcliffe-Maud concedes that the central task in all this, land use planning, has to go to the provincial level and if it is properly exercised, it will determine the use made of the other powers just mentioned. So that any effective devolution in England could not be to the 58 unitary authorities – it would have to be to the non-elected provincial bodies and to the existing *ad hoc* boards, thus at once announcing the emasculation of the elected unitary authorities. When people say the provinces have had no meaning, no impact in their role as planning boards and councils, they are simply pointing to the fact they have as yet had no executive powers and their plans have never got beyond the stage of being interesting suggestions. But had these plans become (as the Scottish plan, The White Paper on the Scottish Economy, 1965–1970 became) government policy, the local authorities would have found that every interesting and important decision had been pre-empted. Planning has been most advanced and effective in Scotland with the major targets accepted by the Government and a series of subordinate plans (for the

North-East, the Borders, Tayside and the South-West) commissioned. If these plans are sound and are put into practice, they decide which small town is to be the conference and cultural centre, which is to have a theatre and swimming pool, where industry is to go, which of the three or four through roads is to be developed and so on down to such detail as the style of lamp posts in the main streets. What then is left for local government? Either rebellion, an expression of irritation that no elected councils were ever consulted when the plans were made, or acquiescence, in which case there is precious little left for the local authority to decide.

It is interesting that Mr Senior, in his *Memorandum of Dissent*, after his brilliant attack on the 58 unitary authorities, mentions a 'second best' alternative in the form of 12 to 15 directly elected provincial units in England (paras. 493–504) but he does not pursue this because the possibility of such a solution would depend 'on how much power central government was prepared to transfer to local government'. He concludes that any positive transfer is unlikely (and in any case must await the report of the Crowther Commission) and so he leaves the important functions which must be handled at a provincial level to a council nominated by the central government working with a Minister of State and a regional arm of the central government. Thus Mr Senior appreciates that these are vital local functions which vary from area to area, that the province is the best unit for settling these issues but since he does not believe that central government will ever hand over these powers, he creates a regional set-up within a UK Ministry of Regional Development.

B. Foreign experience This problem of the degree and form of devolution, whether it is to be bureaucratic or democratic, has arisen in most major European nations. In Italy, for instance, there are five 'autonomous' regions – Sicily, Sardinia and three minority language areas on the northern border – but the Italian Government has decided to proceed and carry through the division of the rest of the country into fourteen provinces with elected councils, each responsible for communal boundaries, urban and rural police, fairs and markets, health and hospitals, vocational training, town planning, tourism, agriculture, forestry and fishing, quarries, regional bus services, roads and other public works. The provinces will receive a quota of central taxes and have powers to levy certain taxes of their own. Coordination with central government policy is to be achieved by the appointment of a commissioner in each province who can ask the Provincial Council to reconsider a law. If it is passed again by the Council, the central government can submit the law to the national parliament and to the Constitutional Court.

The interesting aspect of the Italian case is that in the five regions where elected Provincial Councils were set up fairly rapidly after the war, there were special social, cultural, linguistic or economic reasons for discontent and these sentiments were met by economic aid and by concessions over local self-government. The war ended, for instance, with a Sardinian independence party contesting elections but after twenty years of a local parliament and a combination of central government aid and local detailed economic planning, this sentiment disappeared. But Italian governments were reluctant to grant a similar measure of devolution to the areas of Italy where such special conditions did not exist largely because the Christian-Democratic majorities objected strongly to the prospect of certain provinces being Communist controlled. Civil servants also were dismayed by the prospect of the extra time and energy that would be needed to secure co-operation and to remedy the anticipated incompetence of the regional governments. The tide has turned on these issues in the late 1960s because the Socialists in the central government have insisted on the importance of local democracy and because the civil servants have learnt, particularly from the example of Sardinia, of the value of local co-operation and enthusiasm in regional planning.

In France, as the official press release put it, 'from the end of the Fourth Republic, the complexity of the administration, a source of paralysis and confusion, impressed upon those responsible for the public welfare the need for profound reforms and one of these reforms was a stronger regional element. Decrees of 14 March 1964 made the prefect once more solely responsible for state services, the sole representative of the Government in each of the eighty-seven *départements*. The object was simply increased efficiency, and for the 'vertical' or functional approach from Paris, a 'horizontal' conception of administration was substituted which made the prefect the promoter and co-ordinator of the administrative life of his *département*. The prefect's powers did not cover military services, the law, education, assessment and collection of taxes or factory inspection. But on all other internal administrative matters, such as housing and social security, the senior officer of the ministry in the *département* held his post under the prefect. In practice this meant that there were eighty-seven centres in France for detailed local planning for the kind of joint social service administration recommended in Britain by the Seebohm Committee, for police and for supervision of the local authorities.

But there was also a larger unit, these *départements* being grouped in twenty-one regions, which dealt with broader economic planning. The origin of these was a decree of 7 January 1959 which ordered the Paris ministries to group all their administrative regions so as to create 21 regions with economic affinities which could help work out the local implications of the national plan. The distinction between the *départements* and the regions is almost exactly that between the proposed unitary authorities and the provinces outlined in the Redcliffe-Maud Report, except that in France both were to be levels of delegation from the central government, neither level being elected. But the regional prefect was to be assisted by an advisory body, the commission on regional economic development, almost exactly parallel to the British planning councils. The Government said it 'did not wish the work of this body to take on a political character and to run the risk of overstepping the bounds of its competence'.

These reforms met with some criticism in the early and mid-1960s. Some of the critics wanted regional assemblies elected by universal suffrage. As with the UK, where the pressure has been strongest in Scotland and in Wales and in Italy where regional assemblies were conceded to Sardinia and Sicily, the spearhead of the demand for more democracy was the *Comité d'Etudes et de Liaison des Intérêts Bretons*. There was a real opposition to the attempt to run the regions from Paris and to emasculate such feeling as there was in Brittany and other parts of the West by making the local leaders members of the regional advisory commissions. General de Gaulle felt this pressure and when his régime was threatened by the *évenements* of May 1968, he promised more democracy on three fronts – in the universities, in industry and in the regions. Then the struggle began between those who wanted real decentralisation and regional democracy and those who agreed on local variations of central policies but wanted to leave it all to the prefects. The democrats won and their ideas were put to the voters in the referendum which de Gaulle lost, the tragedy being that the polls showed that the public sympathised with the regional reforms but resented the proposals to weaken the Senate and, indeed, regarded the referendum as a call to show a confidence they no longer felt in de Gaulle.

Germany is the most decentralised of the major European powers and some commentators have said that the system is no longer accepted by many Germans. In fact, this is most superficial. The ten Länder governments are responsible for most internal administration and the Federal Government has no civil servants in the Länder – it can only operate through the states. The merits of the system are that it has created (or restored) real diversity to Germany with a cultural capital in Munich, a journalistic centre in Hamburg, an industrial centre in Dusseldorf/Essen while only the diplomatic corps and the federal civil servants sit in Bonn.

The critics of the system never suggest that Germany should be run totally from Bonn. They argue that the basic law setting up the federation is too hard to change and they would like now, for instance, to alter it in one respect so as to permit a single system of higher education. Also the land boundaries are not satisfactory, the weaknesses being that two of the states, Hamburg and Bremen, are city regions. This is found to be impracticable in terms of planning transport and overspill, so that there is agreement that provinces combining town and country are best and proposals have been put forward to cut the number of states to eight or even five. Then there has been some local criticism of the annual wrangle when the richer Länder have to give up a portion of their revenue to their poorer brethren. But all this does not mean that a decentralised system is disliked. Indeed the most extreme critics simply want to have a smaller number of even more powerful Länder with higher education as a federal function.

C. Horizontal or vertical Thus European experience confirms that there are two central issues; whether medium sized industrial countries find it more satisfactory to organise their detailed intervention in the life of the community on a functional or vertical line of command radiating from the centre or whether it is preferable to carefully set aside certain groups of decisions to be determined locally on a horizontal basis and, secondly, whether the local determination should be by civil servants alone or whether the people of the area should be involved. The case for the horizontal approach in terms both of decongesting the central government machine and of making local democratic participation possible, has already been argued. But critics will say that it is more desirable to make people think about functions – education versus roads, industrial aid versus housing – rather than to encourage them to quarrel over such medieval hang-overs as the shares of public expenditure to be allocated to Brittany, Calabria, Bavaria or Wales.

The point is that no political system removes all sources of friction and the form of institutional organisation plays up some conflicts and buries others. If a country's unity is precarious, and there is a real danger of secessionist feeling arising, forms that emphasise a common national purpose might be most desirable. This is not, however, the case in Britain and most European nations also find that to go in the other direction and to try and submerge local feelings only produces political outbursts which may in time take the separatist form which is regarded as undesirable. There is a paradox here. Countries and continents are becoming more alike. Customs, consumer goods and culture are tending to be less and less local and the room for variations in standards and methods of administration is equally decreasing. But at the same time in all modern countries, government action is having a much greater effect on the life of the various subordinate communities so that citizens, relieved of the immediate struggle to stay alive, are increasingly free to and capable of reacting to, commenting on, even sharing in deciding the form which government intervention takes.

So it is true that regional governments in Britain would bring to the surface disputes about the share-out of resources between the various parts of the UK – but these disputes are going on already and against a background of ignorance breeding suspicion. At the same time, the battle over priorities would be shifted from the national to the regional level, but why not, especially when the priorities do differ a little between regions?

How would a system of devolution work in Britain?

The first point is that it need not be uniform. As in Italy, it might be reasonable to give a Scottish assembly powers over the legal system (which would be undesirable in England) because Scotland has a separate legal tradition. Nevertheless, the major powers of Scottish, Welsh and English provincial units would be much the same, concentrating on economic and land use planning and all the powers in housing and transport that go with planning together with the wider local government powers and the tasks (hospitals, countryside preservation, river purification, etc.) at present given to *ad hoc* boards. It thus seems best to explain the system in a general way rather than to single out special features that might apply only to Scotland or to Wales.

A. But, in considering all the main proposals, it is worth commenting on one that has been made only in connection with Scotland. This is that the Government could review the legislative proposals coming forward for Scotland, decide which were of UK importance and keep these for debate in Westminster but leave to a Scottish elected assembly the task of debating and passing those items which were purely Scottish and raised no issues of principle for the whole country.

This proposal would be both unworkable and undesirable. It assumes that the process of legislation actually takes place in the legislative chamber whereas in fact all the major states in preparing legislation take place previously in negotiation between the departments concerned (often including the Treasury) and the outside interest groups. Thus either subjects would have to be handed over to a Scottish Government *in toto* long before any legislative proposals emerged or else the UK Government would have to make all the major decisions and then hand over what was virtually a finished product for rubber stamping by a Scottish assembly. If the assembly proposed changes in such bills, would they go back to a UK government for re-negotiation or would any changes and their financial consequences be accepted? It would be impossible to set up an elected political leadership in a province or in Scotland without giving them a series of regular tasks for which they were politically and administratively responsible and on which their officials could develop a regular expertise.

B. A second series of proposals have come from the Liberal Party, *The Scotsman* newspaper and other sources suggesting something on the lines of a federal constitution. This could either treat England as a single unit or divide England into a group of provinces, in each case treating Scotland and Wales as separate units. The objections to this proposal have been set out in my book, *The Devolution of Power* (pp. 170–6), but basically they are that it is impossible to make a clear division between functions so that some can be allocated to the central and others to the member governments. It is equally impossible to make such a division of the sources of taxation which would give both governments distinct, equitable and equally buoyant sources of revenue. The idea that this was possible arose in the eighteenth and nineteenth centuries when governments did far less and were not deeply involved in the economy, in planning and in welfare and were not themselves producing and spending a large portion of the GNP. Even in the 1880s, Gladstone and his successors found the task of making such a division for the purpose of the Irish Home Rule Bills almost beyond them. The last attempt was the 1920 Government of Ireland Act which has been so modified by custom and convention as to produce a sharing of powers which were, by the Act, allocated completely to Stormont or to Westminster. Above all, as the continental countries have found, powers of economic planning and of financial policy have to be shared, the public's desire for national standards (with different local applications) tends to increase and all these factors make a federal system with a division of powers and of finance written into a constitution unsuitable.

C. Thus any system of devolution has to look at the existing governmental functions and decide which can definitely be allocated to Scottish, Welsh or English provincial governments. There is the problem that too much rigidity in the division causes trouble but also, the lack of explicit delegation of powers would encourage central governments to keep intervening and resuming powers. In the case of the most important functions, there would have to be a split, certain aspects being retained for the centre and the rest left to the local governments. This happens at the moment in both unitary governments (such as the UK) and in federal governments (such as the USA) but in neither is the line of division made explicit. To take the example of education, in Britain it is allegedly given to the local authorities when in practice they have little except minor discretionary powers while in the USA this is in law entirely a power reserved to the states, but Supreme Court desegregation decisions and federal government money for projects in higher education have introduced some federal guide lines. The task of any new system of devolution in Britain is to look at each governmental function in turn and decide which elements can be best decided and administered by governments representing on average some five million voters and which have to be uniform throughout the country and therefore settled in London.

If devolution was being extended to only Scotland and Wales, it would be possible to make the grant of power a little more extensive in that such small states could not afford to face their electors and fall markedly behind the standards being set nearby in England. It is in this way that the position in Britain has determined the practice in Northern Ireland over a large area of decisions which, under the 1920 Act, were clearly allocated to Stormont. On the other hand, this would apply a little less forcefully if there were provincial governments with the same powers in England, though even here, few would care to get markedly out of step on basic standards in health or education. On the other hand, some explicit areas of decision-making would have to be allocated to the regions in order to make it hard (not totally prevent) the resumption of control by the centre, if a matter became politically extremely sensitive. This problem of division is close to the centre of the paradox already mentioned that while the scope for variation in internal policies is declining and voters keep demanding uniform standards, such issues as where a school is to be built, how the bus routes are to be organised, whether education will be more or less comprehensive or 'modern', do concern voters in each area and they wish to have a direct influence on them.

If a genuine measure of devolution is desired, the principles to be pursued in allocating functions or dividing functions are first to devolve as much as possible, recognising that the central government ministries will still exercise great influence by way of research and advice. The second important principle is to achieve a situation where all governmental decisions fall either to the central or to the (upper or lower tier) devolved authorities. There should be no agencies of government or functions left which are not clearly the responsibility of one or other of these elected authorities. The most difficult functions to divide will be economic planning and overall management of the economy together with the allocation of the powers to tax. In the case of the economy, the central government will wish to determine overall levels of public expenditure. It could be provided that the finance ministers of the regions meet the Chancellor of the Exchequer each year to decide on the overall totals for each region for a rolling five-year programme, just as the individual spending ministries reach the same decisions on a functional basis at present. The overall distribution of industry policy would be a matter for the central government but, as in the case of Italy, provincial governments could be allowed to offer minor extra inducements provided these came within the total of public expenditure allotted to the area. Similarly, some tax rates could be varied locally but only if this did not alter the total of demand in the province. Finally, in the case of taxation, the provinces would have to have a (perhaps relatively small) group of taxes left to their own discretion, there would have to be an equalising grant to aid the poorer regions and then a fixed contribution which could, again as in the Italian case, be an agreed quota of the yield of certain nationally determined taxes.

A Scottish, a Welsh and a number of English provincial governments would, under such a system, be empowered to conduct all local organisation of environmental services, roads, transport, urban redevelopment, the allocation of areas for and some aid to industry, the supervision of forestry, agriculture and fishing, the provision of the main health and hospital services, education up to and possibly even including higher education, police, fire and other Home Office services and the arrangement and allocation of functions to a second tier of more immediate local government. Such provincial councils could be elected every three years on a single-member constituency system with roughly double the number of members each area presently sends to the House of Commons. The arrangements for the internal organisation of the councils would certainly be better, as in Stormont, on a ministerial or cabinet system rather than the present local government committee system. Elected members would be expected to devote considerable time to the work and would have to be paid. At the official level, it would be necessary to have local civil services of the same quality as that in Whitehall, recruited in the same way and with equal pay in the senior posts.

The standard objections

Most of the standard objections have already been dealt with in this paper but it may be worth while to summarise the replies.

1. To grant devolution, in the case of Scotland and Wales, would be to take the first step on a slippery slope that would only lead to more and more demands till there was no escape from the concession of total independence. In reply, all the evidence suggests that an adequate level of devolution to meet local demands for political self-management reduces separatist feeling. Possibly the greatest disaster of nineteenth century British politics was the refusal to pass the first or second Home Rule Bills. Had this been done, Southern Ireland might to-day be a contented part of the United Kingdom.

2. The level of politicians available is not good enough to manage such major governmental tasks. It is true that talent does not exist *in vacuo* but there is every evidence from the levels of persons coming forward (e.g. for the Highland Development Board) when there appears to be real powers available, a job worth doing, that able people can be drawn from the reserves of capacity in the community. They will not, however, come forward for time-wasting or pointless jobs.

3. The level of officials would be inadequate. There are some very able men in local government and if they were supplemented by men seconded from Whitehall (which would need less men, as some of its tasks would be devolved) and if new recruits were collected in the same way as for the central civil service, this could easily be remedied.

4. That to divide public expenditure in part on a regional as opposed to a functional basis would show how much the richer areas are subsidising the less-privileged areas and the latter would be likely to get less. But there can be no reason for concealing the real facts from either givers or receivers and knowledge of the extent of the subsidy has not damaged the case put by Northern Ireland.

5. The other objections are all in fact simply reasons why the objectors dislike any idea of devolution. For example, to argue that this would allow regional policy variations is pointless as that is one of the objectives of the policy. To say that the central government could not impose its policies so readily across the entire country is also true, but that likewise is one of the advantages to those who like the policy. On the other hand, it is probably true that once a region had decided on a development, it could move far faster than the present interminable process of consultation between central and local government bodies and between them and *ad hoc* bodies permits.

6. The concession often made in London, that there may be a case for such curious follies in Scotland and Wales, but certainly not in England has also been answered, but the extra point of parliamentary representation must be considered. Northern Ireland receives less than its proper share of MPs at Westminster because it has devolved internal government. To do the same for Scotland and Wales would, in fairness, involve reducing their representation in the House of Commons. On the other hand, to devolve government throughout the United Kingdom would involve restoring Northern Irish representation to the same level as prevails in the rest of Britain.

Conclusion

Two points seem to stand out from this discussion. The first is that in all the major industrial nations of Europe, the question of how much democracy is to be enjoyed in the rest of this century hinges in large part on the question of whether there is to be effective local democracy or whether the application of national policies is to be determined by officials (located either in the capital or in regional centres). In Britain, as in the European nations, the battle is between those who want a fairly large number of units, big enough to be effective agents of central government but not big enough to have real political standing and force of their own and those who want regions capable, to some extent, of pursuing policies of their own. The second major point is that the answer to this debate in Britain seems to be likely to go by default if this and the next government are allowed to proceed from White Papers to Bills and then to Acts on local government reform without awaiting the pronouncements of the Crowther Commission. For this reason, the Commission is respectfully urged to produce an interim report on this issue by the end of 1971.

2.4 Debate on the economic situation (Hansard, *H C Debates*, 8 Nov. 1973)

When the Commission eventually reported in October 1973 the climate of opinion had changed even if the arguments had not. John Mackintosh rose in the House on 8 November 1973 to urge Parliament not to brush devolution aside. Again he was right: within a week the SNP was to win the most dramatic by-election of all – in Glasgow Govan. This previously safe Labour seat in a typically rundown inner city area fell to Margo MacDonald. She won 41.9 per cent of the vote to Labour's 38.2 per cent.

It is a privilege to follow the hon. Member for Oswestry (Mr Biffen) who always makes such a fresh and candid contribution to our debates. His speech matched in thoughtfulness that of the right hon. and learned Member for Gloucestershire, South (Sir F. Corfield), which I thought was also a significant contribution. I was particularly impressed by his point about people walking the streets in the various by-elections now pending, deliberately appealing to the public's quite genuine sense of disaffection with both major parties.

This was something which impressed me in connection with the report of the Kilbrandon Commission published last week. The Commission detected an undercurrent of disaffection with our political system and its institutions, including the major parties. What bothered me about the reception given to the report by the House and by some of the metropolitan Press was the tendency towards cynicism, to brush it aside and laugh at it. The Kilbrandon Commission may have been wrong in saying that the problem of disaffection and distrust could be cured completely by devolution, but it might well be of some help. In any case, it was wrong to brush aside the Commission's diagnosis and not to treat it seriously.

I feel that a great deal of the trouble, as the hon. Member said, is due not so much just to the machinery of Government but to the fact that both major parties have tried to solve problems and have confidently put up solutions, particularly when in Opposition, but have failed to solve these problems when in office. Nothing would be more utterly disastrous for the political system in this country than that a political party should win the next election and again disappoint the electorate. In fact, in recent years, party after party has won elections not as a result of positive enthusiasm but by default, which in turn has led to greater distrust for the party which then won power. This is a most unsatisfactory situation and a most dangerous one. I feel that we are likely to have this happen again by the way in which we are talking about inflation and the problems it produces.

2.5 'The Report of the Royal Commission on the Constitution 1969–73.' (*Political Quarterly*, 1974, pp. 115–23)

The cynicism of Government reaction angered Mackintosh as he noted in his critique of the *Report* of which only a small part can be reproduced here.

This Report (489 pages of text), together with the Memorandum of Dissent (136 pages), the ten research papers and the selection of evidence published contains a mass of ideas and information which will exercise academic students of British government and politics for many years. It is unlikely to lead to any rapid action or to be a major issue for politicians other than those whose constituencies or entire parties are located in Scotland and Wales. The explanation lies in the origins of the Royal Commission.

In 1966 and 1967 Welsh and Scottish Nationalists won by-elections and by 1968 these parties appeared to mount a serious challenge to the Labour Party in its Celtic strongholds. Within the Labour Cabinet, there was a division over the policy that should be pursued. The Welsh Council of Labour favoured an elected Council for Wales but the Scottish Council of the Party, led on this issue by the Secretary of State Mr William Ross, was strongly opposed to anything of the kind. Among the English members of the Cabinet Mr Crossman spoke favourably of devolution, while Mr Callaghan (sitting for a Welsh constituency) led the opposition. The outcome was a victory for those who wanted to do nothing but to resist the pressure, arguing that by the next General Election, the Nationalist threat would have dwindled. Naturally, other more fundamental arguments were advanced, the chief ones being that elected all-Scottish and all-Welsh authorities would only serve to encourage and provide a platform for the Nationalists and that the correct policy for Labour was to capture control at the centre and then push through policies dealing with the entire United Kingdom.

But, having won this battle, the opponents of any measure of devolution felt they had to have some answer to those who pointed to the rise of the Nationalists, who accepted some of the Nationalist arguments and then asked Labour leaders: 'What are you doing about it?' To meet this, it was decided to appoint a Royal Commission with whom the whole subject could be safely left until after the next General Election. If the Nationalists did win a batch of seats, then the Commission's proposals might be considered. If, as most of the Labour Cabinet anticipated, this did not happen then the whole issue could be forgotten. In fact, the Welsh Nationalists took 13.9 per cent and the Scottish 12.2 per cent of the vote in the 1970 General Election and captured only one seat, the Outer Isles, in rather special circumstances.

As a result, the Labour Party breathed a sigh of relief and put the whole question aside. The Conservatives, who had had far less to lose, had also reacted to the Nationalist tide of 1967–69. The Party appointed a Scottish Constitutional Committee under Sir Alex Douglas-Home which reported in March 1970 in favour of an elected Scottish Assembly to share legislative powers with Westminster. There was strong opposition to this idea (on much the same grounds as in the Labour Cabinet) within the Scottish Conservative (till recently officially called the Conservative *and Unionist*) Party and after the 1970 General Election, these elements appeared to be vindicated. The proposals of the Constitutional Committee were allowed to fade into the background.

For the politicians of the two parties, the Royal Commission on the Constitution had thus fulfilled the purpose for which it was created by June 1970 and it might well have ceased work but the Commissioners decided to go on and complete their task. Further evidence that the Government (and the Opposition) had put the question of devolution out of their minds came from their handling of local government reform. The Redcliffe-Maud Commission had stated that there was a case for an intermediate tier of authorities between a reformed system of local government and central government. If these provincial authorities (as Redcliffe-Maud called them) were to receive extra, devolved powers by taking over some central government functions or the tasks of some of the *ad hoc* authorities, then it might make sense to add on some local authority functions and, in this case, the size and role of these local authorities would clearly have to be reconsidered. This argument received much more force when the Conservative Government turned away from Redcliffe-Maud's unitary authorities to a two-tier system as creating intermediate or provincial bodies would then have meant a most cumbersome three-tier structure. This problem comes out most clearly in the case of Scotland where the Wheatley Commission proposed a two-tier structure of regions and districts, one of the regions, the West-Central or Greater Glasgow region, including a vast territory and over half the population of Scotland.

Mr Heath has always been seriously interested in the question of devolution and I put these points to him when it became clear that the Commission on the Constitution would report just before the Scottish Local Government Reform Bill reached the Statute Book (in October 1973) so that changes could still have been made. He replied (May 30, 1973):

> I have considered what you say about the relation between the work of the Commission on the Constitution and the Local Government (Scotland) Bill. The Wheatley Commission touched on the question of devolution in their report . . . but, as you know, they concluded that this was beyond their

remit. We for our part have always held the reform of local government is a matter of importance and urgency for the people of Scotland and that there should be no avoidable delay in putting in hand the complex arrangements needed to implement it. The question of devolution, while clearly a related matter, has always seemed to us one which should be pursued separately, and later, in a UK context . . .

Is anything likely to come of the Commission's Report? The answer already given is 'no'. But two further factors have come into consideration besides the original function of the Commission which was to tide the major parties over the 1970 General Election. The first is that the majority report pointed out that Scotland and Wales are over-represented and that since 1920 Northern Ireland has been under-represented on the grounds that it had regional self-government in internal matters. If the Commission's proposals were carried through, there might be a case for under-representing Scotland and Wales because they had a measure of internal self-government but there was certainly no case for continued over-representation and no case for different treatment for Northern Ireland. If strict proportion to population was observed, Scotland would drop from 71 to 57 MPs, Wales from 36 to 31 and the number of Northern Irish MPs would rise from 12 to 17. The result would be to give the Conservatives an advantage, as compared with the present situation of about 15 seats.

While this might have made Conservative leaders more favourably inclined to the Commission's proposals, the Conservative Parties in Scotland and Wales have increased their resistance as it is so evident that the Welsh Parliament would be Labour-controlled and the Scots majority, if not under one party, would be an anti-Conservative coalition. At the same time, Labour support for devolution has increased in Wales and revived a little in Scotland. There is still strong opposition in the Labour Party based on the ideological preference for centralisation and a dislike on the part of locally-oriented Labour MPs for any proposal which would remove their chief topics of interest from Westminster.

Besides this lack of enthusiasm on the part of the main parties, thought was stimulated in that only a week after the Report came out, the Scottish Nationalist Party won the Labour stronghold of Govan. Interestingly enough, the SNP victory was not due to a simple preference for a Scots Parliament but owed much to resentment at neglect and to the desire for a more effective handling of housing and urban problems than either of the main parties had evinced. Also the SNP argued that North Sea oil belonged to Scotland and could be used to raise the Scottish standard of life above that of the UK average. The effect of the Commission's Report has been to put this whole question of devolution back into the centre of political controversy in Scotland and Wales, it has made it impossible to tide the matter over with another Commission 'to find out the facts' and it has provided a platform on which moderate nationalists, liberals and any other third party elements can combine. Together they may provide enough pressure to move the major parties. But actual action in the next few years is only likely if this third-party combination, or any part of it, can win a cluster of Scottish and Welsh seats at the General Election due in 1974 or 1975. It is ironic but probably true that whether they can do so depends not so much on the case for devolution as on the degree of success on the part of the Government in running the national economy and on the part of the Opposition in convincing the public that it could do better. If both fail, even to some degree, there may be sufficient victories by third-party candidates to lead to an element of decentralisation in response to their demand for a reform of the existing system of governing Britain.

Part 3

The Labour Government tries to devolve power

The Labour Party was at last forced to take devolution seriously by the Nationalist upsurge in the two 1974 General Elections. The SNP won 7 seats with 22 per cent of the Scottish vote in February 1974. Opinion polls showed its popularity to be still rising. Everyone could see that another General Election would soon be called by the Labour Government since it lacked a parliamentary majority. Between the two elections, when John Mackintosh was out of Parliament, the pressure for change was real, but the detail of Labour's eventual – and ultimately unsuccessful – proposal was not yet set. This was the ideal time for bold and imaginative thinking. During these months Mackintosh wrote a series of three lectures under the general title, 'Setting Up a Scottish Parliament'. They are published here in full for the first time. Framers of future devolution proposals could learn much from them.

3.1.1 'What kind of elections and MPs? Will it make any difference?' (*'Setting up a Scottish Parliament'* 1975)

If, despite all the difficulties, a Scottish Parliament is established with the full powers at present deployed by St Andrew's House, with some of the functions of the UK economic departments and adequate financial resources, is the institution likely to last? Is the position of 'more self-government without total independence' a stable one which can attract public support and retain reasonable stability over a period of time?

The evidence from the various federations in the western world, where the position of the subordinate assemblies or parliaments is often buttressed by special constitutional provisions enforced by a supreme court, is that there is a drift of power back to the centre. The regions find certain functions too expensive for them and accept loans or grants in return for implementing a uniform, nation-wide scheme (for services such as health or the provision of unemployment benefits). It is not always clear that the regions or states produce an adequate standard of political life, though national leaders have come from the states in the United States, Canada and Germany. But is a new Scottish Parliament, created not so much for its own intrinsic virtues but to ward off nationalist pressure, likely to attract the kind of people it needs and will it be able to avoid having its powers sucked back by Whitehall and Westminster?

On the quality of people available, at present there is no group or coterie in Scotland with experience of governing at that level – for obvious reasons. Many in other walks of life have shown an interest in the idea of a Scottish Parliament, but it must be remembered that the candidates who are likely to win the elections will have to come through the political parties. The elections are likely, at least at first, to be lively. Electors will be mobilised by the party machines on the basis of traditional loyalties and it is hard to see many independents being successful. So the question is, how many of those who have an interest in standing are prepared to go through the humdrum work of party meetings and accept the limitations imposed by membership of a party in order to be able to play a part in the Scottish Parliament?

Then there is the problem of which system of election should be adopted. The Labour Party has declared itself in favour of the present single member constituency as it is familiar and would, they think, give them a large majority equivalent to their majority among Westminster MPs (41 out of 71). But the system only just managed to produce this result with the Labour Party getting 36 per cent of the SNP collecting 30 per cent of the votes cast. According to the present timetable, the elections for the Scottish Parliament should take place in the spring of 1977. If, as seems probable, there are two difficult years with living standards not rising (or falling), serious inflation and unemployment, it only requires the SNP to pick up 3 per cent and the Labour Party to drop 3 per cent for the single member system to produce a nationalist majority in the Scottish Parliament.

It may seem cynical to evaluate electoral systems on the likely results but when the main object of creating a Scottish Parliament is to establish a satisfactory political situation short of independence, it would be foolish to proceed in a manner which produced the opposite result, a Parliament whose majority did not seek to satisfy the desire for more self-government but to arouse and stimulate a more extreme passion for total separation. Even if the Labour Party won a majority in 1977, with the SNP clearly the main opposition party, in time there would probably be a reaction against the majority and this would then give the SNP control. Also, part of the object of setting up a Scottish Parliament would be to involve the SNP in the practical task of governing the country. The value would be that the nationalists would then become involved and, it would be hoped, immersed in housing, education, Highland development and so on, so that a combination of arguing about these issues and of visiting London and Brussels to coordinate policies and compare plans might convince them that the days when small countries can maintain the fiction of national sovereignty are over.

For all these reasons, a system of proportional representation would seem to be best. It would mean that the SNP would be likely to be part of the Scottish Government but they would have to share office with one of the parties which was keen to make the Scottish Parliament work and establish itself as a viable institution. At the same time, it would be important to avoid the kind of proportional representation system which leaves the party machines in complete control of the list of candidates. A system of largish constituencies with several members elected on a preference vote or a combination of single member seats plus a national list allocated on a proportional basis (as in Germany) would seem to be best. It would also be important to ensure that Westminster MPs could stand for the Scottish Parliament. Some in the minority parties and some in the major parties whose chief interest is Scottish domestic affairs would want to double up (as Gerry Fitt, MP, did when Stormont was in existence). If there were some Westminster MPs, some regional councillors of the calibre of Geoff Shaw or Peter Wilson, and some of the prominent figures in other occupations who have political affiliations but have not yet stood for office, then the new Parliament would get off to a good start.

The question that remains is whether the Parliament led by the Prime Minister and Cabinet it selected could do enough or have sufficient impact to build up public confidence and become an accepted and valuable feature of Scottish life. It must be appreciated that such a Parliament would not have a markedly greater share of UK resources to devote to Scottish affairs. The Kilbrandon Commission pointed out that if UK expenditure per head on the kind of functions that could, in a maximalist solution, be devolved to a Scottish authority was taken as 100, then Scotland, in fact, got the most of any part of the UK at 129 per head. For political reasons, it might be sensible to earmark part of the revenues of North Sea Oil for the Scottish equalisation grant but, whatever the source, so long as this remained a United Kingdom, no one area is likely to be more than 29 per cent per head better off than the average.

If there were, therefore, no extra resources available so that Scottish school teachers could not be paid more than their English counterparts or more motorways built than had been planned or a sudden leap forward made in the provision of health centres, what could a Scottish Parliament do that was new or distinctive? The answer can only be in terms of its capacity to handle matters better than the present system.

Take, for example, the management of Scottish education. Just now, it is hard to say who takes the decisions or provides the leadership. One thing is clear. The Scottish politicians can contribute little. They have, perhaps, one 2½ hours debate a year on the subject plus some questions. Cooped up in Westminster during the week and running from one constituency engagement to the next at weekends, they cannot really be in touch with all the aspects of the educational scene at home. As a result, Scottish educational policy muddles through as the consequence of English decisions, Scottish local variants proposed by the inspectorate, by the St Andrew's House civil servants with some ideas coming from the Universities, the Colleges of Education and certain influential teachers. But it is a confused process without any central point or focus and with no one responsible for imposing any pattern or coherence.

A Scottish Parliament with a full-time Minister of Education and, it would be hoped, a Select Committee on Education, would provide a centre and a stimulus for thought on Scottish educational questions. Then the unrest which largely escaped public notice and erupted in the recent industrial action over pay might have been understood and the blunders over teachers' pay avoided. In any case, Scotland would have had its own version of the Houghton Committee with the profession and Scottish political leaders fully represented so that our needs and timetable would have been the first priority.

Such examples could be multiplied. The Health Service in Scotland is run by a complex mass of cross consultation between the various professions, the Area Boards and the St Andrew's House Department. Because there is no centre of political authority which can listen to the various arguments and then take decisions, most moves can only take place on a basis of total consensus. So everything is slowed down; the capacity to impose a veto is more important than giving positive leadership. To give one example, to change half a dozen empty and closed maternity beds in Peebles Cottage Hospital to geriatric beds (where there is a queue of patients waiting) takes 18 months of consultations.

But, while it could do many things so much better by having the time and the capacity, a Scottish Parliament could not regenerate the Scottish economy if the UK was in a depression. Much could be better done with existing aids to industry. The Regional Employment Premium, at present, is given to all in industry so that this lavish subsidy is doled out to the oil companies in the North East who do not need a penny of it and less is available for struggling firms in remote areas far from the oil boom. Nevertheless, while existing monies would be better used, Scottish wages, investment and employment rates would still be dependent on the conditions prevalent in the UK economy.

And this is, in fact, the central point. Most of the drive behind the SNP has come not from a desire for a Scottish Parliament but from disappointment over the performance of the UK economy. If there was a continous boom, then the problem in political terms would probably disappear whatever institutional reforms were introduced. Yet it is a pity not to make the best of even the most depressing national problems. If it is accepted that greater self-government in the countries (and English regions) of the UK is desirable then it is a mistake to quibble about the particular conditions that might make the necessary changes politically acceptable.

But it must be appreciated that there are also greater dangers. This policy of devolution could have been carried out easily in the early 1960s. After the Hamilton by-election of 1967, it became harder as it had to be done, in part, as a concession to SNP pressure. Now, after the two 1974 elections, it is even more dangerous as a half-hearted gesture, an emasculated Assembly that pleased no one would not meet the basic objectives of more local self-government and would also strengthen the nationalists. It is to be hoped that there is enough political push and realism to get the problem solved properly as a failure now and a franker attêmpt to find an adequate answer after a debacle at the next general election may be impossible.

3.1.2 Is it just a caper? Who is for and who against?'

('*Setting up in Scottish Parliament*' 1975)

What are the chances of the proposed Scottish Parliament having the extensive powers which would, in my view, be essential if it is to establish itself as a vital and effective governmental institution; as a stopping point short of independence which really satisfies Scottish aspirations for greater self-government?

One must be frank. At the moment, the chances appear slight. The most telling weakness is that no senior or significant Cabinet Minister is committed to this policy. The Secretaries of State for Scotland and Wales are the key figures. Both in the past opposed devolution (Willie Ross did so far more fervently than John Morris) and though now both are prepared to accept some move in this direction, there is no suggestion that they will do battle for the maximalist solution. Nor will Mr Edward Short. On the other hand, a number of English ministers regard the whole exercise not merely as a concession to nationalism, but as an unfortunate tendency where any real changes are likely to have dangerous consequences and must be kept to a minimum. No UK departmental minister will want to lose the Scottish end of his operations and those ministries which are already purely English will want to reduce the risk of a Scottish government engaged on the same tasks embarking on embarrassing experiments or alterations of priority.

With no minister strongly committed to the policy, much will depend on the civil service and it seems likely that the only coherent proposals around which the arguments will take place will be those contained in the papers put up by Whitehall and by St Andrew's House. For a while, Lord Crowther-Hunt was in charge of the thinking of this issue but though he is still playing a part in the preparation of the Bill, his chief responsibility is now in the Ministry of Education. Also, his Minority Report to the Kilbrandon Commission shows that he is a minimalist. He wants the main lines of policy on all issues to be reserved for Westminster and Whitehall. He considers that a Scottish Assembly (as he would call it) ought to operate through committees rather than through a cabinet system and that the Assembly should look more like a large county council than like a subordinate parliament.

Given that these are the views of the chief expert among the ministers concerned, will there be any pressure for a more thorough-going solution from the civil service? It is to be feared that though many in St Andrew's House are as Scottish as a Burns Supper, they may shy away from recommending a maximalist approach. The reason is clear enough. These very able and dedicated men are not diverted by party loyalties or by any idea that they are part of a UK governing elite. They have only one loyalty and that is to the task in hand. They want to see Scotland well governed. When I put my fears about the attitudes of Scottish civil servants at a seminar in Edinburgh University, a senior official rose to correct me. He said neither he nor his colleagues objected to working for a Scottish Cabinet, provided they were satisfied that it could do the job.

And are they so satisfied? There are many reasons why they may well have doubts. First, they may fear that the calibre of those elected will be inadequate. One of the basic ideas of the recent reform of local government was that given greater powers and more freedom from central government control, a new, more capable and more representative people would be attracted into local government. But, in the event, the civil service refused to diminish its power to guide and control the regional and district councils and, looking at the composition of these councils, they may well feel that their caution has been justified. They may fear that the Assembly will be composed of Glasgow Corporation and Strathclyde Regional Council rejects, a few landed gents and a large number of SNP members who would have a vested interest in the experiment failing.

The other source of civil service advice is the Whitehall Departments. Recently, I was invited to lunch by a minister at the Civil Service Department in London to meet his staff. Before any introductions, I asked a senior official what he did. 'Oh,' said he with a grimace, 'I am on the devolution caper.' 'Do I take it, you would define the word "caper" as an essentially silly and meaningless performance conducted simply for the effect it has on those watching?' 'That sums it up perfectly,' he replied. While the advice of St Andrew's House officials is of paramount importance when the transfer of Scottish Office functions to the Assembly and its leaders is being settled, Whitehall's views will be taken into account when those powers currently exercised in Scotland by the Departments of Trade and Industry, of Employment and Productivity, of Energy and of Transport are being considered. Above all, the two Whitehall Departments that will matter are the Civil Service Department which will be commenting on the impact of the proposals on the structure of government and on the civil service itself and the Treasury which will be concerned about the amount of money a Scottish Government will have at its disposal and its capacity to act in a manner which might not fit in with the economic policy in vogue at any particular time in London.

On the first point, if all the powers of St Andrew's House are transferred to the Scottish Assembly and Executive, then does Scotland have a separate civil service with its own recruitment? Will this end the practice, from time to time, of transferring senior officials from Whitehall to Edinburgh and vice versa? But if an attempt is made to leave some overall policy powers in agriculture, education, health and housing with the Secretary of State and the London Cabinet, which civil servants will work for him and which for the Assembly's ministers? And can UK recruited civil servants looking to eventful promotion to top jobs advising the Secretary of State or other UK ministers be loyal to a different set of ministers at an earlier stage in their careers? It seems essential to make a split between the officials responsible to different political masters but such a horizontal cut across the functions and personnel of St Andrew's House would create enormous difficulties.

Then there is the question of the financial and economic powers of the Assembly. It is certain that the Treasury would not concede powers to tax or to spend money which would in any way diminish its capacity, real or imagined, to control aggregate demand. The real question is whether the Treasury would still want powers to assent to or refuse particular items of expenditure in order to ensure certain uniform standards and to see that its concept of value for money was enforced. The problem is that the moneys available to a Scottish Assembly would be enough to maintain existing services. To do something new or different would involve either raising more by taxation or cutting existing services or getting a bigger grant from the Treasury. It is hard to see that Department granting much scope in any of these three directions. The Scottish Assembly would be reluctant to levy higher petrol duties, car licence fees or income tax than the rest of the UK while Whitehall would certainly be unhappy at special Scottish policies designed to save money (such as a reduction in the school leaving age). And if the Assembly asked for a bigger grant, there would inevitably be a demand for close supervision of how the extra was spent.

Besides the St Andrew's House and Whitehall civil servants, many others will have doubts about the merit of a thorough-going policy of devolution. The new regional councils will just have started and they will put up a struggle to prevent the Scottish Assembly having powers to alter the framework of local government. But if the present regional system remains, this reduces the scope of the Assembly very seriously. One would expect an Assembly with a desire to be a really effective force would end the regional councils (it could keep them as administrative units with their staff) and have only one subordinate level of government, the district councils.

In addition, the Universities will fear what some of them will regard as 'local government control' and they will struggle to remain part of the UK University Grants Committee system. The doctors, likewise, having fought off control of the Area Health Boards by the Regional Councils, will certainly fight against direct control by elected representatives in a Scottish Assembly. Scottish industry has shown some fear that such a body would be left-wing dominated and might press for a reduced level of economic powers.

Facing all these real problems in creating an effective Scottish Government, together with the opposition of so many articulate and influential pressure groups, there are no senior ministers determined to see that the policy is carried through for its own sake. No one at that level in the Government would have wanted to push through a Devolution Bill had there been no SNP challenge at the last two elections.

Both Mr Short and Mr Fowler recognise that if the Assembly is to achieve its political objectives, then it is pointless to produce such a weak body that no one is impressed or satisfied. The only virtue of a concession to pressure is if the force behind the pressure is diminished. About 66 per cent of Scottish voters in successive polls say they want 'more self-government' but not total independence. The effort of overcoming the very complex problems involved in devolving adequate powers will only be worth while if this section of the populace do feel they have got what they wanted.

3.1.3 'A glorified county council or a proper Parliament?' ('*Setting up in Scottish Parliament*' 1975)

If, by the end of the decade, an effective and respected Scottish Parliament is an established part of our institutional framework, then 1975 will be seen, in this perspective, as one of the formative years. But the events of 1974, the decision taken by the Scottish Labour Party last August, to create an Assembly, the Labour victory (with the SNP coming second) at the General Election in October and the subsequent creation of a Devolution Unit to frame a Bill, will probably only be regarded as preliminary steps in a long and arduous journey.

While the rise of the SNP and the worries of the major British parties have been enough to start the process, it is not evident that there is sufficient political pressure to overcome the very difficult obstacles that remain. The Devolution Unit itself is built for caution, not for speed. It is headed by two English Ministers (Mr Short and Mr Fowler), neither of whom have hitherto taken any interest in the subject and both of whom were clearly appointed to reassure English MPs that no rash steps would be taken. The Scottish and Welsh Under-Secretaries are both genuine devolvers but neither carry great political weight.

In addition, the instructions given to the Unit are contradictory, creating a confusion which helps to conceal some very serious political problems. The first instruction is that the office of Secretary of State is to be retained. But it is quite impossible to devolve political decisions on any reasonable scale to a Scottish Parliament and also to leave the Secretary of State with his present authority. Two different authorities cannot take the same decisions. A Secretary of State could be kept merely to deal with the annual argument about the allocation of any extra funds to Scotland but this would scarcely be enough work to occupy a Cabinet Minister and the situation would lead to constant embarrassment as the Secretary of State had repeatedly to explain that he was no longer responsible for Scottish health, housing, education and so on. If he did remain responsible for overall policy in these fields, this would mean that the Scottish Parliament was allowed only trivial powers and it would build in a constant source of conflict between a minister supposedly still 'Mr Scotland' and a directly elected Parliament wanting to pursue its own policies.

The second instruction is that the number of Scottish (and Welsh) MPs at Westminster must be maintained. Yet both these countries are now over-represented and while it may be possible to make a case for extra MPs for peripheral areas in a united country, it is hard to do so once a considerable area of domestic policy-making has been transferred to Parliaments sitting in Edinburgh and Cardiff. Moreover, there are signs that English MPs of all parties would not tolerate Scottish MPs casting the deciding votes on English health, housing and education, while they were prevented from having reciprocal powers over Scottish and Welsh affairs. Also, to reduce the Scottish and Welsh representation at Westminster to the same proportion to population as obtains in England would, in effect, cut more Labour than Conservative MPs and, had this been done since 1945, there would have been no Labour Governments in 1964 and 1974.

Not only are there these difficulties in the instructions given to those framing the Bill for the Scottish Parliament but there are other major problems that are only just beginning to be appreciated. There is the key question of the functions to be devolved. On this, on the quality of those elected and on the capacity of the Parliament to make some evident impact on the people of Scotland, rests the political viability of the entire exercise. Bound up with this is the further question of the financial resources available to the Parliament, the methods by which it is elected and the overall British political milieu in which the newly established Parliament will have to operate. Now, when the Bill is being framed, is the time when these subjects should be discussed so that the public can form its opinions and exercise a helpful influence.

If the question of the appropriate powers is taken first, there are two clear-cut positions – the minimalist and the maximalist – each based on a fairly coherent philosophy. The minimalist fears that every concession to the case for devolution is likely to produce demands for more. Some gesture must be made to meet immediate pressures but only enough to give Labour (or Conservative candidates) some ammunition while they wait for the British economy, the country's self-confidence and its prestige at home and abroad to revive. This school of thought also fears that any elected authority will consist of party hacks who have not been able to obtain selection for parliamentary or regional constituencies and so its freedom to do damage both in terms of making the nationalists' case and of general incompetence must be severely limited.

This approach wants to emphasise that the elected authority is merely an assembly; the less like a parliament it is, the better. Thus, it favours the committee system rather than the ministerial system (the latter would produce that dangerous exemplar, a Scottish Prime Minister). The minimalists also want to keep the main lines of policy in the hands of the Westminster Government. Education would be devolved but not the fixing of the school leaving age or teachers' pay and conditions. Agriculture would be assigned to the Assembly but not the fixing of those prices which were outside Brussels regulations and so on. At the same time, the regions and districts would be preserved so that the Assembly would be left a narrow slice of subordinate policy-making sandwiched between a St Andrew's House which settled the broad principles of policy and the regions and districts which actually supplied the services.

The maximalist view considers that to grant such limited powers would be to get the worst of all worlds. The result would satisfy neither the devolvers nor those still opposed to any decentralisation, while it would present the SNP with a wide open target for attack. The maximalists would want to give the widest possible powers to a body to be called a Parliament with a Prime Minister and a Cabinet and all the trappings of Westminster. The objective would be to create a body with such scope that able Scots who had not hitherto contemplated a political career would be enticed into standing. Also, once elected, the members, whether nationalist or not, would be absorbed by the task they encountered and not inclined merely to complain about any limitations on their powers. In time, their inclination might well be to ask Westminster to resume certain functions because these were better run on a uniform basis for the whole of the UK or because they were too great a burden on the finances of the Scottish government. Thus, the objective of this approach is to find a viable level of devolution which would last and, far from being a stage on the slippery slope to total independence, would concentrate the Scots' minds on what was best settled in Edinburgh and what ought to be left to London (or Brussels). This would remove any sense of grievance about remote control and, as a result, in the end confirm the unity of the UK.

In the post-war history of federations, there is no doubt that the maximalist view has some validity. Relations between the central and the state governments have varied, but in all countries where there has been a genuine degree of local autonomy the tendency has been for an acceptance of the need for some powers to drift back to the federal government. This has happened in the United States, Canada, Australia, India and West Germany. On the other hand where, as in France, there has been only a limited concession of purely administrative powers to the departments, public discontent has remained and there has been continued pressure for a more genuine form of regional self-government.

The one example there has been in the UK of a local parliament also supports the maximalist case. The Stormont Parliament created in 1920 was an administrative success (the communal political problem was not the product of this institution), it lasted for fifty years and it established a distinctive local role while voluntarily handing back a number of important powers to Westminster. The minimalists will say 'quite so, but why not accept this and arrange by law for the Scottish and Welsh Parliaments to receive only those powers that Stormont ultimately decided to retain?'

The answer is that in psychological and political terms, there is a world of difference between a subordinate parliament deciding, like the German länder have done, that it would be preferable for higher education to be a federal function and for the central government positively to prohibit the local parliament from considering this function. Also, such an attempt to divide each function between the central and the regional parliaments involves too much rigidity and neglects changes in fashion and in the cost of certain services.

So it is to be hoped that the Devolution Bill is drafted on maximalist lines and that the Scottish Parliament is given all the functions of the Secretary of State, including the Scottish end of regional development powers, the location of industry and the Scottish aspect of the Ministries of Energy and of Transport. With such extensive powers, a Scottish Parliament could have real scope and, therefore, a real chance of being a success.

3.2 'A sound basic structure on which to build'
(*The Scotsman*, 28.11.1975)

In November 1975 the Government, then a year into its new term of office, published its first full proposals for devolved assemblies for

Scotland and Wales in a White Paper *Our Changing Democracy*. The devolutionist camp contained more than a few hotheads who denounced the White Paper, as they would have denounced any White Paper, as 'not enough'. John Mackintosh knew it was not enough but he kept his head and welcomed the proposals as a sound basis.

The White Paper is, on the whole, an encouraging document because it has got the basic structure of the future Scottish Government right. The essence is the transfer of control of the bulk of the Scottish Office's powers from Westminster to the new Assembly together with a block grant to be spent as the Assembly see fit on these functions. In practice, policy-making and administration will be in the hands of a Scottish Prime Minister (he is called a 'Chief Executive') and Cabinet.

So the basis is sound. This is what the bulk of the Scottish electorate, who are dissatisfied with things as they are but are not separatists, want. This said, it is unfortunate that there are some potentially dangerous areas of conflict created by the proposals; conflicts which could and should be eliminated during the discussion and passage of the Bill. There are also an unnecessary number of restrictions on the full use of the powers which are devolved, and there remain some functions which ought to be conceded but which are, as the proposals stand, still reserved for Westminster.

The most serious single area of confusion and potential difficulty is over the role of the Secretary of State. This was always likely because the logic of devolving Scottish government to a directly elected body is that this marks the end of the office of Secretary of State as it is now known. But the Cabinet unit who prepared the White Paper were given two explicit instructions to keep the Secretary of State as 'Scotland's voice in the Cabinet' and to leave intact the existing number of Scottish MPs at Westminster.

To achieve the former (the latter point is not mentioned), the Secretary of State is left with a few Scottish functions running the economic powers of the Scottish Development Agency and aspects of agriculture and fisheries. But these do not amount to much, and to build up the post and to make it the link between the Scottish and the UK Government (and the Crown) the Secretary of State is given all the ceremonial and 'continuity' tasks which normally lie with the Crown or a Governor-General. In addition, the Secretary of State has the highly political duty of watching over the Assembly and of deciding whether any of their Acts are to be resisted as 'unacceptable on policy grounds'.

This combination of functions is highly dangerous. For instance, it is given to the Secretary of State to invite the leader of one of the parties in the Assembly to form a government. If, as is quite likely after the first elections, no single party have a clear majority in the Assembly, this capacity to give one or other party first go at forming a government could be crucial, and will anyone believe that a Conservative or Labour Secretary of State could be totally impartial in making such a choice? Similarly, when a Scottish Act seems unsatisfactory to the UK Cabinet, it is the Secretary of State who has to say so.

There is a real risk that if there was, for example, a Labour majority in the Assembly the Conservative minority would invoke a Conservative Secretary of State as their ally in rejecting measures passed by the Assembly. This provision puts the Secretary of State in the role of the House of Lords before 1911 as a kind of one-man revising chamber, with all the possibilities of conflict that that conjures up.

A major objective of a good devolution Act would be to minimise conflicts between the Scottish Assembly and the UK Government. The way to do this would be first to create an impartial office of Commissioner to the Assembly (like the Commissioner to the General Assembly – a Royal appointee) whose task would be to ask someone to form a government after each election on the same rules as are now applied in the UK by the Queen.

On disallowance of Assembly laws, there is no need to have an explicit and provocative category of laws 'unacceptable on policy grounds' (what, in any case, is 'policy'?). It is sufficient that the UK Parliament can at any time impose their laws on the Assembly, but this should be so rare and so serious an event that the decision to act in this way should not fall to the Secretary of State but should be left to the UK Cabinet as a whole.

To reserve some of the powers of the Scottish Development Agency and parts of agriculture and fisheries to the Secretary of State (that is to London) is probably also a mistake. These powers were devolved to the Northern Irish Government with none of the difficulties envisaged by the White Paper. In any case, if the Scots want to spend more on attracting industry and less on some of the social services, why not?

If these improvements were made the office of Secretary of State would virtually disappear, and this must be faced. It is really impossible to have both a Scottish Prime Minister and a Secretary of State competing for the position of the spokesman for Scotland – particularly when they might be from different parties and would have different power bases. This source of conflict can only be avoided by letting the post of Secretary of State fade away.

The other potential areas of conflict are two-fold – over money and over some of the limitations on specific devolved functions. On finance, again the White Paper is broadly on the right lines. The Assembly will have a block grant of about £2000 million and the power to raise a small extra sum by a surcharge if they so desired. The defect is first that the surcharge can only be on the existing local taxation (i.e. rates), and that the form of local taxation is reserved to Westminster.

It is hard to see any justification for refusing to let the Assembly reform the rating system, which happens to be one of the most unjust and regressive of all taxes. And if the Assembly preferred a local income tax, why should their powers of surcharge not apply in this case? One cannot help suspect that the decision to limit taxing powers to a surcharge on rates, at a time when there is a nation-wide outcry about this tax, either is designed to give ammunition to the opponents of devolution or is at least intended to prevent the power ever being used.

The other financial problem is more subtle. In the arrangements for the annual block grant, it is clear that the Finance Minister for the Assembly will have to make a case for any increase. The danger (and it happened in Northern Ireland) is that the Treasury will say: 'Do not talk in round figures. Justify to us precisely how the money is to be spent'. If this happened the Treasury would resume control of all the policy decisions that are, on the surface, devolved to the Assembly. This is why it would have been better to give the Assembly an automatic allocation of a percentage of the yield of certain taxes (such as oil revenues) designed to produce the same amount as the block grant (i.e. £2000 million), so that dealings with the Treasury would only be necessary if there was any shortfall.

Or the devolved functions, a basically bold and fair allocation to Scotland is marred by occasional fits of nerves. For instance, all housing is devolved except rents and aid to mortgage-holders. But why should not the Assembly decide to boost the private sector in housing if they want to do so? This exception would allow a UK Government to impose something like the Conservative's Housing Finance Act on Scotland, which is the kind of issue, whatever the merits of the case, that ought not to be allowed to become a Scotland versus England conflict.

Whoever wrote the section on the Scottish legal system sat on every possible fence, keeping the Lord Advocate a UK Minister, and keeping the Scots Law Commission, the judges, and the courts part under UK and part under Assembly supervision. There are many other examples of unnecessary restrictions of power. For instance, why on earth should the Assembly be refused authority to improve on the highly restricted functions now given by Westminster to the Ombudsman dealing with Scottish complaints?

One could go on like this through many clauses of the White Paper, but to do so would create too critical an impression. The great task in the next 12 months is to iron out the potential sources of conflict and the imperfections in the plan. I believe this White Paper (suitably improved) has the great merit of establishing the right structure for the future Scottish Government with the minimum powers acceptable, and the proposal is also probably the minimum that can be got through the Westminster Parliament.

Those of us who want any form of Scottish self-government ought to bend every effort to getting these proposals enacted and working effectively.

3.3 'The power of the Secretary of State' (© *New Edinburgh Review*, Feb. 1976, pp. 9–21)

One vexed question for any future Scottish Assembly will be the role, after the Assembly is created, of the Secretary of State for Scotland. John Mackintosh's analysis of the proposals in *Our Changing Democracy* is a good starting point for that discussion. His paper 'The Power of the Secretary of State' was originally delivered at the inaugural seminar of the Unit for the Study of Government in Scotland at Edinburgh University.

Ladies and gentlemen, I congratulate this new Unit for the Study of Scottish Government on organising this conference. I suppose something has come out of the whole Devolution Debate when the Scottish universities take an interest in Scottish government, or will begin to do so, and I hope it does not in any way harm their academic purity or damage their international reputation that they are now taking an interest in these problems on their own doorstep. I think it is very important that all of us in Scotland should do this, because we have got it all ahead of us now in the next year, or year and a half, and that is why I am grateful for this whole conference to clear my mind (as well as other people's) and I will try to be as straightforwardly academic in this matter as I can.

Looking at the power of the Secretary of State, I want to begin by making two general propositions which I hope will be accepted. First, it does seem to me that there is no point in the present situation in taking up the argument as to whether we should have a Scottish Parliament or Assembly at all. My own feeling is that the Tam Dalyell/Ian Sproat position that the whole thing is a mistake and should not happen, is out of date. It is politically untenable and it is the one thing that is not likely to happen. I think we are certain to get something. So for the purposes of the moment, let us assume that we are going to get an Assembly and therefore the sole problem is organising it in the most satisfactory way.

On this question of organising the Assembly and arranging its powers and its constitution in the most satisfactory way, the second point is that any way it is done ought to minimise conflict and particularly conflict liable to be damaging to the political set up in the United Kingdom. I am not trying to say, as some commentators try to say, that it is possible to create conflictless situations. All government is a matter of conflict; one organises and channels the conflict. There is tremendous conflict going on at the moment within the Cabinet between expenditure on a functional basis. People sometimes say to me, 'It would be terrible if the Scottish Government and Scottish Parliament has an argument with the United Kingdom Parliament about the distribution of money.' Of course, there will be such arguments and such arguments, as I say, now take place between Health, Housing and Education. Then there is a sub-argument within these functional awards as to how much of Health money will go to Scottish Health as opposed to United Kingdom Health, how much Housing money will go to Scottish Housing as opposed to United Kingdom Housing. It is not possible to have a conflict-free situation in any political structure with scarce resources being distributed, but what one tries to do is to look at the possibilities for conflict and minimise them and particularly to try and exclude them if they are the kind of conflict which will render the system unstable and lead to disputes and arguments which can only ultimately be resolved by reopening the original settlement. So these are my two 'criteria' – the principal points – that there is going to be an Assembly and that we want to minimise the dangerous types of conflict.

Having said that, I want to turn and look at the actual powers of the Secretary of State and just note them down. I hope you do not mind if I give the clauses in the document because I think it makes it a bit easier. If one goes through this document – the White Paper – and looks at the powers of the Secretary of State, one begins first with his powers as a United Kingdom Cabinet Minister – as a normal politician holding a United Kingdom Cabinet post. The relevant clauses in the White Paper specify half the powers of the Scottish Development Agency (Clause 38); the guilding lines on the Highland and Island Development Board (Clause 39); the Secretary of State has transferred to him now responsibility for the Scottish end of the Manpower Services, Training Agency and Employment Agency Services and parts of the Ministry of Employment (Clause 282). In addition, considerable existing powers are left to him. So there is quite an area within the present St Andrew's House powers and some Ministry of Employment powers transferred to St Andrew's House which remain with the Secretary of State in his role as a United Kingdom Cabinet Minister. I will come back to this because one of the difficulties about this particular role is the separation of function within what are presently coherent departments in St Andrew's House.

Secondly, as one goes through the White Paper, there is a second set of functions which I think, without being rude, one could simply call 'wet nurse functions'. Now the 'wet nurse functions' are first of all that the Secretary of State fixes and runs the elections for the Assembly – not merely the first, but subsequent elections (Clauses 34 and 35). He arranges the date, time and place of the first meeting (Clause 36); he arranges the pay and allowances of the members of the Assembly (Clause 39); he publishes and sets up the Standing Orders for the Assembly (Clause 40) and he fixes the number of Ministers – the total number of Cabinet Ministers or Executive Ministers and what are described as Assistants, who are persons to be brought in from outside if there is no competent lawyer or farmer or other person with a needed specialisation. Such persons can be brought in and called an Assistant. The Secretary of State fixes the number of these Ministers and their pay and allowances (Clause 48). These are what you might call the 'wet nurse functions' and the only one that continues after the establishment of the Assembly is the function of fixing, running and organising the elections to the Assembly.

Thirdly, going through them in order, there are what I call the 'vice regal functions' or in some cases they might be called the 'continuity functions' of the Secretary of State. These are first of all that it is his task to invite somebody after the election, presumably in the initial case the leader of the largest party, to form the Government. If that person can collect a Government which gets a vote of confidence in the Assembly, he formally appoints that person as Chief Executive and then formally appoints or endorses his choice as Executive Members and Assistants.

If the Scottish Prime Minister, because that is what he will call himself (not Chief Executive), makes changes and sacks anybody, or demotes them or gets rid of them, these changes are formally made by the Secretary of State. If anything goes wrong with the Government, if it loses its majority in the Assembly and tries to cling to power he can sack the Government – shades of Fraser in Australia – he can get rid of the Government, but it is an important point to remember when considering this question of a breakdown in the Assembly that the Assembly has a fixed term. This is why the Secretary of State is empowered to appoint a caretaker Government while he looks around and tries to find somebody else to become Chief Executive and form a Government.

Not many have realised this feature of these 'vice regal' or 'continuity functions'; namely that they will be more frequently exercised than in the British Parliament at Westminster because this is a fixed-term Parliament. In Scotland, it will not be possible to get out of a difficulty by having an election. The person responsible for continuity has to guddle about inside the Assembly to try and create a new Executive if the existing one loses the confidence of a majority of the members. The question of setting up a caretaker Government and of finding somebody else to take over and form a Government is a very real possibility which could quite conceivably occur several times, or once or twice within the four-year life of an Assembly. Then again, these 'vice regal' functions include the provision that it is through the Secretary of State that Bills go from the Assembly to receive the Royal Assent. The clauses on these functions are Clauses 44, 45 and up to 57 which deal with the Secretary of State's 'continuity' and 'vice regal' functions.

Now there are the fourth set of functions that the Secretary of State has which can be called the 'veto' functions or the 'disallowed' functions – the kind of 'one-man-House-of-Lords' functions. These come chiefly in Clauses 58, 59 and 73. Clause 58 is where it says that if a Bill of the Assembly comes up and is *ultra vires* then the Secretary of State pronounces on this fact and sends it back to the Assembly, asking them to remove the *ultra vires* sections. In Clause 59, which I think in some cases has been picked on by the media as the catch or key clause, it says that if the Bill is unacceptable on policy grounds, the Secretary of State specifies the policy grounds on which it is unacceptable and sends it back again to the Assembly. If the Assembly is not prepared to make the Bill *intra vires* and/or acceptable on policy grounds, then the Secretary of State lays it before the United Kingdom Parliament and asks Parliament to override or annul the action. Now we know that turning to Parliament is a formality because the Secretary of State will be in the majority party, he will have a majority at his command and the whips command the House of Commons, so in effect it means that it is the Secretary of State who disallows bills either on grounds of being *ultra vires* or on grounds of being unacceptable for policy reasons. One key point to look at, and I think this has been missed by some of the commentators, is that it is not merely bills that come under this 'disallowance' power. There is also Clause 73 which provides power either to take over and do or remedy executive acts of the Chief Executive or the Scottish Government – to take over and do them if they are not done, or undo them if they are done wrongly, on behalf of the Scottish Government. That is to say, the Secretary of State can take direct executive action.

This is very, very important because there are a number of functional reservations in the chapter dealing with powers where the Chief Executive of the Scottish Government could extend this power simply by doing what Nixon used to do when Congress tried to get him to do things he did not like – he simply said, 'Right, it is the law, but I am not going to do it'. To give an example, I can imagine a Scottish Government being told that one of the things it could not touch was the Land Commission legislation passed by the United Kingdom Parliament and the White Paper does specify that this aspect of land and land use planning is not to be within its powers. Then the Scottish Government might say, 'that is fine, but we are not going to appoint the civil servants to carry out this policy', or 'we are not going to provide the money to do it'. 'We would rather spend the money in more sensible ways; this legislation can sit on the United Kingdom Statute Book, but as far as Scotland is concerned it is just not going to be carried out.' That is clearly one of the things the Scottish Government could do in this situation and Clause 73 gives the Secretary of State power then to step in and do it for them. He could set up and appoint the necessary civil servants to carry out the Land Commission administration.

There is apparently some doubt in the minds of the people who produced the White Paper as to how frequently this kind of 'disallowance' or 'intervention' power will be exercised. Gerry Fowler has been going around now saying that all this is only a power of last resort; that it would only be used ('disallowance') in the case of a breakdown of relationships between the United Kingdom Government and the Scottish Government. But that is not exactly the position stated throughout the White Paper and I would like to draw your attention to Clause 27 in the centre of the clause where it is talking about the 'disallowance' powers, where it is stated that 'the use of these powers should not be regarded as a last resort or implying a serious confrontation'. So there is a suggestion in some parts of the White Paper that these powers could be used and one could see situations where they might be used, not frequently, but at least not only as a matter of last resort.

I want to mention two other functions of the Secretary of State before I turn to the question of how much conflict his position will cause and what can be done about it. The fifth function is that the Secretary of State is the channel for all communications with the EEC. I do not think that this is terribly important but it is again using the Secretary of State as the main intermediary between the Scottish Government and all external agencies. This is the case in dealing with the United Kingdom Government and it includes all relations with the EEC at Brussels. The final function, and I do think this is important, is tucked away in Clause 285 where it states that the Secretary of State will be the chief person giving advice to the United Kingdom Government on all aspects of Scottish affairs. I think the key point to notice here is that when the block grant comes to be renegotiated each year for risen costs, it is clear that the Secretary of State is going to be deeply involved in this whole question of Treasury control of Scottish expenditure. Any increase in expenditure will have to be justified and the Treasury will want to know whether last year's expenditure was sensibly made on this or that or the other item. In this case, they will turn to the Secretary of State because he will have the civil servants, the advice, the information to give to the Treasury.

He will be partially the spokesman for the Scots, helping the Scottish Assembly and its Executive to get whatever increase in their block grant they want. He could also do an about turn and be the chief person saying to the Chancellor of the Exchequer, 'Don't give it to them for this, don't give it to them for that – they misused it, or overspent this amount last year, or they didn't do the following properly'. So the final function to look at is 'general advice' on Scottish affairs but especially on the block grant allocation, because that is when this function will be exercised in its most acute form.

So there are the six functions that the White Paper gives to the Secretary of State as it stands and you can see that they are very elaborate. What I want to do now is to go through them with you, pointing out the possibilities for conflict and then I want to finish up by explaining how, with one exception, it would be possible to reorganise the whole thing to minimise conflict, to reduce enormously, without substantially altering the distribution of powers between the United Kingdom and the Edinburgh Government which this present Government have set out in the White Paper.

First of all, it is worth examining the possibilities of conflict. I think they are fairly obvious and I do not need to stress them to any great extent. However, notice that as a United Kingdom cabinet minister, the Secretary of State will be running a United Kingdom policy for all parts of Scotland with civil servants in St Andrew's House under his direct control. Presumably there would be some attempt to segregate them from the Assembly's officials. I think it might be a good idea if they were separated because it will be very difficult to have an office where the person in one room is responsible to the Secretary of State who might be a Tory in London while the person in the next room is responsible to the Chief Executive, who is a Labour Minister at the head of a Labour government in Edinburgh. If this happened, they might be suspected of saying, 'Tell your minister in London to stop my minister in Edinburgh doing this and that . . .' I can see all sorts of conflicts of loyalty and difficulty for the Civil Service in St Andrew's House, particularly in ministries like Agriculture and Fisheries which is divided, or in other divided departments such as regional and economic affairs. I think the division of the SDA is highly likely to cause this sort of trouble because the Scottish Government may say, 'We would like to bring certain factories to West Central Scotland', while the United Kingdom Government may not agree and may tell its section of the SDA 'We would rather these factories went to Dundee or to the east coast.' In such a conflict, the Scottish Government has the power to refuse the Land Use plan and to refuse the permission to locate the factories in the east. So there are real possibilities of conflict built in when the White Paper proposes to take what are at present administrative functions totally devolved to Scotland and cut them in half – or cut them in parts – giving one part of the office to the Secretary of State in London and the other part to a Scottish Executive. So those are the possibilities of conflict in the way in which these powers have been allocated.

The 'wet nurse functions' are not important. I do not think they are very significant; I merely think that they emphasise the Secretary of State's role as a sort of 'nanny' of the Assembly and I think they could be unfortunate. As I said, the only one that will continue after the first year is the power to run elections and I think it is not basically appropriate or suitable that these kinds of powers – to run and to look after the conduct of elections – should be with a United Kingdom party politician, or with any United Kingdom cabinet minister. I will come back to this. I think it is a mistake, but I do not think this function is as liable to cause conflict as some of the other functions.

Now I turn to the functions that I think are going to cause most trouble – the 'vice regal' or 'continuity' functions and the 'disallowed' or 'veto' functions. Consider for instance this situation: it is highly likely in my opinion (but whether it is likely or not does not matter), that when the first election for the Scottish Assembly takes place, the result will produce three strong parties in the Assembly and it is certainly conceivable, and one must think of all possibilities, that no party will have an absolute majority. So the election will result in parties A, B and C being returned each with fairly strong representation in a Scottish Assembly, but none with a clear-cut majority.

I think it is very unsatisfactory and even dangerous for the man who has to decide 'do we ask the leader of party A, the leader of party B or the leader of party C to form a government', if this man is himself a United Kingdom politician, who is a close party colleague of the leader of one of these three parties. Supposing the parties draw roughly equal numbers, does a Tory Secretary of State do his job properly and go and ask the Labour leader to form the Government if the Labour party is one or two seats ahead? Maybe he does. Suppose he asks the Labour leader to form a government but Labour has to ally either with the SNP or with the Conservatives in order to form a working majority inside the Assembly and supposing the Secretary of State is a Conservative, may he not indicate a preference for a coalition which excludes the SNP. Even if the Secretary of State is totally silent on this point; if I was the Conservative leader in the Assembly, I would be tempted to say to the other parties – 'Look here, you would get on much better in negotiating the block grant if we were included in this government, because the Secretary of State is one of us. We have got access to the Cabinet and therefore to Whitehall and you have not. If you form a Labour/SNP coalition, you are asking for frightful trouble when it comes to the block grant. Do you think Secretary of State Campbell will go and plug a good case for you when it comes to the block grant if we are in opposition and tell him it is all rubbish?'

That is the kind of problem that is going to arise and it will not merely occur when the Government is being created. It will occur if, at any time during the four-year life of the Government, the coalition breaks up. Supposing there was a Labour/SNP Coalition running the first Scottish Government, I would think it is quite feasible that after a year or two some of the people in either the Labour or SNP parties in Scotland would start to say, 'Look here, what are we getting out of this? It is the other party which is getting the credit and our party is going to pieces. So come out of the coalition at once.'

Remember that this is a fixed term Assembly and it is not possible to have an election to resolve a breakdown. As a result, one of the two parties then has to team up with the Conservatives. But this whole 'continuity' function of setting up a caretaker government and of arranging the negotiations is being done not by an impartial figurehead but under the control or supervision of a United Kingdom party politician. The possibilities for conflict in this situation are enormous and very, very dangerous.

I hope I have illustrated some of the problems of the 'vice regal' or 'continuity' functions and these difficulties get worse when the 'disallowance' or 'veto' functions are considered and it is remembered that the Secretary of State is a United Kingdom cabinet minister, possibly of a different party from the majority in the Assembly. I do not think I need to emphasise the difficulty too much, but let us assume again, for the purposes of argument, a Labour/SNP government with a Conservative Opposition in the Assembly and a Conservative minister as Secretary of State (or it can be postulated the other way round, it does not matter). Then anyone running the Conservative Opposition in the Scottish Assembly would fight fairly hard, but would inevitably be inclined to say, from time to time to the majority, 'You pass this and I will see that the Secretary of State disallows it'.

If the Secretary of State does not disallow it and says, 'I am behaving like a constitutional monarch. This is a disgusting piece of legislation but to veto it would cause a political row between the United Kingdom Government and the Scottish Government – it is not worth it.' What then will the Conservative Opposition in the Assembly say? There will be a terrible row in their party. They will say, 'What do we have you there for; why have we elected a Conservative government; do you mean to say you are going to sit there and leave us to put up with this left-wing legislation?' There will be the sort of row which occurs when the Glasgow Council does not raise rents as the Conservatives would like. Then the Tories from Glasgow pour down to Westminster and demand action. One gets this reaction in both parties. I find in the Labour Party this is a fairly normal situation. If a Conservative local authority does something in Scotland and it is disliked, the Labour minority on the council come to the MP and say, 'For God's sake, John, tell that Secretary of State to step in; what do we have him there for; what have we chosen him for; why is he letting these local Tories get away with it?' That is the kind of situation and the problem is that if the Secretary of State does step in, either on executive grounds under Clause 73 (Executive Acts) or to disallow a bill, then the argument will not just be about the merits of the bill or the action – there will be a conflict about the powers of the Assembly – just the thing one does not want to happen. What must be avoided in a conflict between the Edinburgh Government and the United Kingdom Government in which the Edinburgh Government will say, 'Look, it is not a problem of whether the Bill was a good one or not, the problem is whether an elected Scottish majority is entitled to do the job it was elected to do.'

I do not want to put ideas in Ian MacCormick's head, in fact I know him well enough to know there are plenty there already, but if I was the SNP in a Scottish Assembly and if by any chance on the 'first past the post' system, the SNP got a majority, it is clear what they ought to do given this set-up. The temptation would be to pass lots of jolly laws, doing all sorts of lovely things for the Scots, and then sit and watch them being disallowed by the Secretary of State. Then after they had been disallowed for a year the SNP could say, 'Enough of this damn nonsense. You electors elect us to do a job and we do A and we do B and we do C. Then what is the response of London? – they veto them. This is intolerable. The UK had a Referendum on whether the country should stay in or out of the Common Market. Now we are going to run our own Referendum on whether Scotland should stay in or out of this unsatisfactory union.' This is the kind of conflict that is being set up if the powers of disallowance in the White Paper are put into the Act, this curious mixture of powers given to a person who is a political figure in Westminster and who has also to deal with a political Assembly in Scotland.

So these are the conflict possibilities of the 'disallowal/one man veto' section. I do not think the proposal that the Secretary of State should be the only channel to the EEC matters so much, although it would clearly be better if the Scottish Assembly dealt directly with the various sections of the British Government that were in fact putting the UK case in Brussels. After all, the Secretary of State – and I am not wishing to be personal – probably knows less about the EEC than any other British Cabinet Minister and it would make more sense if the Scottish Government, when it had to deal, say, with Fisheries, dealt with the Fisheries section of the UK delegation at Brussels, because these people would be putting the United Kingdom Government case. It would be more sensible if the Scottish Government dealing with, let us say, a transport matter, dealt with the Ministry of Transport in London, giving the Scottish version of the situation and then the Transport Ministry official or minister would put the case for the whole of the UK in Brussels including any special points which covered conditions in Scotland. I therefore think that putting all the connections through the Secretary of State is clumsy and serves to over-emphasise his position, but it is not of tremendous importance.

The last of the Secretary of State's powers wraps up the others; it covers the 'disallowance' powers and the 'vice regal' powers. This is the advice-giving function. The Secretary of State and the civil servants working to him would give advice to the United Kingdom Government on those matters of Scottish policy on which the central Government should exercise their authority. In particular, I think it will breed trouble between the Secretary of State and the Scottish Government when he becomes involved, as he would be, in fixing the annual block grant, especially if he did not support the Scottish Government's case on this, that or the other request. So I can see enormous seeds of conflict when all these functions are put together in the hands of a politician in the United Kingdom Cabinet. One man is going to be exercising all these powers and his relationships with the Scottish Government are going to be constant, complex and potentially dangerous.

I come to the last section of my talk and I will be as brief as I can. How could one minimise these conflicts? As I said, at the beginning – and I will qualify this at the end – I do not want at the moment to argue for any substantial alteration of the powers allocated between Edinburgh and London. All I am saying is that one could, accepting the White Paper's allocation, arrange the functions in a manner which minimised conflict and allocated these tasks in a way which made it easier for the Secretary of State to perform what was left. Let me deal with the easiest reallocation first.

I begin with the 'wet nurse functions'. These are, I think, entirely inappropriate for the Secretary of State. What I would do with these would be to set up a commission under the Speaker of the House of Commons because such tasks as drafting the Standing Orders of the House, fixing its pay, its conditions, its time of meeting and the conduct of elections are traditionally the kind of things that one gives to an impartial body. I would create a commission under the Speaker and dissolve it after the Assembly got going, leaving the conduct of elections to the various bodies who provide the administrative cover for existing general elections.

Turning next to the 'vice regal/continuity' functions. I think these ought not to be performed by a politician for the reasons I have given you. I find that when I have argued this case with Edward Short, he is particularly insistent that the Queen should not perform these functions because it is she who performs them for the United Kingdom Parliament and he is particularly keen that the Assembly in this case ought not to be on the same footing as Westminster. This is all part of the attempt to stop the Assembly looking like a full or proper parliament. This is why the head person is called a Chief Executive, not a Prime Minister, it is an Assembly and not a Parliament and all the rest of it.

I think that none of these attempts to downgrade the body that is elected in Scotland will work. It will call itself a Parliament. The leader will call himself 'Prime Minister'. If the Assembly has any sense, it will rig itself out with maces, Black Rods and the lot and try and look like a Parliament. When the Assembly is set up in this way, I think that the question of who should perform the 'continuity' functions becomes simpler and I would have thought that if there is an insistence down south that the functions cannot be performed by the Crown (and there will be more to these tasks because of the fact of the fixed term point that I have made), then all that is necessary is to appoint somebody who is clearly a senior, impartial person.

The Crown manages this perfectly satisfactorily when a Commissioner is appointed to watch over the General Assembly of the Church of Scotland. I would not call the person a governor, or a Governor General, because that suggests executive functions which are out of date, plumed hats and all that sort of thing, but I would just appoint a Commissioner. A senior person, presumably an ex-politician now accepted as a non-party figure would meet the case. The Commissioner's function would be to ensure continuity. He or she should be free from any charge that in asking A or B to form a Government, that he was acting in a manner designed to benefit his own party in Westminster or its political position. So I think these functions can be easily taken away and they are not normal functions for a Cabinet Minister to exercise under any circumstances.

Now there are the 'disallowance' or 'veto' functions and I am not suggesting, as I say, for the moment, that there should be greater scope given to the Assembly – although one can of course argue this case. I am simply considering an alternative to having these powers exercised by the Secretary of State. First of all, as the White Paper admits, United Kingdom law passed by Parliament will be superior to any Scottish law passed by the Scottish Assembly, so that there is no need for a 'disallowance' power. Just as the United Kingdom Parliament abolished the Stormont Parliament when things had reached breakdown point by simply repealing the Act of 1920, so any United Kingdom law which says 'this law applies to Scotland' applies to Scotland. Thus there is no need for them to take a special power of 'disallowance' on policy grounds. The whole issue can simply be left out and that would make such a veto much more definitely a matter of last resort.

On the question of *ultra vires*, Professor Mitchell is going to say more about this when he comes to make his remarks, but it seems to me that this is much better left to a court. This is a question of law – is the power in the Act or is it not in the Act? So the solution is to leave *ultra vires* to a court and to leave policy disagreements just to the fact that United Kingdom law is supreme. When it comes to the question of interfering with executive acts of omission or commission of the Scottish Government, I think that it has simply to be cut out. It is not desirable to intervene in this way or there will be constant political crises between Edinburgh and London. On this particular matter, on the omission and commission of executive acts, I think the way to solve this is to clean up some of the present functions of the Scottish Office that have been split. These are cases where there has been an unnecessary reservation of functions – particularly minor subsections of functions – to the UK Government.

On the sixth function, particularly giving advice on the size of the block grant, I think this can be avoided by doing what the Kilbrandon Commission recommended and setting up an Exchequer Board. I think unless you set up an Exchequer Board which mediates between the Scottish Government and the United Kingdom Treasury and particularly stops the United Kingdom Treasury supervising expenditure down to minute details before it is prepared to increase the grant for the following year; unless that is done, there is no real freedom of action given to the Scottish Government and the scene is set for constant conflict.

I have tried to show that it is possible to reorganise these functions without changing the basic structure of the whole plan. All these functions can be taken away from the Secretary of State, leaving him purely as a United Kingdom cabinet minister and that I think is the one function which he should have. The only question therefore that remains is whether it is desirable to keep the Secretary of State as a United Kingdom cabinet minister? This is the one area where it is open to argument whether the distribution of functions is correct and I now want to consider this point. I do consider that the powers reserved for the Secretary of State are unnecessarily large and as I tried to indicate at the beginning of my remarks, will cause great difficulty when they necessitate the sub-division of a department or of an agency. Relations would be particularly difficult if there was a difference between the policies of the Assembly and the UK Government since the latter could use its powers to thwart the operation of the Scottish section. I think this is most unsatisfactory. It does not make sense to me to have a group of functions which administratively are devolved to a Secretary of State, but are not considered suitable for political devolution to the Assembly. The general principle that if something can be run separately for Scotland as an administrative package, then it makes sense for this to be transferred to the Assembly. The chief weakness in applying this principle, which appears throughout the White Paper, is its assumption that if certain things need to be done uniformly throughout the UK then it is unsafe to leave such matters to the Scottish Assembly. I think this fear is misplaced because the pressure for uniformity in these matters is a real pressure, a pressure from consumers, and such pressure will affect the Scottish Government as much as it will affect the Secretary of State. For example, I think it is wrong not to devolve the whole of Agriculture and Fisheries; that is the whole of the St Andrew's House Department; simply because agricultural prices have to be uniform. Of course prices have to be uniform, but that will be as clear to Scottish farmers and Scottish administrators and to the Scottish Minister of Agriculture as it is clear to anybody else. The whole of agriculture was devolved in the case of Northern Ireland and there was no problem; they adopted the same prices not for political reasons but for sheer practical administrative reasons. They had to keep level with Britain step by step in the matter of prices. But what devolution did leave them free to do was to run a coherent Ministry of Agriculture and to adopt slightly different policies in those aspects of land holding, of small holding, of agriculture research, of agriculture marketing and agricultural advisory services which were special or which they wanted to run differently in Northern Ireland. I think that is the much more sensible approach. I prefer it to what the White Paper does which is to extract those specific aspects of policy which could be separate in Scotland, or different in Scotland, and give these sections of the present Department of Agriculture to the Assembly, while keeping back the bits that have to be uniform to the Secretary of State. The general principle should be applied – 'If it is reasonable to run a Scottish department now, devolve it, and then let the Scottish Government run any aspects of policy on a similar basis with London departments when these policies are better organised in an identical way'. If this policy was applied throughout the White Paper, it would not lead to great changes but it would lead to the removal of those little reservations that crop up all the way through the document, reservations that look small in the White Paper, but which are politically very dangerous.

So ladies and gentlemen, the changes in content I would propose would in fact remove the Secretary of State's functions as a United Kingdom Cabinet Minister because in fact everything that could be done for Scotland on a separate administrative basis is a suitable subject for devolution to the Scottish Assembly. So the conclusion of this exercise is to abolish the post of Secretary of State. To do so, in my view, would make the position of the Assembly and its Executive as the Government of Scotland much clearer and much more satisfactory. If devolution is to work, there is no place for two governments in Scotland, one by the Assembly and one by the Secretary of State. The former could work reasonably well with a UK Government carrying on what were clearly UK functions in Scotland. This would minimise conflict while to retain a second level Scottish Government in Scotland with its direct functions and the task of supervising what would in this case be an essentially subordinate Scottish Government is only creating unnecessary and potentially dangerous conflicts.

3.4.1 'Making Scottish Parliament more effective than the Commons' (*The Scotsman*, 10.5.1976)

The proponents and opponents of devolution had many arguments to use. Few, if any, however, went as far as John Mackintosh in exploring the ways devolution to Scotland could open the way to reform of the entire UK constitution. The Assembly might have been the forging house of democracy. He explored this theme in the two articles in *The Scotsman*.

One of the exciting aspects of Scottish affairs at the moment is the prospect of creating new institutions hopefully without the blemishes apparent in some of the models presently operating. For instance, there is considerable public criticism of or disquiet about the working of the House of Commons. It is not good enough just to talk about creating a Scottish Parliament. What is needed is careful consideration of the kind of legislature which is desirable, which would attract public support and engage the interest of able people who might then stand as candidates. Ultimately the public's willingness to obey laws depends on the confidence they have in the process by which the laws are made.

It is hard to single out the reasons for the public's lack of enthusiasm about Westminster. Probably the chief explanation is simply the failure of successive governments to provide economic stability and success. But part of the trouble is the procedure of the House of Commons. People are coming to realise that Parliament is so tightly bound to the party battle that it has virtually ceased to affect government proposals, at least by any public process of amendment.

This pattern, that the Government makes its case, the Opposition puts its objections and then the Bill is pushed through, has become totally ingrained in the minds of those in charge at Westminster. This is why last week the Government Whips struggled so hard to resist the argument that standing committees should reflect the composition of the House in which case the Government would have only half the members.

It must be emphasised that these committees do not do committee work in any normal sense. They are miniature replicas of the full House with a Government side, a Minister and a Whip making the political case for a measure, while the Opposition team with its Shadow Minister and Whip batter away and all votes exactly reflect the numbers of each party in the committee. So it was assumed that if the Government lost its majority on all committees, its legislative programme would grind to a halt.

These examples will illustrate the inflexibility of those in control. In my own case, I had taken an interest in the reform of the Scottish licensing laws recommended by the Clayson Report. I took two-all party deputations to the Secretary of State to urge the case for reform. I spoke in every debate on the subject and when the committee was to be set up I wrote to the late Hugh Delargy, Chairman of the Selection Committee, asking to be nominated. But I was exlcuded. 'Sorry John,' Hugh Delargy told me, 'but the Whips seem to think that if you were on, you would vote against them on one or two amendments so you were kept off.'

This attitude is particularly obtuse on an issue like the licensing laws which have never been in any party programme and where members of the legislature ought to be free to act on the merits of the case. Yet those in charge of government business feel it would be a humiliation if they were not able to push the measure through in whatever form the government wanted.

Another example was the Government's proposal for scrutinising laws or regulations coming from Brussels but which were not important enough to be put before the full House of Commons. The obvious solution (adopted in most EEC legislatures) is to have committees on the major topics – agriculture, industry, transport and so on – with powers to collect evidence and then these committees examine the Brussels regulations dealing with their subject.

The British Government would not consider such a solution as these committees might use their powers to probe domestic policies in order to be sure of the impact of EEC regulations. So the Leader of the House made an amazing proposition. He would draw MPs' names out of a hat and thus set up a new committee for each regulation. The committee would sit for an hour and a half and debate the regulation and then be dissolved, fresh names being chosen whenever another regulation came up for scrutiny.

When this scheme was put forward, every MP who took part in the debate except one said it was hopeless. The Leader of the House was begged from all sides, including an ex-Foreign Secretary on his own Back Benches, to take the proposal back for reconsideration. But he refused to budge.

When the vote was called, all those who had heard the debate (64 MPs) voted against the Government but enough members came in from the tea room, their offices and the library to put through the Government's proposal. Again, this was not a party issue. It was purely a House of Commons matter but the Government would not concede an inch.

If a Scottish Parliament is to have vitality and win respect from the public, it must be seen to have some independent life of its own. It must be less dominated by the Government. If this happens and if measures are amended and MPs are given some scope, then the outside pressure groups will not (as in London) prefer to negotiate directly with government departments. They will also seek to influence MPs. If the process of legislation thus returns, in some measure, to the legislature, then the Scottish Parliament will be reported in the media and will come to play a meaningful part in public affairs.

Some may argue that the best way of achieving this is to adopt proportional representation. While they may be right, it is also possible, since the effect of PR is to produce a coalition, that coalition MPs will be as rightly held to a common line as at present simply to prevent the coalition being defeated. Also the proposal in the White Paper for fixed terms is a help as the Scottish Prime Minister cannot then threaten MPs with a snap election if his Government loses a vote. But the real answer is to allow some flexibility through the procedure of the House; to permit probing delays and defeats, at least on matters of detail, without assuming that this is a disaster indicating the imminent collapse of the Government.

The way in which this is achieved in other legislatures is to supplement debates on the big issues on the floor of the House with an effective committee system. The House of Commons is the only major free legislature with no Foreign Affairs Committee, no Defence Committee, no Economic Policy Committee and so on. It is interesting that though successive Governments steadily rejected proposals from the House of Commons Select Committee on Procedure for a proper committee system, this has largely been conceded (in Clauses 76 to 79) of the White Paper in the case of the Scottish Assembly. When I commented on this to a senior Minister, he replied 'you know that these committees will try and pin down the Executive and we don't mind Scottish MPs pinning down Scottish Ministers but we are not having it happen to us.'

Whatever the motives, as far as the Scottish Parliament is concerned, the result is admirable. Permanent committees should be set up to cover each of the major devolved functions such as health, agriculture and education; probably ten or eleven in all.

These committees would have power to call Ministers, civil servants, and outside witnesses before them. They would meet regularly and consider any issues coming up in the area they were covering. When legislation was contemplated by the Government (or by a private member) the first step would be a motion in the House asking 'leave to introduce' a Bill. The need for legislation would be explained in general terms before any measure was prepared or negotiated. Then, if accepted, the proposal would go to the relevant committee which would hear the Government's case for legislation and get the reactions of those citizens and pressure groups who would be affected. If the Committee agreed that action was necessary, then the process of drafting and arrangement of details would take place.

Once the Bill was ready and printed, there would be a debate on the principle in the House, normally with no time limit so that the debate could continue as long as MPs wished to contribute. If passed the Bill would go back to the same committee which would have power not only to inquire into the way the measure was prepared (who got what in the bargaining process) but to amend or pass the Bill clause by clause. Then there would be a final debate and vote on the finished product.

Drawing on recent experience in the House of Commons, one further safeguard is essential. At present members are put on or struck off committees by the Whips who also choose the chairman. It is essential that a method should be found by which those who have won recognition as specialists or as having valuable contributions to make, can become and remain committee members (and not, as at present, often find themselves excluded precisely because they have these qualifications).

The answer is to provide for the election of committee members, in proportion to party strengths, by all the members of the House. This would not only take the matter out of party control but allow a degree of bipartisan appreciation of members' qualities to count in the selection. The committees would then choose their own chairman.

Many other aspects of the procedure of the House of Commons could be improved on when the Standing Orders of the Scottish Parliament are drafted but if this Committee procedure is established, this will be the most important single step towards the creation of an effective, and therefore a respected, Parliament. MPs will have to give time to the committees and there will have to be 'committee days' when the House itself does not sit.

The process of legislation will take longer in the House than it does at Westminster, but some of the time which is now spent preparing Bills in great detail before they reach the Commons will be saved as this work will be done during the passage of the measure. Restoring some freedom in legislation to Parliament should not cripple the Scottish Government; it must still be able to conduct its affairs and be held responsible for the policies it has pursued.

But it does mean that much of the process of arranging new measures at present conducted in secret with the various pressure groups will, in this system, be open to scrutiny by the elected representatives of the public and they will be in a position to see that the views of the unorganised, the citizen, the taxpayer and the consumer, are heard at a formative stage. Governments will still have to govern but they will have to persuade the legislature step by step rather than bang a Bill on the table and ring the division bells. If this can be done, it is even possible that the Mother of Parliaments might be prepared, in time, to learn a few lessons from her youngest offspring.

3.4.2 'Scottish Government must reform government'
(*The Scotsman* 21.6.1976.)

There is no point in creating a Scottish Parliament and a Scottish Government responsible to that Parliament if the result is not an improvement in the running of the country. Scottish government must be more effective, cheaper and more responsive to public opinion.

The tragedy of the recent reform of local government is that (together with all our economic failures) it has induced a mood of total scepticism about institutional changes. All around the country people now say that any change must be for the worse, that increased bureaucracy costing more and doing less is unavoidable. So alter nothing or the result must be worse than the present situation.

The precise reasons why local government reform had such an unfortunate outcome (in England as well as in Scotland) would need a long and careful analysis. It is only fair to spare a thought for those often able and dedicated people who stood for the new councils and suddenly, despite real and exhausting effort on their part, found themselves so unpopular. One major source of the difficulty is that local authorities have had to raise any money they needed over and above the rate support grant. In a period when the national income has declined and the cost of services has shot through the roof, the local authorities have had to cover these costs through the rates. . . .

There is no need here to go into the full explanation of the failure (so far, at any rate) of the local government reform except to make two points. The first is that it has nothing to do with the personal qualities of those elected, most of whom are quite as capable and genuine as either the councillors in the old authorities or the bulk of MPs. The second is that it is a counsel of despair to say that because this and so many other aspects of British management have produced disappointing results in recent years, all change should be abandoned; that there should be no attempt to learn from the mistakes of the immediate past.

In reality, Scottish government at the moment is in a great muddle. It is slow, cumbersome, inefficient and costly and this is due not to the personal capacities or incapacity of those involved but to the application of certain conventions, and to the difficulty of getting the old structure to perform new tasks.

It is essential for those creating the Scottish Parliament and Government to think carefully about these points as the system they are setting up will be judged by how far it can produce better results. And since the Scottish Government will be on a combination of block grant and certain local taxing powers, its financial position will not be able to be sustained by endless borrowing. It will have to cover its costs, and the only way extra money will become available for improving Scottish services will be through higher taxes or administrative economies.

What, then, has caused the difficulties in Scottish (and, almost equally, in British) government? First, there has been the contention that central government – and in our case, the Scottish Office – ought never to operate on the ground. It must supervise, guide, plan, control, show the way but never actually run anything. So the Scottish Education Department does not build schools or hire teachers. This has to be done through an agency; in this case, the local authorities.

From this, several consequences follow. One is that if the local authorities are not suitable either because the areas they cover are inappropriate or because they are not trusted, then new agencies have to be created to do the job. So when countryside problems proved to be too extensive for the old county councils or it was evident that rivers flowed across local authority boundaries, it was thought that special agencies were needed, and the Countryside Commission and a series of river pollution boards were set up.

In the case of health, the local government units are now of a suitable size to do the job but they were not regarded as entirely trustworthy in the health field, so district and area health boards were created.

A further consequence of these developments was that since central government (St Andrew's House, in our case) did not trust this array of agencies, it was felt necessary to employ civil servants to watch over, check and authorise all the decisions which had been delegated to these agencies.

Then there were further problems stemming from democratic theory and from the recent increase in the desire for 'participation'. It was not thought suitable to set up all these bodies spending public money (although always under central government supervision) unless there was some popular voice in their management, some questioning on behalf of the public. This could not be done by parliament as the House of Commons lacks the appropriate committee system. Councils had their elected councillors but what about all the non-elected agencies?

The solution in this case was to appoint *ad hoc* extra committees for consultation and advice. These are nominated, usually by the Secretary of State, and consist of an over-worked trade unionist, a clergyman, an academic, an active woman, a retired army officer, and some people interested in the special activity of the agency. These bodies have meetings, expenses, lunches and so on. They are worthy people but they can contribute little as they are neither full-time professionals on the job, nor do they represent any electorate. So they can offer only a few helpful suggestions.

Finally, on the democratic side, desire for an element of involvement and participation means that the professionals running the services get put on to all sorts of consultative committees whose approval is needed before action can be taken. This has two effects. One is that the more senior people become in any occupation, the more they become involved in something which they should not be doing and are not trained for – administration.

Secondly, when there is a mass of these consultative and professionally involved committees and no clear-cut political lead, no-one at the top to say 'we have heard the arguments and the decision is x; now get on with it,' then it becomes impossible to proceed on any basis other than total consensus. Determined opposition at any point in the system can bring action to a virtual standstill.

What are the results of the kind of administrative pattern which has been built up on the basis of these contentions? The chief result is that it is desperately slow. In part, this is simply because of the number of agencies that have to be consulted before anything can be done. Any decision on tourism, for example, requires the consultation of the district leisure and recreation committee, the regional leisure and recreation committee, the Scottish Tourist Board, the Sports Council and the Countryside Commission as well as the appropriate section of St Andrew's House. Even when the number of agencies is limited, delay is imposed by the need to refer decisions up to St Andrew's House for approval.

For example, recently I was told that the Government had decided to go ahead and build a new district general hospital for the Borders at Huntleyburn. The decision was taken in late 1975 and, it was said, the necessary planning and administrative procedures for a small, non-specialist, local hospital of four wards would then take until December 1980, when building could begin. I was appalled by this, but the special agency set up by the Government (the Common Services Agency for the Scottish Health Service) came up with the following timetable:

1 Schedule of accommodation: March 1976
2 Development control plan: Sept. 1976
3 St Andrew's House approval: March 1976

4 Cost limit documents: March 1977
5 Approval of this by St A. H.: June 1977
6 Preliminary drawings: July 1978
7 Approval of St A. H.: Oct. 1978
8 Completed drawings: Oct. 1979
9 Completed contracts: Feb. 1980
10 Out to tender: March 1980
11 Tenders in: July 1980
12 Approval of St A. H.: Sept. 1980
13 Commence work: Dec. 1980

Besides these interminable delays (and in part because of them), the system is far more expensive than it need be. Time is money in government and it is safe to say that these six years planning for this little hospital will mean that it will cost far more than putting up a pre-fabricated four unit hospital, which would take six or nine months in all. Also all these agencies – there are 60 categories of agencies solely operating in Scotland listed in Appendix E of the White Paper – have to have headquarters, offices, typists, doorkeepers, cars, and most of them have consultative committees with all the expense that they involve.

A last feature is that while the public frets and fumes under the delays and the costs, there is still no feeling of real participation. To have a sense of self-government, the public must know about one place where the important decisions are debated; they must hear about the arguments on television and in the Press and they must know who to blame (and sack) if the decision is unacceptable.

The present arrangements are so complex and private that no-one knows quite how or where decisions are taken and the only recourse is protests, sit-ins, or general dismay once the news percolates out.

What should those constructing the new system of Scottish Government dependent on the Scottish Parliament do about this? Space only permits the listing of a few main lines to be observed.

First, the two-tier system of local government must be abolished. It would be a great mistake to offer another blanket solution – all regions or all districts must go. It will be necessary to look at each area of Scotland and devise a single-tier system of local government that will be suitable for the kind of communities in that area.

Second, the Scottish Government itself should act as a tier of executive government; that is combining the present policy-making function of central government with much of the work of the regions and of the agencies which it currently supervises but does not itself conduct.

Third, the mass of agencies should be abolished, not in the sense that their work should stop or their expertise should be dissipated but they should be gathered into single ministries (for tourism and recreation or for Highland development) each run by a minister in the Scottish Parliament.

Fourth, all consultative boards, commissions and so on would also be abolished, the democratic control coming from Scottish MPs sitting on select committees, one to watch over the work of each ministry.

Finally, this would enable the restoration of a clear distinction between political debate and control (by the Scottish Parliament), the running of the service (by the full-time civil servants) and the professional conduct of the service (by the doctors, teachers, etc.). The latter would give their advice to the politicians so that the public debate would be well informed but the bulk of their time, expertise and energy would be devoted to those receiving the service, the patients and the pupils.

It is vital that devolution does not run into the cul-de-sac of frustration and disappointment that has gripped local government reform. This great step will only be a success if it releases the energy of the Scottish population and ushers in a more constructive, confident and satisfactory period in our national life.

3.5 'Do some Scots dread democracy?' (*The Scotsman*, 13.3.1978.)

The Scotland and Wales Bill failed in February 1977. It was ground to pieces between proponents who did not really know why they wanted this Bill and opponents who had ceased to fear the nationalists and who had always known they did not want devolution. The Government tried again with separate Bills for Scotland and Wales, each of which contained a number of small, but useful, improvements over the earlier Bill. The Scotland and Wales Bills eventually became Acts of Parliament but the Government was forced into undertaking to implement them only if the peoples of Scotland and Wales approved them overwhelmingly in referenda. As the referenda drew closer, the opponents of devolution increasingly made the running and the Government and its allies were short of arguments. In March 1978 John Mackintosh put his finger on the essential weakness in the devolutionists' arguments and the mainspring of the anti-devolutionists' case.

Are people genuinely frightened of democracy, of the kind of representatives their fellow-citizens would elect? One had hoped that as styles of dress became a matter of age-group rather than of class, with widespread opportunities for entertainment, as more and more people could have holidays, buy cars and decorate their houses as they liked, that social harmony would become more evident. And there are signs that this has happened, as when the miners recently rejected pressures from their leaders to fight it out on wages with the Government and insisted on accepting a productivity scheme. The old gaps in our society seem to be narrowing, to everyone's benefit.

Yet, going round Scotland, whenever the subject of devolution comes up, I encounter a major divide or gulf between the reactions of different groups. Most audiences reflect the opinion poll findings of two to one in favour. Too many reforms have been disappointing, too many 'economic miracles' have failed to materialise for people to be unduly optimistic and changes of Government seem remote and mechanistic. But the bulk of electors agree that to devolve policy-making in specifically Scottish matters such as education, the structure of local government or housing makes sense.

But when one encounters businessmen or professional groups, middle or upper middle class people who are in practice running precisely those activities which will be devolved, there is an almost universal hostility to the whole idea and sometimes what appears to be a dread of the outcome. The reasons given are not uniform or clear but concentrate on criticisms of the kind of candidates who would, it is alleged, be elected to an Assembly. It would be bound, these people say, to consist of those with low ability, poor versions of councillors (unnamed) elected to authorities in the Strathclyde Region who might either be extreme Left-wingers or Nationalists, but who, whatever their views, would do enormous damage.

Trying to sort out and understand these fears is extremely difficult but if one begins with an account of the present structure of government in Scotland, there is a broad measure of agreement. Those who express these fears do not want Scotland administered from Whitehall. They accept the case for a Scottish Office with its 11,000 civil servants doing the work of nine English ministries. They accept that over a large area of internal administration in Scotland there are special features which are best determined in Scotland. Then most of them who have had any experience of public administration are prepared to accept two further points.

They realise that a single Secretary of State, even aided by a few juniors, cannot possibly do the forward thinking, encourage and listen to discussion and then take the necessary decisions in all these different branches of activity. Many are prepared also to agree that the mass of nominated executive and advisory bodies (on which numbers of they themselves serve) do also complicate and increase the cost of administration in Scotland enormously. Provided the word 'devolution' is not mentioned, they are often prepared to complain about the structure and say that too many decisions are taken by officials in St Andrew's House.

One can carry the assent of businessmen heavily critical of too much bureaucracy and of professional people who feel that the machine both consults too much and concedes too little. But if there is any suggestion that these problems could be better handled under an Assembly, all the alarms and fears I have mentioned reappear and suddenly the audience stops any criticism of the present set-up; it becomes perfect in contrast with the horrors that devolution could bring.

Why should this be? Every other major industrial country in the Western world runs a devolved system of government except France. At this point, some say: 'It would be all right if it was a federal system and the same powers were devolved in England.' This ought to end the discussion for, in a federal system, the Scottish Assembly would probably have more powers than proposed in the present Bill (it would certainly have same revenue-raising powers) and would be elected in the same way. Those who would be happy about the quality and modus operandi of a Scottish Assembly in this situation cannot object to such an Assembly working on its own until the English decide whether they, too, want devolution to their regions or not.

But it quickly becomes clear that this does not get to the root of the objection. This is a fear of the kind of people who would be elected to and who would run the Assembly whether Britain had a federal system or not. Again this is curious because it cannot be held that the Scots are inherently incapable of the kind of self-government enjoyed by the inhabitants of Bavaria, Sardinia, California or Queensland. Indeed, the Scots in the imperial years ran many other countries, so why not their own?

Clearly the business and professional groups who express these fears believe that whoever was elected to the Assembly, it would not be them. Who do they imagine would be chosen by the voters? The usual answer is to point to the existing MPs and regional councillors and then to say that the Assemblymen would be 'even worse' or more to the Left or more nationalistic or more dedicated to the problems of Glasgow which would dominate the business of the Assembly.

Let us consider these fears in turn. It is sometimes alleged that Labour would control the Assembly and that the Labour Party would be Left-wing dominated. This is really a throw-back to the 1920s and shows no knowledge of the current position in the Labour Party. In October 1974, 41 out of the 71 Scottish MPs elected were Labour, but of the 41, only nine belonged to the Tribune Group or to the Left in any sense and this was a lower proportion than among UK Labour MPs.

Also, this degree of Left-wingism cannot be held to produce policies totally unacceptable to non-Labour voters. Four of the nine Left-wing MPs are or have been Ministers and no-one can say that Mr Carmichael or Mr Robert Hughes exhibited tendencies in office that spelt danger, while the most Left-wing, Mr Buchan, was a highly competent and capable junior Minister of Agriculture.

As far as businessmen's fears are concerned, they ought to accept that the Scottish Assembly, however limited its powers in economic and industrial matters, will be desperately anxious to encourage investment and growth in Scotland. Indeed it is significant that the fears of Labour MPs representing the North of England are the opposite (and certainly more realistic) ones that an Assembly would do too much to aid expanding and incoming business and thus damage the chances of the remoter parts of England. The experience of Northern Ireland is also instructive. There, despite all the political tensions which existed even before 1969, Ulster got a good share of incoming industry and one reason was that a local Parliament and Ministry could provide a faster and more personal service for businessmen than the various regional development agencies in the UK.

Then there is the worry about Glaswegian domination. Glasgow will have 30 and the Clyde conurbation some 50 of the 142 seats in the Assembly but these are bound to return some Conservative and SNP members. It is very difficult to see the equivalent in the Assembly of Mr Teddy Taylor combining with Mrs Margo Macdonald and Labour members to thwart the overall Scottish policies of the other Conservative, Nationalist and Labour MPs. In practice, the bulk of Conservative and SNP seats will come from outside Glasgow as will a fair proportion of Labour seats and it will be party policies, not civic or regional loyalties which will dominate the Assembly.

Whether these arguments are cogent or not, in my experience they calm but do not totally convince the groups whose worries I have described. The objectors fall back on anxieties about the quality of the people likely to be elected. At this stage, one seems to get closer to the truth. Scotland is at present run, despite long-range control by the UK Cabinet and despite or through all the complex processes mentioned above, by these groups of business and professional people. They sit on the boards, commissions and advisory bodies together with the same few former Labour councillors and trade union officials.

At bottom, any criticism of the results of the system is a criticism of them and they feel sure that any new elected body would reduce their influence. When they express fears about the quality of Assemblymen, they are really talking about the difficulty, for them, of imagining a system of Scottish government from which they were excluded.

To this there are two answers. First, they are partly correct in that most of these with ability and an interest in public affairs are already being consulted by government and it would be a great loss if all of them gave up any contribution. But, and secondly, there is no reason whatever for them to contract out or for them to imagine that the electorate has no respect for their abilities or experience. There are probably few communities in the Western world where training and capacity are more respected than in Scotland. The few lawyers, doctors and teachers who have stood for office in Scotland have not lost public support because of their prior qualifications and certainly these skills will be as badly needed under devolution.

The only thing that could make the remaining fears of those professional, business and middle-class groups come true is their own actions. If they exhibit such a lack of confidence in the democratic process and such a lack of interest in the future of Scotland that they all contract out of any involvement in the Assembly and in the devolved system of government, then it will be impoverished but it will be nobody's fault but their own.

Part 4

Nationalism: threat and ally

There have been three stages in the relationship between devolutionists and the National Party in Scotland. First of all the SNP was a nuisance and a threat to be combated. Secondly, from Winifred Ewing's by-election victory in Hamilton in 1967 (Labour losing a seat held by a majority of 16,576) until Margo MacDonald's failure to win the seat in another by-election in 1978, the SNP – or rather the Labour and Conservative Parties' panicky reaction to them – provided the spur to change. John Mackintosh lived through these two stages and his reactions to the SNP reflect their changing fortunes. By the time of the referendum the argument had been lost, the SNP was becoming more openly separatist, and so their support for the Act was a mixed blessing. After the 1979 General Election, the devolutionists in the SNP lost their hold and the Party turned its back on devolution. John Mackintosh did not live to see the reversal – though he often warned against it and against the threat it could prove to the union of Scotland with the rest of the United Kingdom.

4.1 'A bed of thistles' (*Socialist Commentary*, December 1967, pp. 11–12.)

In 1967 Mackintosh warned both against the Nationalists and Labour's uncomprehending reaction to them.

Everything possible went wrong at Hamilton; literally everything. To take the more apparent mistakes first – the Labour candidate was not selected for six weeks *after* the Scottish Nationalist (SNP) was in the field; time for one complete canvass of the constituency by the Nationalists. Then, when the Labour Party's belated selection conference did take place, the choice fell on a fifty-five-year-old miner, Mr Alex Wilson.

It must be emphasised that Mr Wilson was a worthy and well-liked nominee who would have made a useful addition to the miners' MPs in the House. At a General Election there would have been no problem. But this was a by-election where the candidate is subject to quite special pressures and publicity and where it was already known that the SNP had a capable, news-worthy, photogenic candidate. At the Labour Selection Conference there were at least two young and very brilliant men, able as speakers and politicians, tried in previous contests and one at least had all the necessary West-of-Scotland local knowledge. Yet Mr Wilson was chosen, and part of the reason was that the Party in Hamilton had always been used to sponsorship and he was backed by the National Union of Mineworkers. Hamilton was once a miners' seat but now there are only 2000 miners in the constituency. The result was to confirm Labour's Scottish image as an elderly party of special interests stemming from the old and declining heavy industries.

All this could have been minimised if Mr Wilson had had a capable organisation and sound political guidance during the campaign. He lacked both. The local party had managed its own elections in the past, and, with a 16,000 majority, saw fit to reject the services of the Scottish Regional Organiser and his team of professional agents; they were only called in at the last stages when it was too late. Nor were there many volunteers. As a result, on the afternoon and evening of polling day in a working class area some distance from the polling station, with the rain pouring down, there was *only one car* in operation worked by myself and another MP while the Nationalists, operating a proper pull-out system, had cars in every street.

Faced with attacks from two fronts and in a difficult political situation, Mr Wilson had no senior Labour politician posted to advise him, no press agent, no one to help with the tactics of the campaign. The decision to ignore the Nationalists was a mistake and no attempt was made to expose any of their often fallacious arguments and statistics, or to press them on their weakest point – the merits of total independence. It would have been of great help to Mr Wilson had the previous member, Tom Fraser, who was widely known and greatly admired, returned to give a hand or at least to commend the new candidate as a worthy successor.

Yet even if there had been a proper organisation, the ideal candidate and effective propaganda, and even if Labour had held the seat, there would still have been a huge SNP vote which would have to be explained. It was fashionable before the result (and even now in certain quarters) to say that this was just a protest vote, a by-election fluke. While it is true that many Labour supporters could both protest by voting SNP and still know that a Labour government would remain in office, and while thousands of Conservatives could vote SNP as the only way of beating the Labour candidate, there was more to the protest than this. Hamilton's majority should have been big enough to withstand such pressures.

Going to Nationalist meetings, talking to their supporters, it was clear to me that this was not just a mid-term mood of disgruntlement produced by the economic difficulties of the Government. It is probably true that with full employment and a 4 per cent growth rate, Labour would have won Hamilton. But about a third of the student audiences and youth fellowships I speak to in Scotland wear SNP badges; an age group which knows nothing of unemployment.

Listening to SNP propaganda, it is a curious mixture of contradictory arguments. There is the theory that Scotland is governed from London by Englishmen who either do not understand the problems or do not care. There is the view that Scotland fails to get a fair share of the defence contracts, the science-based industry, the government offices that help boost the economy of the South-East and the Midlands. More extreme, the argument is advanced that Scotland pays more into the National Exchequer than is received back, so that the industrious Scots subsidise the English.

An extension of this argument maintains that Scotland exports more per head than England and that with whisky, woollens, ships and tweeds, a separate Scotland would have no balance of payments problem, no need for periodic deflations. Finally there is the case that as a separate country the national culture, the special traditions in the church, in education, and in the law and in local government would flourish. Scotsmen would have more pride, more self-confidence, and would play a proper role in world affairs.

It is hard to say which of the items in this programme really wins votes. Much of it is complete rubbish and the use of patently fallacious propaganda explains the low calibre of SNP candidates and leaders. For instance, the Scottish Office in Whitehall, which is supposed to govern Scotland, is a small set of rooms for the Scottish ministers in attendance in the House of Commons. On health, housing, education, roads, agriculture, fisheries, Home Office matters and economic planning Scotland is administered *by Scotsmen from Edinburgh*. The Revenue and Expenditure return for 1952–53 (Cmnd 9051) shows quite clearly that Scotland contributes in revenue a smaller proportion than the ratio of Scottish to English population merits, and receives more – as would be expected from a poorer area requiring higher social service payments.

Yet none of this worries SNP propagandists. They can run together the idea that Scotland lacks adequate new industry with the idea that it is the result of 'London rule' and that Scotland would be better off on its own. Normally the appeals are simpler and seldom stress future policy in an independent Scotland; middle-class audiences are told that the SNP is opposed to idlers loafing around on swollen social service benefits; the working-class audiences that their wages are lower than English wages 'and Labour have done nothing about it'.

Behind all this, there is a widespread but elusive feeling that modern government is too complex, too remote. Accepting that while the important decisions are taken by Scots civil servants in Edinburgh, it does seem peculiar that the administration can be devolved but not the machinery of democratic control, and it is true that the Scottish Office is much less supervised because the MPs spend their time in London away from both the Ministry and the problems.

What should the Labour Party do about this? At the more superficial level, the reforms are obvious. The old notion that the Secretary of State for Scotland and the Parliamentary Party should keep clear of all electoral questions must go. The Secretary of State is the leader of the Party in Scotland. He should entrust a colleague with watching over the candidates' list and steering the right men to the right places, particularly in by-elections. In such a case, he should be able to send in all the available organisers and see that the politics of the operation are properly handled.

A Parliament for Scotland

At the broader level of policy, the objective should be to separate those who want more local democratic control (70 per cent of the electorate in a recent poll) from those who wish total independence (a mere 18 per cent). As a democratic socialist party, there is no reason why Labour should not accept the idea of a council or parliament for Scotland to undertake the major local government functions, many of the tasks not given to *ad hoc* regional boards and some of the central government duties at present devolved to the Scottish Office. With a second tier of councils below it, such a body (with a permanent Labour majority) could draw the real enthusiasm and idealism aroused by the SNP into constructive channels. Seventy-one Scottish MPs could be left at Westminster to look after those Scottish issues that are better settled on a UK basis, and at the same time, to play a full and distinctive part in British national affairs.

4.2 'Why I cannot join the SNP' (*Typescript summary of address at the North British Hotel, Edinburgh, 7.30 pm 28 February 1977, prepared as if for a press release*).

Some maximalists left the Labour Party because of its foot-dragging over devolution. But John Mackintosh stayed and fought. In February 1977 the Government lost its fight for its first devolution Bill (the Scotland and Wales Bill) and some devolutionists nearly threw in their lot with the SNP. In a speech to the Andrew Fletcher Society (an SNP study group) the following week John Mackintosh sought to maximise the pressure on his party short of actually leaving it. The call in the last paragraph to 'join the SNP' can be mistaken for a call to become members of the SNP. From the context, it is clear that he merely wanted to work alongside the National Party.

Professor Mackintosh said that the SNP had had many good effects on Scottish politics and had broken up the traditional two party mould and he had many sympathies with the drive behind the SNP but he could never join them because he did not believe in exclusive nationalism. For over 200 years there had been a Scottish tradition fostered by the law, education, separate Church and local government, but the Scots were also British and had taken pride in British traditions. It was quite wrong to attempt to make the Scots deny either half of their dual nationality. On the other hand, it was wrong for the English to refuse to allow political expression of the Scottish dimension and this was what the Devolution Bill had sought to do.

It was quite fantastic for the small handful of anti-devolvers to argue that institutions could not be devised by which Scottish traditions and interests could be presented and given full expression within the United Kingdom. It was precisely this obstinacy of English nationalism which had led to the creation of an Irish Republic when all the Irish had wanted was Home Rule within the UK. If it was possible for Britain to have a special identity within Europe, it was possible for the Scots to have a separate identity within the UK. Thus he sympathised with much of the SNP's idealism but it was odd that they should be calling for a withdrawal of Scottish Members from Westminster at the same time as they were proposing to take part in European elections. Just as it was possible to accommodate different states within the European Community, it was surely possible to devise institutions that would satisfy Scottish aspirations without denying them the right also to be British.

The terrible problem of the defeat of the Home Rule Bill last Tuesday night was that it cut the ground from under the feet of those like himself who had wanted expression for the dual nationality of the Scots. The anti-devolvers, with their adamant insistence that one could only be in a unitary country or opt for total independence, had won the day. In fact, the message from the House of Commons was that if the Scots wanted devolution the only hope of getting it was to vote SNP.

The Sunday Times leader had asserted that unless there were more SNP Members after the next election it would prove that devolution was rubbish. This presented people like himself, who had argued the case for 20 years, with a stark alternative of going along with the SNP, though he was not a Nationalist, or else accepting the status quo.

If faced with this choice he could but seek a working accommodation with the Nationalists and he feared that many in Scotland would do the same, although it would be with reluctance. Still, on the polls, only 20 per cent wanted independence but all the devolvers and those who wanted some form of Home Rule for Scotland were driven into collaboration with the SNP who had now pushed up their total support in the country to 36 per cent.

The only solution now was for all those Liberal, Tory and Labour members who favoured devolution to join the SNP and insist that as a first stage after the next election there must be a federal solution and they must trade their votes in Westminster for some solutions of this kind with whichever Government was prepared to cooperate. The anti-devolutionists had driven all those in Scotland who wanted some measure of self-government into cooperation with the SNP. This might be regrettable but there was no alternative to the position in which they had been placed by the defeat of the guillotine last Tuesday night.

4.3.1 'The trouble with John P. Mackintosh', by Stephen Maxwell (*Question*, 18 March 1977).

Mackintosh's statement to the Andrew Fletcher society provoked an attack on his nationalism from SNP theoretician Stephen Maxwell (*Question*, 18 March 1977). Maxwell's critique provoked Mackintosh in turn to reply with the fullest statement of his 'dual-nationalism' position.

No MP contributes so consistently and so notably to the Scottish debate as John Mackintosh himself. No other commentator is so readily accepted as an authoritative voice on Scottish developments by the Scottish media.

Yet the somewhat plaintive tone which informs this acknowledgement of the growing autonomy of Scottish political debate illustrates an ambivalence which runs through John Mackintosh's prolific pronouncements on the state of Scottish politics. He is by no means the only Scottish MP to display such ambivalence. Indeed some of his colleagues – Norman Buchan and Denis Canavan spring to mind – display raging schizophrenia. But he is by far the most prominent, and he is certainly the one most respected by the Scottish Establishment.

Mackintosh's ambivalence may be due partly to that sense of isolation from the crowding events of Scottish politics to which many Scottish MPs in their enforced weekday exile in London, testify. But it is surely also due in some measure to the peculiar role John Mackintosh plays in Scottish politics. No other Scottish MP or political pundit can boast a consistent record of support for devolution in some form or other going back to 1957. Yet his contributions to the debate have always been made from the margin, as a gifted commentator not as a man of power or a maker of policy. He has been right about Scottish politics more often than any other Scottish MP, yet he has lacked the gift of identifying with any of the distinctive currents of Scottish opinion which intellectually more fallible politicians such as Norman Buchan, Jim Sillars and even Willie Ross have displayed. Lacking a political base either in the Labour Party or in an identifiable popular constituency of the sort cultivated by Teddy Taylor, John Mackintosh has found both his political allies and his intellectual peers in English politics, among the now dwindling ranks of Labour's social democrats. Similarly, as a political commentator he has found his most sympathetic and responsive audience among the readers of the *Observer*, *The Guardian*, the *New Statesman* in its long decline from the noncomformist radicalism of Kingsley Martin and of specialist periodicals like *Political Quarterly*.

The high regard in which the English Liberal Establishment holds John Mackintosh as a political writer and analyst has undoubtedly increased his attractions as a political pundit to those still numerous managers of the Scottish media who crave metropolitan approval for their editorial decisions. But it serves incidentally to obstruct John Mackintosh's influence among the new political public in Scotland, for it presents him, not entirely unfairly, as we shall see, as a symbol of Scotland's continuing cultural dependence on England.

The source of John Mackintosh's ambivalence is most clearly revealed in his own considered contributions to the Scottish debate. These are at once superbly lucid and hopelessly flawed in their assessment of Scottish nationalism. Although John Mackintosh has been ahead of opinion in both England and Scotland in interpreting Scottish developments, his interpretations have usually been couched in terms which are familiar and reassuring to conventional wisdom. In the shock of SNP's Hamilton by-election victory, John Mackintosh warned Labour's social democrats through the *Socialist Commentary* that the result was not a fluke nor merely a mid-term protest against the economic failures of the Labour Government. Behind all this, he revealed, was the 'elusive feeling that modern government is too complex, too remote'. He recommended that the Secretary of State for Scotland should exercise more leadership in electoral matters, that the extent of administrative devolution to Scotland should be more vigorously publicised and that a Scottish council or parliament should be set up to undertake the major local government functions and some of the central government duties devolved to the Scottish Office.

With some modest amendments, these remained the chief elements of John Mackintosh's diagnosis and of his prognosis until 1974. In the *Devolution of Power* published in 1968, he joined his analysis of Scottish developments to a general account of the weaknesses of British government. He repeated his warning that nationalism was not purely, or even mainly, about economic deprivation. Many of the voters who supported the SNP belonged to a generation which had known only prosperity. Their concern was more with the quality of life and with their capacity to influence a system of government which too often presented itself as remote, indifferent and hopelessly complex. As part of a scheme of elected regional councils throughout the United Kingdom, he recommended the creation of Scottish and Welsh assemblies, in the Scottish case with additional powers over the legal system, the courts and other Home Office functions. Even in *The Government and Politics of Britain* published in 1974, Mackintosh attributed nationalism to dissatisfaction with remote bureaucracy and with the poor economic performance of London governments.

Mackintosh's consistency in analysing Scottish nationalism as a precocious reaction, or over-reaction, to general defects of the British system has been watched by his constituency in denying it the status of a genuine Nationalism. To Mackintosh, Scottish nationalism has been 'neo-nationalism', a response to problems Britain shares with other highly developed political systems, but sharpened by Britain's peculiar post-war economic history and by a residual sense of Scottish identity preserved in the traditional Scottish institutions of law, church, education and local government.

The reason for Mackintosh's refusal to admit Scottish nationalism to the company of the classic European Nationalist movements appears to be his belief that it lacks a foundation or cultural nationalism. One must be cautious here for Mackintosh has never claimed to be a cultural historian and his references to Scottish culture – or to culture of any sort – are invariably brief. If, however, he intends to draw attention to the lack of a literary-cultural base for contemporary Scottish nationalism of the sort which sustained the Nationalist movements of the nineteenth century; he is undoubtedly correct. (The nature of the relationship between the literary nationalism of the 1920s and 1930s in Scotland and contemporary political nationalism is a complex question so far almost untouched by Scottish historians.) And in the absence of a vital literary nationalism, Mackintosh is right to refuse to be impressed by whatever claims might be made for Scotland's traditional institutions as untapped reservoirs of cultural energy.

Yet his implicit definitions of culture may be too restrictive. Cultural identity need not depend on literary culture alone. It can draw sustenance from other areas of culture, from social institutions or even, as the case of Switzerland demonstrates, from 'distinctive political ethos or institutions.'

As a political intellectual John Mackintosh might be expected to be alert to the possibility of just such an alternative cultural base for Scottish nationalism. Indeed, in an article in the *New Statesman* at the beginning of last year he hints at the emergence of a distinctive Scottish political culture. What blocks John Mackintosh's vision is a quite, explicit belief that the Scots have a dual identity – that they are both Scots and British – and that this is demonstrated above all in their political attitudes.

His pamphlet *A Parliament for Scotland* published in 1976 by his East Lothian Constituency Association includes one of Mackintosh's rare attempts to argue this thesis. He identifies the Parliamentary tradition as 'purely British', and cites the rejection by a majority of the Scottish public of the 'It's Scotland's Oil' slogan in favour of sharing with the rest of Britain and SNP's failure to persuade Scotland to cast a tactical 'No' vote in the EEC referendum. He concludes by quoting opinion polls showing a large majority in favour of Scotland remaining part of the United Kingdom.

Such flimsy evidence will appear less than convincing to those whose political formation and commitments are less directly British than those of John Mackintosh. He offers no defence against the obvious response that these attitudes are the residue of a rapidly wasting sense of British identity. Even a brief excursion into Scottish cultural history would suggest to him that his British political identity would draw little support from the general culture. If such a hybrid as British culture ever existed it was surely only in the nineteenth century through such Anglo-Scottish figures as the Mills, Macaulay, Carlyle and Ruskin, before it guttered to an inglorious end with Robertson Nicoll and *The British Weekly*.

Equally lacking from Mackintosh's assessment is a developed appreciation of the historical conditions making for a revived sense of Scottish identity. On rare occasions he has himself hinted at the possibility that the parallel decline in the traditional Scottish inhibitions and in the prestige of British political institutions has released the ambition to establish new – or rediscover old – reference points for Scotland. In a *New Statesman* article in 1974 called 'The New Appeal of Nationalism' he acknowledged that Scots might feel more at home in Oslo or Copenhagen than in London and recounts how, when invited to comment at a European conference on the shameless special pleading of a British Minister, he declined with the words: 'I am from Scotland and I must dissociate myself from all that you have just heard'. But he concludes the article by reasserting, if less confidently than usual, Britain's claim. 'Only one thing will halt or reverse the onward march of the SNP – a period of government in London which is really successful so that it ends with a satisfied electorate eager to vote positively for a country that once again restored the feeling that Britain is a successful, worthwhile country to belong to . . .'. The absence of any suspicion that such long-term, and irreversible, changes as the abandonment of Empire may be the crucial factors, not short-term changes in governmental performance is entirely characteristic.

Even if Mackintosh is right in arguing for the dominance of a British identity, that identity would not necessarily provide a secure date for the continuation of the United Kingdom. The Scandinavian example demonstrated that some sense of common identity, even common political identity, can co-exist with constitutional separation.

Mackintosh's intellectual position in a Britain facing the problems of Scottish and Welsh nationalism perhaps bears comparison with that of Pierre Trudeau facing the challenge of Quebec separation. Like Trudeau, Mackintosh represented a new reformist element in his immediate provincial context. Mr Trudeau believed that Quebecers should adapt themselves to the role of French Canadians, Mackintosh believes that Scots have a dual Scottish British identity. As Trudeau sought to reform Federal attitudes to accommodate Quebec's non-separatist ambitions, so Mackintosh has laboured nobly to instruct English political opinion in the new Scottish realities as he saw them. As Trudeau began by patronising the Quebec separatists as narrow-minded chauvinists only to learn that they had as keen a sense of the international context in which both Quebec and Canada must operate as he himself, as John Mackintosh once scorned the Nationalists as political kailyarders only to learn that even if they were not familiar faces at Königswinter conferences and the other gathering places of the new self-regarding European élite, they had their own perhaps more catholic view of Scotland's international links.

The comparison takes added point from the fact that it is not long since Mackintosh was prepared to cite Quebec's role in Canada as a reassuring example of the viability of Federal systems. Perhaps over the next few years Mackintosh and Trudeau will be witnesses of a practical demonstration that in an interdependent world of multinational corporations and international competition for natural resources, neither the economic nor the cultural survival of small societies can be secured within the political limits imposed by the classic Federal division of powers.

4.3.2 'The trouble with Stephen Maxwell' (*Question*, 15 April 1977).

Stephen Maxwell has done me the courtesy both of taking my views seriously and of reading a large part of my writings over the last decade and I appreciate his analysis. There are, from my angle, only one or two actual mistakes or misunderstandings; any other disagreements are over Stephen Maxwell's own assumptions or the position from which he judges other people's arguments.

It may be worth going over these points because I do consider the differences between Maxwell and myself to be significant and they lead to consequential differences about what ought to be done in the immediate future of Scottish politics.

In my description of the position of Scots over the last two centuries as one in which they have a 'dual nationality', I am not, as Maxwell seems to think, either decrying the Scots or saying there is something incomplete about their outlook, nor am I making a recommendation. This is a statement of fact. It is, for instance, factually the case that since 1707, the Scots have operated in a British political system with elections to Westminster, the parties have been British and the Scots have taken part in so many other British institutions, notably the Empire. (One of Maxwell's few mistakes is to say I ignore the decline of the Empire as a reason for the declining pride or value in 'being British' – this is explicitly cited in all my major articles on the dual nationality.)

This participation in so many British activities and a sense of loyalty or identity with these activities and institutions may or may not be desirable; the point I am making is that it exists. I also argue that being British for certain purposes has never removed the sense of being Scottish for other purposes, a sense fostered and maintained above all by certain distinct Scottish institutions. Moreover, throughout the last two centuries there have been fluctuations in which side was uppermost, the Scottish or the British. Much depends on the role which the Scot is playing at the time and who or what he is contrasting himself with.

Thus a Scotsman can belong to a Scottish regiment within the British army; both loyalties can and do exist together. One can play for Scotland and for the British Lions. This sense of a dual consciousness or loyalty is true of most periods and of most people in Scottish life. Again, to say so is neither to praise, to blame nor to recommend, it is simply a fact. When Burns, who thought of himself as a Scot so often when contrasting his outlook and conduct with that of the English turns to consider the possibility of a French invasion of these islands, he becomes British. In his address to the Dumfriesshire Volunteers recruited to resist a Napoleonic landing he says:

'Be Britain still to Britain true
  Amang oorsels united,
For never but by British hands
  Maun British wrong be righted.'

At an institutional and professional level, this has been our experience increasingly in recent years. Are the Scottish universities part of a vertical pattern of Scottish education or are they part of a horizontal tier of UK higher education? The answer is that they are both. If forced to choose which connection matters most, differences arise even among Scottish teachers, but both aspects are there. There are so many examples of this situation. One finds Scottish trade unionists thinking of themselves as part of the STUC but also as part of unions whose headquarters are in London and whose basic demands are made for workers throughout Britain. No-one could be more Scottish in some senses than Willie Ross yet no-one fought more bitterly against any separate Scottish political dimension. The same goes for the judges, those conservative custodians of Scots law who put up Lord Wheatley to say that they (apart from Lord Hunter) passionately objected to a Scottish Assembly having control of the Scottish legal system. They were determined, at that level, to remain British.

Once again, I have deep objections to some of these views. But I am not commenting on this situation at this moment. I simply report that this duality has existed in varying degrees over the period since the union.

For Stephen Maxwell, this description of Scottish history and current experience is in the first place, some kind of slight on the Scots. It is to deny them 'the status of a genuine nationalism'. Secondly, he seems to think he must find a personal or psychological aberration underlying my motives for reporting in this way. It must be due to a 'sense of isolation' derived from living in London or a lack of cultural values or, in other places, a desire to please English readers, or to be accepted among 'the new self-regarding European élite'.

On these personal points, I have only one comment. In my experience, there are two ways in which one can feel Scottish and I think I have experienced both. One (which seems to predominate with Stephen Maxwell) is to feel a resentment against the assumptions of superiority, of absolute standards, so evident in the older English universities, in London media circles, among Whitehall civil servants and so on. The other, when one has been in and through all these groups and their activities, is to be reasonably confident that the best of what is done in Scotland and by Scots is as good as anything that these custodians of proper standards can produce. The latter is, I believe, a happier and healthier stage to be at but it inevitably exposes one to charges of having 'sold out', of having joined the enemy on the part of those who remain apart from and resent these people and what they do. Thus Stephen Maxwell indicates his Scottish distaste for the kind of writers, industrialists, trade unionists and politicians who gather at the annual (note the title) Anglo-German Conferences. My most vivid memory of the last of these conferences was the confidence and success with which Margo MacDonald not only addressed the group but led the singing of 'Flower of Scotland' later in the evening.

On the other point, which is that to describe the dual nationality of the Scots is to deny Scottish nationalism its status as a full or proper nationalism, Maxwell is correct in one obvious sense. Scotland has not been independent and therefore has not had that form of nationalism –

the kind which can arise in France or Germany. But what he appears to be arguing is that there is a 'full' or 'proper' or 'complete' nationalism which is discernible even when the institutional preconditions do not exist.

Historically, I do not think this is correct. The sense of identity (which is closest to the core of nationalism) has varied in almost every case of a nationalist movement. And thank God this is true as some nationalisms have been vile and evil forces. Sometimes, national movements lacking a political or institutional expression, have based themselves on language, sometimes on colour, sometimes on that more elusive concept of race, sometimes on common historical experience. No-one can survey Zionism, recent German nationalism, black African nationalism and the movements of self-determination among the peoples of the Austro-Hungarian Empire and conclude that there is a single set of feelings or conditions or objectives which can be said to exist and that when they exist, there is a 'genuine nationalism'; otherwise there is some spurious phenomenon. Since there is no isolatable Platonic essence of nationalism, the sentiments which do exist and have existed in Scotland are neither proper nor improper. The only question is whether they have been accurately described and assessed.

It so happens that my account of the dual nationality experienced by most Scots fits with a mass of current political evidence. Stephen Maxwell describes all the poll material that has been collected over the last decade as 'flimsy evidence', but there is a great quantity of it and there is no evidence to the contrary. The major finding, in this respect, is that the bulk of Scottish electors want more self-government but within the United Kingdom; they understandably want to express both the Scottish and the British aspects of their nationality in appropriate political forms. There are many other findings that support this central point. One is that only about 50 per cent of those who vote SNP say they want independence. Another is that a majority (even among SNP voters) reject the 'its Scotland's oil' proposition and agree that the oil should be used to benefit Britain as a whole.

Nothing in all this means that the SNP are not entitled to fight for independence and, given sufficient depression of the British side of the dual nationality, and sufficient stupidity on the part of UK politicians, they may win. But it does suggest that there may be difficulty in nationalists pushing their support beyond a certain level as so many Scots may be unwilling to abrogate the British aspect of their consciousness. It also makes the demand for an effective Scottish

Parliament and Government harder to push if it becomes accepted that this, which a majority do want, is only a stage on the road to something which a majority of Scots do not want.

I also believe that there is a basic validity in the preference of the majority for home rule (I prefer these words to devolution) within the UK because I consider that there is an unreality about independence for any state (other than a super-power) in the modern world and especially for a small country closely tied by economics, communications and recent history to a larger neighbour. The UK itself has only a degree of independence, the Republic of Ireland, Belgium and Luxembourg have less, so Scotland would come somewhere on this spectrum if it was technically independent. I feel our control over what happens to us (this is what self-government or democracy is about) is greatest not when one chases unreal notions of independence at either the UK or the Scottish level, but when appropriate political forms are devised to give us as Scots the maximum self-determination first at the Scottish level, secondly at the UK level and thirdly within Europe. It also so happens that this accords with the history of the Scots. We have only to recognise or to add a European dimension to the dual nationality to fit the realities of modern political life.

Part 5

Agriculture

John Mackintosh's interests are not easily separable. He applied a rigorous consistent mind to all the subjects he discussed. He was not solely concerned with constitutional reform. No MP or political thinker could be. In this and the succeeding sections, some of the most pressing political issues affecting Scotland to which John Mackintosh turned his mind are reflected.

The politics of agriculture became very important to him as his seat contained rich farmland as well as old mining villages. Indeed, his interest in agriculture became so compelling that he brought many votes and not a few activists including his successor in Parliament John Home Robertson – himself a farmer – into the Labour fold.

5.1 'Political pressures on agriculture' (*Report of the Twenty-fifth Oxford Farming Conference*, 1971*)

Mackintosh's contribution to this subject and indeed his flair for public speaking is epitomised in this address to a farming audience.

The task of a political system is to provide a method of arbitrating between the pressures within and from outside upon a society; it arranges a process by which conflicting pressures are resolved so that some kind of compromise emerges as public policy. Where the system is an open one with all pressures known and observable, it is still difficult to assess the precise weight to be attached to each pressure. Many influences are at work and it is often hard to say what would happen if one source of pressure was removed or intensified. Usually an estimate can only be made if there is an element of conflict and even then many of those involved and well informed will make different estimates. The problem becomes much harder where the system, as in Britain, is partially or largely secret. At present, year by year, agricultural policy is settled by the Annual Review and Determination of Guarantees, but no-one has been able to examine the process and set out just how much NFU pressure influences the result as compared, say, with the effect of the overall economic situation as put forward by the Treasury, or to weigh the contribution of the Ministry of Agriculture as compared with that of the Ministry of Trade and Industry.

* Subsequently reprinted as Unit 14 Open University Course T273, OU Press 1978.

What makes the subject particularly interesting at present is that we are on the eve of a major change in agricultural policy from a situation where just under a half of the public money put into the agricultural industry comes in the form of deficiency payments to a system where (it is hoped) prices will be maintained by levies on imported foodstuffs. This new policy was devised by the Conservative Party in opposition and will now be worked out by the Ministry. But although it was devised out of office, the process by which it was evolved is not much easier to examine because it went on inside the Shadow Cabinet, in private negotiations with interested bodies, and those concerned may not want to put a precise weight on the various considerations which affected their decisions.

In this paper I want to consider the pressures that are brought to bear in agricultural decision-making in these two types of cases, the one being the regular annual process of farming policy within the established procedures as laid down in the 1947 Agriculture Act and the other the rarer special case when a major new departure in the basic policy is initiated. In both cases the process is so largely secret that all that can be done is to depict the major forces at work.

But before beginning this exercise, which does involve so much groping in the dark, it is worth noticing that the process was not always so obscure. A similar turning point occurred in British agricultural policy in 1846 when the Corn Laws were repealed. This was in our era of open politics and vigorous public discussion. The Anti-Corn Law League was organised to put pressure on Parliament, the agricultural interest dug in its heels, pamphlets poured out, there were mass meetings, by-elections were fought on the issue and, finally, as the free trade arguments won, the Conservative Party split and the Repeal Bill was passed. Almost sixty years later, an attempt was made by Joseph Chamberlain to persuade the country to return to a system of partial protection in the form of imperial preference in 1903–5. Once again, the argument raged in public, within the Conservative Party and inside the House of Commons. Thus the details of Chamberlain's struggle (which he lost) can be readily discovered and an assessment of the various forces arrived at.

It is not so easy today for two reasons. The first is that Parliament has been largely cut out of the process and the second is that the arguments have become so very complicated. Parliament has been cut out because major new policies are worked out by the parties and then launched on the public rather than discussed in the House of Commons or, if the policy changes are not so extensive, they are the product of discussions between the Ministry of Agriculture, other sections of Whitehall and outside interests and again are announced to the House only when actual legislation or money is needed. So, when the Conservatives had prepared their recent change of policy inside their various committees, it was outlined at a Conservative Eastern Area Agricultural Conference in March, 1968, taken away and modified and reissued in four public speeches by Mr Godber in January 1969, but he never saw fit to explain his ideas to the House of Commons. Aspects of the levy system have been debated, for instance by this Conference last year, and I debated them with John Hill, MP, at the Farmers' Club in November, 1969, but they have not so far been debated in the House. Nor will this happen till the first Bill embodying the new system is presented and by then all the negotiations will be over, all the pressures will have been at work and MPs will only see the end product and hear the complaints of organisations who are not entirely happy about the final result. Even then these bodies will not want MPs to push their points of reservation too hard in case they prejudice their negotiating position with the Ministry. Whatever the merits and defects of such a political system, it does mean that pressures are not exercised as publicly as they were in the days when each interest had its spokesmen in the Commons and the case was made there. As a result, it is much harder nowadays to estimate the degree of activity and strength of these forces and how much each contributed to a particular decision.

The other reason that has been mentioned is the complexity of the arguments. The Conservative Party has far more resources to deploy, both in financial and in human terms, on agricultural topics, yet one of the weaknesses of Mr Godber's proposals in opposition was that he had not been able to estimate some significant effects of the change to a levy system; he simply lacked the staff to do so. To have an effective political debate now will be even harder, for the details will be being filled in by the expert staff of the Ministry, while the Labour Shadow Minister, Mr Cledwyn Hughes, for whom I have the greatest personal and political respect, has virtually no support in the way of staff or specialists. One man with two parliamentary assistants, with their own constituencies to manage and other political issues to consider, cannot possibly keep track of all the important aspects of this new policy, study the academic and technical material, talk to various bodies involved, see the experts and extract from this (as is the politician's task) the salient issues affecting the industry, the taxpayer and the consumer, placing these in a provocative and interesting way before the public and in the House of Commons. Incidentally, this is why the fertiliser companies and the farmers' unions have such an advantage in modern conditions, because they alone can afford the kind of counter-bureaucracy that is needed and they will therefore be able to highlight the issues affecting their members, but they have no other wider responsibilities and it may be in the interest of all these bodies to have no discussion of some of the most important aspects which should be concerning the public and the House of Commons.

At the same time, it must be remembered that though the process is secret and damages the quality of public debate, the executive is not in any way subservient to particular pressures. The fact that the Cabinet is backed by a solid majority in the House and can normally get its way with little trouble, insulates it very effectively against vested interests. The next election is usually several years away and in this strong position a government can spend most of its time, if it is so inclined, on the overall problems and well-being of the country. Indeed, some Prime Ministers have not only felt very free to decide what value to attach to particular pressures but have positively felt the electorate responded to the sight of special interest groups being slapped down.

Having made these reservations and complaints about our current political system, I will try and estimate the political pressures on the formation and conduct of agricultural policy. The estimate has no fact-based validity. The only way this might be achieved would be by an elaborate series of interviews with all concerned in the formation of agricultural policy. But even this would not be very satisfactory, as there are so many factors in the various currents of opinion about which people find it hard to be explicit or to estimate in their replies. As a result, I am not sure that one could ever produce an account of pressures in such a sensitive and complex field which could be measured like the pressures on a physical construction can be measured. This is not, then, so much an apology for an impressionistic approach as a recognition that this is an impression, a personal set of guesses and, though the guesses could be better informed, more carefully collected and be derived from more direct experience, at the end of the day there would be a subjective element in any account.

This list of pressures is not in order of importance but I will try to give a weighting at the end of the discussion. The first important political pressure is that of inertia. There is, at the moment, an accepted way of supporting agriculture which everyone is used to operating. A huge Ministry with many subordinate statistical sections, research stations, advisory centres and so on, is geared to working this system. Also the outside groups, particularly the Farmers' Unions, which have a privileged place within the system, are familiar with current methods and find them part of their normal life. Thus, it becomes very hard to change things and this is especially true in Britain.

Moreover, in the case of agricultural policy and administration, as so often happens in Britain, mere longevity brings veneration. We have become accustomed to boast about our system and its alleged great virtues despite constant grumbles over the day-to-day operations. Indeed, the pattern may alter and even the overall policy be adapted out of all recognition but still the myth of what the policy used to be survives and is venerated. For instance, it is commonly supposed that this country's main method of agricultural support is through price guarantees and deficiency payments when, in fact, these techniques now play a very restricted role. Again, a system devised during and after the War to encourage production and expansion was altered after the 1957 Act to become one of restriction and, later still, steps were taken to encourage farmers to give up the occupation, yet many commentators speak as if virtually one policy had been in force since 1947.

So there is the first powerful force – inertia; a tendency to go on with existing patterns because they are there and have acquired the support of habit and familiarity, they have been theorised about and praised and, in part, the process of change is made harder because sometimes people have forgotten precisely why the various key features of the policy were originally devised.

The second force to be reckoned with is the prevailing climate of ideas. It is not so much a pressure as an enveloping fog which makes it harder for all concerned to see the landmarks and to steer a course other than the one on which they are already set. Also there appears to be one major paradox in the prevailing climate of opinion about agricultural policy. On the one hand, there appears to be a general acceptance that the industry should have support. Since agriculture was boosted during the First World War, there has been one kind of government aid or another and this has settled into an accepted pattern since the 1947 Act, the present proposals for a levy system being a further step in the direction of government protection. One sometimes, in politics, can draw conclusions from the fact that something does not happen and it shows the degree of acceptance that Mr Enoch Powell has not made an attack on agricultural support a main theme in his campaign for a return to free markets and open competition.

On the other hand, there is also a widespread, if vague and ill-informed, sentiment that agriculture is inefficient and over-subsidised. This idea comes out in many ways. Take for instance the opening remarks in an article by a Mr Richard W. Howarth on 'The Political Strength of British Agriculture' (*Political Studies, Dec. 1969*). He says:

> in the period since the decontrol of food in 1954 the taxpayers of the UK will have spent £4204 million on . . . agriculture . . . This represents an average annual sum larger than Government expenditure on universities and scientific research and is roughly equivalent to the yield of one shilling on the standard rate of income tax or a subsidy of over £1000 per full time farmer . . . The economic case for continuing the present system and level of agricultural support is held to be weak by many agricultural economists . . .

Mr Howarth then sets himself to try and solve the problem which his assumptions have created of how agriculture has been politically strong enough to maintain such an indefensibly large subsidy.

In this respect, opinion in the House of Commons may well be reasonably representative of opinion in the country. On the Labour side there is a tendency to regard farmers as men who are or want to be petty gentry, who drive large expensive cars, send their children to fee-paying schools, whose wives still get domestic service or constant help in the house from the wives of the very poorly paid workers on the farm and who are constantly demanding money from the taxpayer to pay for all of this. Labour MPs who take part in agricultural debates and who argue the case (obvious in all developed countries), that incomes in all sectors of the agricultural industry are depressed, are regarded as peculiar and it is assumed must be doing this for constituency, i.e. vote-getting reasons. This also is regarded as a sign of poor judgment as a further common belief is that the more Labour Governments subsidise farming, the more solidly the farmers vote Conservative. I must emphasise that this is not a universal attitude but it is a widespread one in a Party whose core is the industrial working class and whose chief interest is in cheap food.

On the Conservative side, though, there are fifty or more 'regulars' in agricultural matters and though farming is regarded as being close to the heart of the Conservative Party, the case for financial support for agriculture also encounters obstacles. One of the arguments which helped to persuade some reluctant Conservatives to accept or tolerate the official line in favour of a levy system was that more money could never be got out of the Treasury. This was a most curious argument as MPs with farming interests had accepted the case for expanding agriculture; they believed that extra resources put into agriculture would yield satisfactory returns but, apparently, they also believed that they could not, given the attitudes among the public and the rest of their Party, convince a Conservative Chancellor of the Exchequer of the validity of the case.

One suspects that there is something of the same general atmosphere in Whitehall. Discussing the various approaches which characterised the major departments, I have on several occasions noticed bright young civil servants shrug their shoulders about the Ministry of Agriculture and lament departments that are over-sold on the area of British society they have to deal with; indeed, I have even heard the Ministry dismissed as merely a pressure group for the industry. There were whiffs of this in the evidence put before the Select Committee on Agriculture when the Treasury witness indicated a mild disbelief in the claim that the returns to agriculture had been too low and recounted his experience that squeezing the farmers only made them work harder. Similarly, the Board of Trade, as it then was, made it clear that it thought extra resources put into industry brought better returns and that in trade deals with other countries, it was usually worth offering easier access to the British food market in return for tariff concessions on British industrial exports. The then DEA suggested that while economic growth was their main concern, their chief worry about agriculture was that an increase in farm workers' wages might produce a round of claims in industry to maintain existing differentials.

There is something of this paradox in the Press. When farmers are hit by special problems, as in the bad harvest of 1968 or the collapse in fat stock prices in 1967, the leading articles – though few and far between – often accept the need for aid, though some papers, particularly *The Economist*, are prepared in general to maintain the position that subsidising agriculture is inefficient and overdone.

Before leaving the attitudes prevalent in circles which could have some marginal effects on agricultural policy, it is worth noticing two special areas of opinion. The first is that agriculture has benefited recently from some of the doubts about modern industrial society and its values, evident in such books as E. J. Mishan's *The High Cost of Economic Growth*, and in the general campaign against pollution and in favour of preserving the countryside. As more people go into the countryside for holidays and for weekends, the importance of preserving rural life, its practices and values is easier to put across. People are worried about the taking of attractive farm land for airports, motorways and housing estates, although this loss to agriculture is, from an economic or statistical viewpoint, insignificant.

A second and contrary current is the hostility which can be aroused against some of the practices associated with intensive livestock and poultry production. I get a regular small correspondence asking when the recommendations of the Brambell Committee are to be implemented and this type of pressure can sometimes damage farming. In the last Parliament on one day when the subject was being debated every member got three pieces of string in an envelope. One showed the wing span of an adult hen, the next the current width of battery cages and the third the width recommended by Brambell, and this undoubtedly helped to create a feeling that if farming was to be factory farming, then farmers could pay the same rates on these buildings as industrialists do (and this has happened) and, in general, that there is no point in getting emotional about the value of agriculture as a way of life.

Turning from the weight of existing practices and the general climate of opinion to the actual institutions designed to apply pressure on questions of agricultural politics, clearly pride of place goes to the NFU with its Scottish associate union. The NFU is always regarded in text books on British politics as one of the most powerful and effective bodies in the pressure group category. It is alleged to be the envy of the others, the model on which they wish to base themselves because the NFU has its bargaining rights as a producers' organisation built into the 1947 Agriculture Act. Also, none of the other bodies concerned with agriculture has these privileges. Thus the NFU leaders take part each year in the Annual Price Review and put their case before the Government fixes its prices. The NFU, as a result, knows far more than MPs for agricultural or any other constituencies. In return the NFU preserves the confidentiality of all negotiations, it helps the Government to keep in touch with the industry and, if the policy for that year can be agreed with the Government, it helps put across the official case by saying that it is an 'agreed Review'.

In a paper which I gave to the Agricultural Economics Society (printed in the *Journal of Agricultural Economics*, Vol. XXI No. 1, 1970) I doubted whether it could be established that the farmers had been able to exert as much pressure on governments as a result of the efficiency of the NFU as was often supposed. The answer on this point will probably never be known, but it is known that the Government spokesmen open the final round of negotiations with a bid which is under what they think will ultimately be a fair settlement. They are prepared to go up in return for NFU agreement, as this has a positive value, but whether they are prepared to go, or do go, further than the figure they had originally decided upon as an appropriate final offer cannot be said. But it is important to remember that pressure group bureaucracies have their inertia as do government departments. The leaders get used to the system, they like its known routine, they like the sensation of being 'on the inside', they learn to respect the officials and want, in their turn, to be regarded as 'sound' and 'responsible'. Thus it is quite possible for a serious gap to arise between the leadership and the members, the sort of gap that recently led to a breakaway movement under Mr Wallace Day and the defeat of the then President of the NFU who was replaced by a more militant figure. It is at least arguable that the privileges of constant consultation and confidentiality can draw the teeth of a pressure group and that it might mount more actual pressure by operating entirely from outside the governmental machine.

But this discussion throws the problem one stage further back. However effective the NFU may be, on what is its bargaining power based? No-one takes the possibility of a farmers' strike seriously, nor are mild farmers' demonstrations and disruptions of traffic the kind of thing to make ministers change their minds. Mr Howarth, in the article I have already quoted, says that the farmers' influence must rest on the political power they exercise. He looks at the agricultural vote at a general election and on the most generous calculation finds that in only 60 seats was the farmers' vote larger than half the simple majority at the 1966 election. But no-one imagines that half the farmers would change their votes simply for agricultural reasons and he accepts that the most that could be contemplated would be 1 in 4 swinging in this way. If this were to happen, 15 seats could change hands but, again, the swing on grounds of farm policy would all be one way – presumably to the party offering more to agriculture, so both parties could not gain. Thus, if 25 per cent of the farmers had swung to Labour in the 1966 election, the Conservatives would have lost six seats. On the other hand, if 20 per cent swung to Conservatives, Labour would have lost three seats (mine being one of them).

Mr Howarth, having extracted these figures, I am sure is correct to conclude that this is not any source of strength to farming. He does not add in the incalculable factor that, irrespective of the small number of seats involved, few politicians on either side believe that given generous policies they could produce a 25 per cent or 20 per cent swing among farmers. Mr Howarth says: 'agriculture's political strength lies in its less tangible influences'. I am not sure what he has in mind, but I am sure he is right. The strongest influence, I believe, though it cannot be proved and it is somewhat old-fashioned to say so, is in the merits of the case as it appears to the informed, opinion-making sections of the public. Thus, the reason why farming was so powerful in the 1940s and why the NFU was granted such very favourable terms in the 1947 Agriculture Act, was not fear of adverse votes or of any other kinds of muscle-flexing by the farmers, but the fact that food had been desperately scarce in the war; the nation had dug for victory and realised the tremendous importance in siege conditions of a vigorous agriculture.

The strength of agriculture declined in the late 1950s because people began to talk about world food surpluses, because it was clear that production in most western countries was rising faster than demand and that resources would have to be withdrawn from the industry. When this is the actual situation, the income of the industry is depressed and people wonder whether it makes sense to take fertile land in easily worked situations with a good climate out of production while paying special aids to hill sheep farmers struggling in the most difficult conditions on the tops of hills in Scotland and Wales. On the other hand, the greatest strength of agriculture in this weak bargaining position is simply that it is accepted that no worthwhile section of the community can be expected to take either an absolute cut in living standards while the rest of Britain gets richer or that there can be too drastic a gap between levels of growth of income in the various industries.

The tide changed somewhat in favour of farming in the 1960s for two reasons. One was that Britain's recurrent balance of payments problems made the performance of the industry in saving £250 million worth of foreign exchange in the decade 1956–66 impressive and the prospect of further savings attractive, and the other was that in terms of comparable incomes and of return to capital, the industry had a strong case for more income.

Before applying these arguments to the situations outlined at the start of this paper, it is necessary to mention the other organisations and sections of the community in Britain and abroad which can have an effect on agricultural policy. There are such bodies as the National Union of Agricultural Workers, the Country Landowners' Association and many specialised groups such as the National Growers' Association, the National Poultry Association of Great Britain and the National Sheep Breeders' Association. While these bodies perform useful functions and help concentrate ministers' minds on problems, and prod departments into examining special cases, again much of their success depends on the reality of the situation. Pressure groups in the sheep industry have had difficulty because the demand for mutton has barely risen, the price has stayed fairly level and therefore producers have been in considerable difficulties. There has been less trouble and therefore less organisation in the cattle side of livestock because the demand for beef and its price have both increased and show a better income elasticity than most agricultural products.

There remain two other sources of political pressure on agricultural questions, both of which are extremely difficult to assess. One is the influence of external suppliers of food to the British market together with the support they can gain from British exporters interested in reciprocal trade and there may also be some generalised sentimental support for certain Commonwealth countries whose economies have become heavily dependent on the British market. There is no doubt that New Zealand, the Sugar Islands and Eire all have made agricultural trading treaties with Britain which are advantageous to them and make life difficult for competing British producers (though the guaranteed price system is a form of protection both in the returns it offers to British farmers and in the way it keeps down import prices). How far these countries are able to use bargaining power in offering to maintain or create tariff preferences and how far Britain has the dominant voice because of the value to them of the British market is something that is barely calculable. But, to me, it has seemed that the major factor in determining the shape of these trade treaties was the theoretical one that the British negotiators accepted the economic theory that it was in Britain's interest to expand her exports of manufactures and also in Britain's interest to import cheap food.

The other source of pressure which is hard to assess is the most generalised one of all, the desire of British consumers for cheap food, and of taxpayers for reduced taxes. While both are important sentiments, the specific effect on agriculture tends to get lost because food prices are rising for many reasons and the impact of higher guaranteed prices (or even of a levy) may get lost in the overall secular trend. Similarly, there are growls in the Commons and among the public when those unfortunate words, 'an award to farmers of XX million', are announced each year, but no-one knows just how much of their tax bill goes on agricultural support. And there may be a dim realisation that if farming is not supported by the taxpayer, an alternative method will have to be found which might well be equally or more unpleasant.

Summing up these pressures and trying to give some weighting to their effects in each of the two kinds of situation described at the start of this paper is hard and must be largely a matter of guesswork. However, it would seem that in determining the annual level of support and its distribution, the economic situation of both the country and of agriculture are the primary factors. The Treasury has the main role in explaining the former and the Ministry of Agriculture (with the NFU at its back) the latter. But once the overall level is settled, then the NFU plays a larger part in dealings with the Ministry of Agriculture in settling the form of the shareout and its distribution between commodities. Even here, however, the Treasury may take over and, as in 1970, insist that extra money must not be put merely on the end price but made dependent on extra investment and efficiency. Other, more general, factors and the minor pressure barely come into the reckoning.

In the case of the major change of policy (to levies), the overall balance of forces is surprisingly similar, though the broader considerations appear to have been political rather than economic. The Conservative Party leadership was scrutinising public expenditure looking for public expenditure that could be abolished or the burden transferred direct to the consumer. Agricultural support was an obvious candidate. Also, the Party wanted to reduce the amount of government and agriculture is one of the most highly administered industries (the cost of running the support system is over £10 million a year). Thirdly, the Party leaders wanted to get agriculture in line for joining the Common Market. All these three pressures pointed to a radical change towards a levy system.

The Conservative agricultural interests were probably unhappy about this at first but reflected that they were a small minority in the Party and that by this method they might be able to get both extra resources for expansion and achieve the political aims of their party. (On the first point, it was never proved that more resources would be available, but this was accepted as likely by these farming MPs.) It is interesting that in this calculation, general objections to increased food prices were not considered a serious political obstacle and, indeed, Mr Heath managed to make his central theme in the 1970 general election an attack on rising prices with a farm policy in his manifesto (which was barely mentioned) which would have the effect of pushing these prices up even further.

At this stage the NFU, who apparently had not been consulted, were told about the policy (in a speech by Mr Godber at Cambridge on 23rd March, 1968) and reacted so strongly that the Shadow Minister took the policy back and talked it over with them. The main lines were not open to negotiation, as in the Annual Review, but the detailed application was and Mr Godber came back in January, 1969, with a new account of how prices would be stabilised by a 'fallback' guaranteed price. He did not spell out the details, but the NFU was sufficiently placated to let the policy be announced without making any formal hostile statement. Thus, as in the Annual Review negotiations, pressure by the NFU obtained alterations in specific points of application but it was overall political and economic considerations, the facts of Britain's position and the prevailing beliefs in Whitehall and the parties, that determined the course of agricultural policy.

This discussion of political pressures in the formation and conduct of agricultural policy can be summed up in several ways. One is to look at the converse. What is the main weakness of agriculture when its claims for support are being weighed by the final arbiters, the Treasury and the Cabinet; that is being weighed against the claims of higher education, defence east of Suez, the motorway programme or the popular acclaim that follows cutting sixpence off the income tax? I suspect, and this is, like the whole of this paper, just an impression; I suspect that the chief weakness like the major strengths listed above lies in the realities of the agricultural problem, in the real question marks that lie over the merits of the alternative policies.

When one turns, then, to these weaknesses, what are they? The sort of problems I have in mind include the following. It is hard at present to measure the value in terms of national wealth of switching resources from agriculture to industry and *vice versa*. Then, while the value of agricultural production as an import saver is clear, does it make sense to expand British production when in Continental Europe and North America great efforts are being made to take land out of production and to cut the resources going into agriculture? Again, is it possible to get farm amalgamations and the extra efficiency which comes from larger units while aiding agriculture to a level which encourages the marginal man to stay in the industry? Would it not be better to try and keep up the income of the industry, not by ploughing in more resources, but by encouraging withdrawal, thus sharing the returns among smaller numbers? Then, even if the objectives of agricultural policy were agreed, there are severe technical problems in achieving them. It is, for example, impossible to say what level of farm income will rise from a given level of deficiency payments. Moreover, miscalculations are inevitable where factors such as weather and animal diseases play a part, and in an industry where small changes in supply affect demand very little, but can have a catastrophic effect on price, farmers are often complaining that the costly support system, painfully evolved (whatever it may be), is not working and they want more money at once. These technical difficulties are not avoided by the levy system. For example, no one can say how much of a higher market price will find its way back to the producer. It is hard to forecast whether such higher prices will or will not produce a shift of resources into agriculture. And, in terms of the balance of payments, who will pay the levy – the British importer in higher import prices or the foreign supplier?

In my view, the difficulty in reaching agreed policy objectives in agriculture and the technical difficulties in costing and bringing about these objectives when they are determined, constitute the greatest political weaknesses of agriculture; they are the greatest handicap to those arguing the case of the industry on the occasions when the major policy decisions are being taken.

The moral of this paper, if there is one, is that more work needs to be done on agricultural problems and that the quality of public discussion should be raised by every means possible. This is why I so lamented the untimely end of the Select Committee on Agriculture. It is why I think it is madness that we in this country do so little to equip our oppositions to study problems, to carry out their own research so that they are equipped, not merely to oppose, but to raise the level of the argument and to contribute ideas of their own. Although my unscientific approach can only have lowered the tone of this conference, I am nevertheless glad to be here and to participate because of the Oxford Farming Conference's pre-eminent record in tackling the sort of problems that we must thrash out in the interests of agriculture and of sensible public policies in Britain.

Discussion

Mr W. Sternfeld (Lincs.): I would congratulate Mr Mackintosh on a beautifully unbiased and fair paper. He said that he wondered what effect the NFU had on bargaining, but I don't think he is quite as naive as he made out. Would I be right in thinking that, in the battle between the Ministry of Agriculture on the one hand and the Treasury on the other, the Minister of Agriculture might be delighted at any time to have any ally, such as the NFU, as long as they don't start blocking streets with tractors, and that such an ally would help him with his case in the negotiations with the Treasury?

Mr Mackintosh: I think the Minister of Agriculture likes any ally he can get, though again I think it would be dangerous for him to say too strongly to the Treasury, 'The farmers don't like it,' because you remember what happened to the girl who said 'My mother wouldn't like it,' and the boy said, 'Your mother isn't going to get it!' (Laughter.) I rather feel that might be the response if it were pushed too hard, but I quite accept that any support that they can get is welcome, and judicious pressure by the NFU clearly helps very much to create this atmosphere. I think also that the reverse can happen, that the NFU can say that if certain things aren't done then production will fall, and you could carry your argument one stage further that the NFU should welcome Mr Wallace Day and his organisation, because they can then say to the Minister of Agriculture, 'Persuade the Treasury to be nice to us, or you'll have to deal with them instead of us!'

Mr F. C. Mannell (Devon): I would like to congratulate Mr Mackintosh on a wonderful paper and I am reluctant to get up to criticise anything, but he kept referring the whole time to support for farmers, while on the other hand to the fact that the cost of living would increase considerably if we shifted the emphasis of support to the levy system. Surely nobody is going to let him get away with this, for it is blatantly obvious that the support is to the housewife and towards keeping the cost of living down? You only need to go across to the Continent to see what the housewife over there pays for equivalent produce in her shopping centres, and the fact that they come across in droves on the Channel steamers to buy cheap food to carry back to France.

Mr Mackintosh: I hope I didn't give the impression, as I obviously must have done to you, that I am a keen supporter of the levy system, as I have always criticised it for the reasons that you give. I prefer the money on the end price, and the guaranteed price system as by far the superior method of agricultural support, and I use the word support though I know that one wants to be careful about catch phrases of this kind, because different forms of support exist and one has to work out which sections of the community benefit. On the whole, I would always prefer a guaranteed price system and I would myself oppose a levy system very strongly if it was just introduced by itself. I would take it as part of the Common Market package deal, because I think other benefits would be greater by going into the Common Market, if you want my opinion on these matters, but I do also think that in a few years' time, when the Common Market is virtually self-sufficient in all major temperate food products, then a levy system will cease to be effective. It only works if you import and have to get over a levy. If you become self-sufficient, then you must drop your price, and I think we might see the Common Market in the late 70s producing the type of agricultural support system much more like the one we have in this country now, so I don't think we're committed for ever to the levy system if we go into the Common Market.

Mr J. M. Johnston (Oxon.): I was absolutely fascinated by Mr Mackintosh' paper, which covered the ground in almost every detail. He did list amongst the pressures which tended to play a part in forming Government decisions, the chemical industry, but there are a number of other industries which are ancillary to agriculture which are of extreme importance in that they are industrial in nature, such as agricultural engineering, rural building, rural transport, agricultural merchanting and even banking. Would he agree that no Government can allow farming to decline and thereby injure these industries, and would he agree that perhaps they lend great support to agriculture in any negotiations with the Government?

Mr Mackintosh: I did think about this, but it is very hard to be specific about it. My impression would be that when agricultural policy is being decided, these industries do not make separate representations to the Government or to the Ministry of Agriculture. They are deeply affected by whatever happens to agriculture, but if you take each of them, they are branches of a major industry which has so many other consumers, and so many other people it deals with, that I do not think you will find them making special representations about agricultural decisions affecting them. Take, for instance, banking. The banks have lent a great deal to farmers, but they have lent to many other people, and on the whole the banks dealing with the Government have not, I think, categorised agriculture as being different from other industries, though at times there has been pressure for the banks to give special treatment to farmers. But this hasn't come from the banks, it has come from the agricultural industry through the Government to the banks. Similarly with engineering, tractor-making, fertiliser provision, building and so on. These are in all cases important, but agriculture is only one of a number of consumers and they may make representations, but I have never come across actual evidence of them doing so. Where I myself have made representations on behalf of my constituency is when, in a purely agricultural area, there is a serious drop in the well-being of farmers and in their income level, which affects all these ancillaries. You find that the suppliers have bad debts, and wait a long time to be paid; you find the local small building contractors falling off; you find all the other side industries feeling the pinch in that area, and the accumulative effect in a purely rural area is therefore very serious indeed. This is the sort of situation where actually the member of Parliament plays a more useful role than the managing director of any of these industries, who sees it as a small part of a big industrial pattern, other bits of which may be booming or doing relatively well, whereas the person representing the geographical area sees the total accumulation of impact of these things on that one community. I think that this is a very strong argument which one tries to put, and I would like myself to go back to more open bargaining, and to be able to visit the Minister of Agriculture during such periods and tell him about these points.

Part 6

Reforming Calvinistic drinking habits

Drink is the curse of Scotland. Scots drink more, and suffer more from alcoholism than any other British nation. The traditional responses to this excess are either to ban the sale of drink or to make the place and time of its consumption as nasty and inconvenient as possible. John Mackintosh deplored both.

6.1 Debate on the Clayson Report on Scottish Licensing Law (Hansard, *H C Debates*, 18 April 1975, cols. 38–44)

When the Labour Government began to move haltingly towards reform, Mackintosh made common cause with the Licensed Trade Association in pushing for more liberal and more civilised drinking laws.

I am glad to take part in what has been a useful and helpful debate.

I should like to make my position clear. One of the residents in my constituency is Mr Arthur J. H. Squair, the chairman of the Scottish Licensed Trade Association this year. When he became chairman, he asked me to help to push the case for enacting Clayson in the House, and I said that I should be glad to do so. I have no other connection than that of conviction. There is no question of any sponsorship or association with this organisation – with which I disagree on a number of major points. But I said that I would do what I could to get the report considered and to push for legislation.

I therefore took an all-party delegation to see my hon. Friend the Under-Secretary and to ask about what was happening. He told us that some work was being done, and I think every member of the all-party delegation will be extremely grateful to the Under-Secretary for the very helpful way he received us and the useful information he gave us.

Turning to this debate, an important point has been made by several Members. We are legislating for conditions in Scotland, but the tourist trade is important to many of us. To try to change licensing laws on the excuse that tourists want change but we do not is not very satisfactory. We must produce a situation which is adequate for our own people and which fits the conditions of the day. We all recognise the problem of alcoholism, but we do not know enough about it.

One of the few points where I disagree with the hon. Member for North Angus and Mearns (Mr Buchanan-Smith) is that I do not think enough research has been done. I occasionally look at the research on this matter to find out the connection between alcoholism and other activities. It is easy to say that in 90 per cent of cases – which is the figure someone quoted – there is a connection between crime and alcoholism. It is by no means clear whether the crime would have been committed without the alcoholism and whether the alcohol only triggered off behaviour that would have taken place under other stimuli and in other circumstances.

Recently when students in universities with which I am connected took to drugs in large quantities, I saw the dean in one of them who said that he wished they would stick to the drink as 'we' used to. It is not always clear in these cases what causes what and when I look at a recent study of the definition of an alcoholic I find that no one is very clear. I had the strong impression that the definition of an alcoholic was someone who drank as much as oneself and whom one disliked intensely.

One thing which is clear to me is the point made by the hon. Member for Roxburgh, Selkirk and Peebles (Mr Steel). The law as it stands has not prevented alcoholism. The law cannot be said to be a safe guide or a bolstering up of good behaviour because we have not all the good behaviour that we would want.

We have had a great deal of change. We ask where the present Scottish licensing law originated. It is interesting to look back and see that it originated from the kind of quotation that the Secretary of State gave dating from 1915. Present licensing laws and practices date from the turn of the century and the immediate pre-First World War period when the temperance movement, very powerful indeed and closely allied with left wing progressive movements in Scotland, was clear in its mind that alcoholism was a great problem – greater, I believe, than now. They intended to stop this by making it clear that if a person was going to drink, it was to be under certain circumstances in restricted areas and in conditions that were so unpleasant that no one could do it unless, in the Secretary of State's words, he 'had a real need'. People should not be attracted to these places.

Therefore, there was legislation restricting hours, closing on Sundays, forbidding adequate number of seats, entertainment, people under a certain age, creating the conditions we remember in the pubs of our youth when it was done behind frosted glass in uncomfortable premises, with a tray of sawdust around the bar, where people leant against the rail and merely consumed.

I remember going into a pub with a friend in Partick when I first worked in Glasgow. We started conversing with the men in the bar and they said that they would like to talk to us but it was not the place for conversation. They drink and talk when they are put out at 10.20. That sort of approach to drinking created a certain environment and atmosphere which persists in places.

I understand the Secretary of State and others when they ask whether we want more of this and want to let children into that kind of atmosphere. Of course, the answer is 'No.' I remember when women were not allowed into that kind of atmosphere. When I was a student at Edinburgh, there were 10 pubs – my hon. Friend the Member for Glasgow, Queen's Park (Mr McElhone) talked about 100 pubs being in one ward – in one block near Edinburgh University and they all carried the notice in the window, 'Women not served', for the simple reason that they were so sordid and unpleasant that the only women who would go in were undesirable and they wanted to protect their customers from them.

That is the sort of situation we had in the past, and I think we are moving away from it. Clayson is absolutely right about licensing being a restrictive and negative process playing only a strictly limited part. The next sentence in the report gives the clue to the whole Clayson Committee approach:

'The part' the law should play 'should be that of strengthening social control by helping in the formation of public attitudes to alcohol and modification of practices in its consumption.'

We have witnessed a strong movement in parts of the country along this road. In my constituency – and unlike most Members, who appear never to touch alcohol in their constituencies, I go into pubs and clubs in it – a great change has occurred in the past 10 years in working class areas where men now take their wives, particularly to the clubs.

Previously they left them at home on Saturday nights. The atmosphere is far more pleasant. There are attractive lounges, fitted carpets, and entertainment provided of all kinds. This has now become a social occasion, a place where the women and even the parents and grandparents can be taken. The whole atmosphere and conduct is better.

This is very much a circle. If the behaviour is bad and the atmosphere is wrong and one intensifies it, the situation becomes worse. If, on the other hand, people are enabled to behave better in a better environment, they begin to think of the whole process in a different fashion and one has a different attitude to drink. It seems to me that this is what the Clayson Committee is trying to introduce with its various proposals.

At this stage we should not discuss details, but I should like to make the point that there is a strong public opinion in Scotland now for change in our laws to bring them up to date with the best practices and to reinforce the good practices that I have described. One simple example that I would urge upon the Secretary of State is that if the law falls behind social practice people find ways around it. We remember the old '*bona fide* traveller' law for drinking on Sundays. If people wanted to drink, the buses went three miles out of Edinburgh. Everybody had a drink and then they went back again. It was a complete abuse. Because people wanted a drink on Sundays they got round the law. In my view, it is better then to change the law and support good practices.

The same is happening today. The burgeoning of clubs is in part because a person cannot go into pubs on Sundays. I know of alleged clubs. There is a mining club – not in my constituency but next door – which takes £100,000 a year. The pit was closed four or five years ago. It exists simply as a method of allowing people in that area to have a drink on Sundays before lunch or in the evening.

It seems to me that if this is what the public wants, we should keep pace with them in our legislation. What we do along this line – to urge that the places people go to should be pleasant places, places where they would like to be seen, to spend an evening and where they go not simply out of a primitive need which must be satisfied – will induce the kind of social behaviour which all of us would like to see more uniform in Scotland.

This brings me to one or two simple examples of the kind of difficulties we are in. People have spoken about the question of children. The Secretary of State is right about the traditional Scottish bar. The answer is clearly 'No' to the question whether we would want children in them. It would be disastrous. On the other hand, when one thinks of the pleasant restaurant, the situation in Banff described by the hon. Member for Roxburgh, Selkirk and Peebles (Mr Steel) –

Mrs Winifred Ewing: And Morayshire.

Mr MacKintosh: And Morayshire – where children were with their parents on a social occasion, a satisfactory and proper occasion, this is entirely desirable.

I had the opposite experience from the hon. Gentleman when I returned from holiday abroad and was taking my family on a shopping expedition. We went for a meal into what appeared to be a restaurant in the West End of Edinburgh. After I had helped them to food, the proprietor appeared and said that he was sorry but the room was defined as a bar since drink was served in it. He said he regretted it, but we had to leave.

The same occurs in my constituency where there are some beautiful villages and pubs which are attractive and delightful to go into. There are suitable adjoining rooms to the bar, yet on chilly days one's children must sit outside on the pavement clutching their Coca-Colas because the landlord is not prepared to take them in. They should have a nice room similar to their living rooms at home and an atmosphere which encourages them to behave in a proper way. It seems to me this is the kind of progress that we want.

When my hon. Friend the Member for Glasgow, Queen's Park and the Secretary for State talked about 'need', and said they disliked commercial assessment this again expressed an old-fashioned view because it tended to regard the desire for a drink rather like the desire to relieve oneself. It sounded like a decision on the number of public urinals to be sited: what are the 'needs' of the people in this area? It all depends what is being offered and what is being provided.

I can remember when there was almost no restaurant eating in working class parts of my constituency. People did not go out to eat because they ate at home. Now that they are better off and there are good restaurants providing a good meal, people want to go. If people are providing an attractive place to spend a night with one's relatives, friends or social acquaintances, then the need is created. I do not think it is a bad need, and I would much rather people did their drinking in this kind of social atmosphere with other people than that they did it at home.

This brings us back to the children question. My hon. Friend made a good point when he said that people can get drink if they want it. If children under age want to drink, they can get an over-18-year-old friend to bring it to them. There is no problem about this. The real problem nowadays is whether one wants teenagers to drink at parties in their own houses with drink bought by those who are over age, or whether it is better to have them in social situations where adults are present, where there are other people whom they respect who see them and watch how they are behaving. Which is the more desirable situation? I appreciate that this is a most difficult and complex problem and that there is no easy answer to it. What we want is progress along the lines I have suggested.

I hope, therefore, that the Government will consider this and agree to bring in legislation. As for several other hon. Members, the one thing that has disappointed me is that, although the Secretary of State suggested that the Department was working on some sort of Bill – he let slip the words, 'Committee stage' – I did not perceive an actual commitment to legislation or to the timing of this legislation. I hope we shall receive a commitment before this debate is finished. No one is to blame, but it seems to me that there is an element of delay. The Committee was appointed in 1971, it reported in 1973, it is now 1975 and it will be 1976 before anything is done. If one goes much beyond five years from the appointment of a committee, the actual evidence and the opinions put to the committee become out of date. The whole thing slips back even further behind social practice than it is today. This would be most unsatisfactory.

I would also make a point which will not have escaped my right hon. Friend. I hope no one will suggest that it is a question of parliamentary time, because I feel that being told continually that we have no time for divorce reform, for law reform or for licensing law reform in the present legislative framework constitutes a powerful argument that the legislative framework for Scottish affairs is not adequate. If this is the case, I would not want to see this argued. If there is a case for the Bill, and if it is, as I believe, demanded by Scottish public opinion and by a majority of Members of Parliament from Scottish constituencies – in the *Sunday Mail* poll 53 Members indicated a desire for some degree of reform and a change out of 71 – then I hope the Secretary of State will find time for this in the next Session and that before the debate is finished he will give us a commitment.

Part 7

Education and the Scottish intellect

If drink is a Scottish curse then education is an obsession. Education became the Jacob's ladder by which many Scottish youngsters climbed out of poverty. And criticism of the educational system, now feared to have lost its superiority over the English, is a constant theme in public debate in Scotland.

Few people have contributed to that debate as wittily as John Mackintosh. Perhaps his most telling contribution is the previously-unpublished lecture 'Teaching if nothing better offers' which lights on both the best and some of the worst aspects of Scottish education.

7.1 'Teaching if nothing better offers' (*Unpublished lecture delivered between 1954 and 1961*)

As a lecturer in history, I have always considered that I am a member of the teaching profession. Part of the work is reading and research (that is, preparing material for others to use in their thinking and teaching) but all teachers have to keep refreshing their minds and adding to their experience in this way. If the task were purely research, one would have a research fellowship or be employed by a body like the History of Parliament Trust. It is interesting and perhaps rather sad that some of the university staff have remonstrated with me for describing myself as a teacher. They would prefer the title 'lecturer' or 'historian' though the job entails many kinds of teaching other than just lecturing, and not all history teachers at universities can claim to have written history while some school teachers are historians in this sense.

There is a tendency within the universities to resent any suggestion that they have close connections with the outside world. The fact remains that teachers in the universities form a link in the country's educational system. We have to work with young men and women and accept not only a certain standard of technical ability on their part but a whole attitude to learning, acquired at school. A fair proportion of those who then return to teach in the schools owe their academic standards and their concept of what constitutes an educated person, in large measure, to their experience at a university.

In this situation, the level of university work is often discussed, the effect of entrance regulations on the schools is well known, and, up to a point, the requirements of the schools are considered in framing degree courses. But if one believes that education is important and teaching worthwhile, ought the university teacher to encourage students to enter the teaching profession? It may be said that this is none of our business – teach, but leave the students to decide their own future. Obviously this is broadly correct, but one's advice is often sought. The tutor comes (or ought to come) in constant contact with the student and his attitude to teaching, his values, though seldom or never explicitly mentioned, convey a sense of what he considers to be worthwhile. To put it at the simplest level, almost all honours students tell their teachers in the final year what they intend to do – does one approve and encourage if it is teaching? I remember that in my own first visit to the university as a freshman, even before the start of the term, the Director of Studies asked me to fill in a blank in my matriculation form entitled 'intended occupation'. When I said I had no fixed intentions, he put down 'teaching if nothing better offers'.

Facing this problem, I thought it best to have some idea of the attitude of the students. I asked eighteen students entering their final year of the Honours course in History whether they wished to teach and to give me their reasons for and against. The number consulted was insignificant and the result was only a guide to the feelings of that particular group, but I found it useful. Three wished to teach, eleven did not and four would accept teaching if they could not get into the Civil Service, journalism, or start on full-time research.

The reasons for not wanting to teach were interesting and depressing. In almost every case, low pay was not the most important deterrent, though many mentioned it and several added that the annual increments were too small. The chief reason for turning elsewhere was a feeling, expressed in different ways, that the profession lacked confidence, lacked pride in itself, was unexciting, contained too many discontented or dull people, produced small-minded men and women who stood on their dignity or, as one summed it up, 'I have seen what it has done to my father'. Four replies concentrated more on what the public thought of teaching and complained that its social status was low. Several found the year at a teachers' training college a disincentive, repeating criticisms they had heard from friends at Moray House. Other points which featured on a number of lists were control of promotion by a non-professional board which, it was said, led to canvassing and extraneous considerations in promotion, and three mentioned large classes and poor conditions in some schools.

Turning to the reasons for teaching (and all who did not wish to teach nevertheless mentioned those aspects which did attract them), the major one was that it was a socially useful and rewarding occupation. Next came long holidays and security, the chance to keep up with one's subject, and time for outside activities.

One factor which stood out was that the students knew much more about teaching than about any other job and had given the matter considerable thought. It soon became evident which aspects of a profession tend to appeal nowadays. The full page advertisements in *The Guardian* and *The Observer* dwell on the same points. Reasonable pay is usually assumed; what matters is status, security, yet combined with this must be a sense that there is variety of experience, wide possibilities for advancement and making your own mark. Of these the only one that teaching offers is security.

Given this background what should one reply to the student who says 'Next year? – Moray House, I'm afraid'. In my own case, I have always thought that teaching has tremendous attractions. There can be little more satisfying than bringing on a good sixth form – or winning the confidence and exciting the imagination of a junior secondary class. And in the holidays one can write, travel, start a PhD or stand for Parliament. On the other hand, visiting schools, I have doubts. There is a terrible status – or rather 'lack-of-status' – consciousness among teachers, and the visitor listens to an endless round of complaints about butchers who can afford better cars, about lack of respect from children, parents, and the public – and yet there seems to be little *self*-respect in the first instance. What is perhaps worst is the lack of unity in the profession. Being shown round a school, the headmaster often pauses outside the classroom door and slips one the vital clue to the inmate – not, 'good teacher' or 'very interested in theatrical work' – but, 'this man has a second', 'only an ordinary MA,' or 'one of our few non-certificated teachers, I'm afraid'. These divisions are reflected in the various organisations whose conflicts prevent teachers presenting a unanimous case on educational questions. Heads of departments will explain that they have problems, but that everything is fine for the non-graduate women teachers. Divisions of this kind are reinforced by the superiority of senior over junior and secondary over primary schools, and together they are bound to have a deteriorating effect on morale. In dress and manner, in the conversation in the staff room, the visitor often gets the impression of a discontented, clock-watching group of men (less so, perhaps, among the women) whose chief interests are focused on their private lives when they are away from work. If all teachers could be miraculously offered a 'free transfer' to the job of their choice, how many would choose to remain in the same profession? How many recommend their children to follow them?

This question of self-respect or *élan* in a job is extremely important, especially to the new arrival. Whatever the attitude of the average university student, my impression is that by the time the young graduates have completed their teachers' training and found themselves a job, they are enthusiastic. It is their first responsible task, their first chance really to do something on their own, their first pay packet. Yet there is nothing more dampening than to join a group in which cynicism or lack of constructive interest prevails. Some time after a student of mine was appointed to the staff of a large junior and senior secondary school (not really comprehensive) in a mining area, I met another member of the staff and asked if he knew the man in question. 'Oh, yes', he said, 'a do-gooder'. He is the only one who stays behind to help with the football but we will soon break him of that'. It transpired that the rest of the staff all rushed for their cars to get back to their wives, bungalows and the security of middle-class Edinburgh.

On the more cheerful side, morale seems to have risen a little from an all-time low in the late 1940s and early 1950s. Yet if, as appears to be true, British society is adopting the practices and values that have become most evident in modern America, the improvement seems likely to be temporary. In the United States, even after the worries about Russian scientific achievements, school teaching is regarded as scarcely fit for men who have an iota of ambition. Even career women steer clear of it. It has become a suitable occupation for young women and spinsters who do not want to tax themselves and who enjoy plenty of spare time. In a year in America I travelled in every sort of conveyance over most of the continent, but whether the person giving me a lift was a dirt-farmer, long-distance lorry driver, oil tycoon or fellow undergraduate, when I said I intended to teach, the response was the same – 'But you look as though you're fit to do a proper job'. Indeed, in any society where status and earnings are as important as in modern Britain and America, where elections are won not on wise or good government but on slogans like 'You have never had it so good' (coined first by the Democrats in the US in 1948) teaching is likely to suffer. It is significant that when the Royal Commission on Doctors' and Dentists' Remuneration carefully investigated the median income of comparable professions, they considered accountants, actuaries, barristers, solicitors, architects, surveyors, engineers, *university* teachers and graduates in industry, but not school teachers.

What, then, is one's attitude to be? Is it fair to recommend young men and women to enter an occupation whose long-term prospects seem so poor? The answer will vary, but must depend on one's values. If one believes that the constant praise of acquisitiveness and cupidity indulged in on all sides today is not just misleading but harmful, if one believes that awakening the imagination, producing a greater adaptability and understanding in even a handful of children is worthwhile, then there can be no doubt.

But besides a personal belief in the value of teaching, it is still possible to envisage measures which might maintain or even improve the position of the teaching profession. The first, and most important, step is to create a greater measure of unity. The nation appears to have accepted the need for education up to the present age and even beyond, yet there is a shortage of some 3,000 teachers in Scotland and 16,000 in England and Wales. As has been said so often recently, if the country wills the end, it must be prepared to find the means. But the existence of these gaps gives teachers no greater bargaining power or scarcity value while they are divided. There is no shortage of applicants of tolerable standard for the senior secondary schools – the vacancies are all in junior secondary work, and these can be filled with partially or hastily trained people for whom current pay and conditions are an adequate, and perhaps the only, attraction. What is required is not an insistence that only people with given certificates should be taken. The profession makes itself look ridiculous if men of known educational attainments and teaching ability are kept out just because they have not been to a Scottish teachers' training college. The task is to exclude men and women who have little interest in their subjects and cannot show any capacity to teach, and this might well involve the exclusion of some with university degrees.

A second expedient for creating greater unity and self-respect would be to devise a common source for all teachers. At present there is an unnecessary distinction between graduates and those from the training colleges. (I remember a student of mine who came up to visit me while he was at Moray House and complained that 'They treat you like children'. I asked for some instances and he said 'You know at the Union here, there is no distinction between staff and students – you can sit anywhere in the dining room. On my first day at Moray House, I sat down at a table and was shoo'd away – Reserved for staff only'. 'Very poor', I agreed. 'And what made it so much worse, I had to sit with some non-graduates'.) This division bears no relation to intelligence or capacity to teach. A fair proportion (usually given at about a third) of those entering the training college could have entered the university and in some cases the preparation at the training college is deeper and more valuable for a teacher than that undergone by ordinary M A students at the university. I am making no claim that the universities are superior bodies, but as graduates tend to feel superior to non-graduates, this might be diminished by making the training colleges part of the universities and awarding their students a minor degree. A single source of recruitment would do much to increase the feeling of common background and unity. The body awarding the degree in teaching could also perform the function mentioned above of deciding how to train, or whether to allow older persons from other occupations or teachers trained in other countries to teach in Scotland.

A unified profession could then demand that appointments should be by merit and lie with a purely professional committee, rather than with a lay body. At the same time the feeling that there was no route for the able to advance, for the enthusiastic to push along, could be reduced by pressing for proper sabbatical leave and for more exchanges (and for credit for such extra experience) with other countries. The universities could offer intermediate degrees involving some course work to be done in vacations or in a sabbatical period and some research so that promotion could be hastened by getting extra postgraduate qualifications. It would make a tremendous difference if a man knew that ability as a teacher, a B.Litt., and a year's teaching in Canada were more likely to bring him a headmastership than knowing the members of the education committee and being a pillar of the right church. This unity should be carried further and some teachers be asked to take a turn as assistants in the universities while lecturers could benefit from a spell of school teaching at occasions during their careers.

The more one reflects on the situation – the acceptance that children must be taught and a severe shortage of teachers – the more evident it becomes that the remedy for any weaknesses lies in the hands of the teachers themselves. If they were prepared to stress the importance of the ideals they serve, to unite and get control of the criteria for entry to and promotion in their profession, there is little they could not achieve. The constant failure to make use of such opportunities suggests that they have always been too ready to accept that it was 'teaching if nothing better offers'.

7.2 Debate on education (Hansard, *H C Debates*, 18 Nov. 1971, cols. 702–5).

Education is a difficult issue for Socialists to handle, more difficult than is commonly realised. The difficulty arises because education provides a means of individual salvation from ignorance and poverty which can be used by some members of the working class to rise and then betray their class. The pain of this betrayal is incomprehensible to many Tories, who fail to understand why Socialists insist so fervently on equal access to education and an end to all privilege. The Socialist in John Mackintosh burst out when the House of Commons debated a proposal from the Secretary of State for Education (Mrs Thatcher) that university students' unions be accountable to their universities for the public money they spent.

Mr John Mackintosh (Berwick and East Lothian): The hon. Member for Wellingborough (Mr Fry) says that hon. Members on this side of the House who are interested in education are bothered by envy. I agree with him. I am envious. I am envious of people in my constituency who live in small towns where there are perfect comprehensive systems. They need not think about standards, the quality of education or fees. They simply send their children to school. They think about the quality of the education, of course, and they think about the lessons. But they do not experience the misery which afflicts so many people in big cities who feel that they cannot send their children to schools created by ghetto housing and wonder what alternative they have, twisting and turning, this fee or that fee, up a grade or down a grade, will there be a uniform or will there not be? They do not experience all the wretchedness and misery brought into our education system by the class pattern of education that we have in our big cities. I find it the most repulsive and reprehensible part of our educational system.

I envy rural areas like my constituency and the Highlands of Scotland where there is one good school for the whole area for all classes. Parents have no second thoughts about the matter. Their children go to the school and they can concentrate on their happiness, well-being and development. I do not wish to be drawn into this theme, attractive though the curious remarks of the hon. Member for Wellingborough were.

This evening I want to raise points on one special aspect which has been raised, namely, the financing of student unions. I listened with considerable interest to what my right hon. Friend the Member for Sunderland, North (Mr Willey), the Chairman of the Select Committee, had to say and to the hon. Member for Chertsey (Mr Grylls). I was bothered about what the hon. Member for Chertsey said. It seemed to me that there was a basic contradiction in his speech. He said that he wanted the maximum autonomy for student unions. I would agree with this. At the same time, he welcomed the proposal in the consultative document that the entire financing of the buildings, the organisation and the running of student unions should come from the university authorities and be open to their financial control in detail because they, in turn, would be responsible to the Comptroller and Auditor-General for the spending of that money. I can think of no method of financing student unions which is more likely to cause trouble for the universities. I can think of no method which is bound to destroy the autonomy of university unions more clearly and decisively than placing them under the accountant of the university who will always be frightened of the Comptroller and Auditor-General who will in turn take him to task for how the unions spend their money.

An inevitable tendency, if we then give the unions in this detailed financial way to the university authorities, will be that the day-to-day running – because that is what the expenditure of money is – of the unions will be drawn into the hands of the university authorities. Every major dispute which arises between the students and their committee about how money should be spent, instead of being a matter for themselves, will be a conflict between themselves and the university authorities. This is a recipe for creating the maximum trouble and difficulty inside the universities. I hope that the Secretary of State will look at this point very carefully before she contemplates giving it her approval.

The right hon. Lady's proposals inevitably produce a series of peculiar contradictions. She says, for instance, that, on conscience grounds, she would like students to be able to withdraw from membership of the unions. At the same time she says that they should have equal use of the facilities of the unions. How does this work? How can a student say, 'I do not wish to be a member, but I can use every facility in the union'? What distinction does this make?

There is a subordinate idea that certain special funds should be given to students to join this or that society, but often these facilities are available inside the unions. Therefore, we would have three categories of membership: those who are members, those who can use all the facilities but are not members, and one cannot tell the distinction, and those who pay certain extra subscriptions and go into special rooms inside the unions for special purposes. This is a muddled, unthought-out approach and is liable to cause great trouble. Therefore, the right hon. Lady should look at this matter carefully before continuing with it.

Mr Edward Short: If students are allowed to opt out they will not be able to use the bars in the unions because of the licensing laws. There is a contradiction here. They cannot use all the facilities if they opt out.

Mr Mackintosh: This will create further difficulty inside these buildings. I think, therefore, that this proposal of giving a conscience clause of this kind is unsatisfactory.

I suggest a somewhat different approach to the right hon. Lady. I know that the difficulty is compulsory membership of the union. Without this, the local authority will not pay the subscription. This could be got round by saying that all students should get an addition to their grants to enable them to make use of the kind of recreational facilities which ought to be provided. I suggest that students ought not to be obliged to join a particular organisation with this money. I know that certain friends of mine who belong to student unions, as all who went to universities did, might be worried and might say, 'If you allow people to opt out with their cash they will use it for themselves and this will undermine the student unions as organisations.' This is true and it would happen. But I should like the Secretary of State and my friends to consider that many of the larger universities contain several organisations of this kind.

There is not one union. Indeed, for a university in a big city with 10,000 or 11,000 students, it would be a grotesque horror to think of a single organisation providing facilities in one vast building for those numbers. What happens in practice is that there is a main union and there are outlying facilities for students at the agricultural college on the edge of the city, for the medical students at the hospital, and for the science students who are often some distance away from the arts block. One gets a union more useful to a section of the university and subordinate facilities for others.

I suggest that there should be compulsion on the student to join union facilities, but not necessarily the one union in the university. We might allow students to choose from a variety of possibilities and thus encourage the creation of adequate facilities for different sections of universities which often feel under-privileged because they are not near the administrative centre of the university where the one major union facility is provided.

I should like to emphasise this point. If the universities and colleges provide one vast union building or try to encompass all the students in this way, they will produce a huge, impersonal curious sort of cafeteria-cum-jungle. I have been in such establishments recently. They have the air of the waiting room at Heathrow Airport at the end of a long day's use. I sometimes wonder why, when I was so happy at university, there are so many students who are not really happy and enjoying university life. They do not feel that this education is a privilege and they are worried about the situation.

I was at a small university and in a union maintained totally by subscriptions. It belonged to the students and was under their control. They operated under no supervision of any kind. By Jove, I should like to have seen anybody attempt to take any of our funds and give them to purposes which we did not want. We ran the place well and efficiently and provided better facilities than the university did in its refectories and various other ways. In that establishment there was a sense of identity and self-government, which we valued. Yet, just across the road there is now an amenities centre built by the university on a throughput basis of so many students per seat per hour, eating so many mutton pies, beans and chips per hour. Because there is a shuttle conveyor belt system, there is an air of lack of responsibility, lack of possession and lack of identification. I am not surprised that in these circumstances some of the students feel ruffled about the situation.

Sir G. Nabarro: Is it not a fact that when the hon. Gentleman was an undergraduate his fees to the student union came out of his own pocket. They were a private subvention. Was that the case? Today we are paying for it, and we ought to have some control over it.

Mr Mackintosh: That is not the case. I was entirely maintained by a body known as the Carnegie Trust for the Scottish Universities. This maintenance consisted of £9 per annum in those days. The rest I provided from work which I did. My point is that students are entitled to some support for these facilities. I do not believe it does students a great deal of good to be distracted from their studies by having to do outside manual work. The learning value of that kind of thing can easily be overdone. Students should be allowed to concentrate on qualifying in the subjects they are supposed to be taking. Therefore, a legitimate element of grant for this purpose from public funds, from local authority or central Government funds, is satisfactory. I think that the hon. Gentleman's point is that, if the student is given this money and is told to use it as a subscription to maintain his union, he will then watch over the expenditure of that money with the greatest of care. This is indeed a correct approach to getting responsibility.

I support what was said by the hon. Member for Chertsey. I think that in any case this whole business has been grossly exaggerated. Out of £3 million per annum spent by student unions, misappropriations have been trivial in terms of the total amount, and I should like to know how many local authorities could club together to spend £3 million with as little argument about how the money was spent, or how many private organisations have never had any instances of misappropriation when such a large sum has been involved.

It is wrong to condemn the students for wishing to give more to charitable causes. Students are idealistic. Many of them want to give money to these causes, and they should be congratulated on so doing. They should have autonomy in deciding how they do it, but I agree that the money should come out of subscriptions which they would otherwise retain for their own benefit and purpose.

I am worried about the consultative document. It seems authoritarian and paternal in approach, though I am not necessarily attacking anybody for that. It is a recipe for increased trouble at the universities. I wish to see students given greater autonomy. The decision on how to use grants provided for their purposes should be in their hands. They should be given the chance to develop responsibility in applying the grants to their own needs.

7.3 'The case for traditional teaching' (*The Scotsman*, 26.4.1976)

John Mackintosh was usually on the reformist side of an issue. But in his article 'The case for traditional teaching' he spoke for many.

There are times when one's personal experiences, the cases and complaints from the constituency and evidence from friends and former colleagues seem to add up and suggest the existence of a real problem. This had happened to me in recent weeks over education.

My eight-year-old son (at an Edinburgh – or rather Lothian Region – school) was groaning over his homework recently. I asked him what he was doing. 'I am drawing five baskets with 25 pineapples in each and it takes such a long time.' 'What on earth for?' I asked. 'To show that 5 × 25 equals 125,' he replied.

It reminded me of a situation some years ago when I visited a primary school in the constituency and got a little confused trying to do sums with coloured bits of wood. The youth I was talking to helped me: 'It is easy if you understand numbers,' he pointed out.

The recent evidence from my constituency came from some primary schools in Berwickshire. There the parents, or some of them, had become disturbed about the standard of education. When I asked what they meant, their replies revealed a worry that their children were not as far on with reading and writing as they, the parents, had been at a similar age. The cases quoted were, for instance, of a parent asking a nine-year-old to look up a number in the phone book and finding that this was impossible because the youth had never been taught the sequence of letters in the alphabet.

The final comment came at a recent British-French conference held in Edinburgh where I was talking to a lecturer in French at Edinburgh University. He complained that nowadays it was much harder to teach French language because boys and girls coming to the university had not been taught the rudiments of English grammar and so this ground work had to be laid before it was possible to go on and teach them French grammar.

What then is the Member of Parliament, the parent or anyone else outside the school teaching profession to make of this kind of evidence? Has something gone wrong in our educational system? Are standards falling or do such standards of technical achievement matter anyway?

Considering these questions, the first lesson I learned is that most people, including those with a real concern for education, have little or no idea what is going on in the schools. If one asks one's children, they regard this as an inquisition and take refuge in non-committal replies or just disappear. Even the talkative among them usually only recount anecdotes about the teacher or their friends. If the question is put during visits to schools, the headmaster will say, 'we have adopted X or Y modern methods,' but it is hard to be sure that this does mean that these methods are actually being practised once the classroom door is shut, particularly when the teacher was trained long before these methods were invented.

Secondly, it is a complete delusion to imagine that certain categories of schools are synonymous with certain types of education. Many people talk as if comprehensive schools are all permissive, anti-streaming, 'learning by discovery' and so on, while direct grant schools cling to older, more didactic forms of teaching.

This does not follow. A tremendous amount depends on the staff, particularly the headmaster and on the director of education. Some local authority schools retain the older methods while some fee-paying schools with young staff or a recent appointee as headmaster may be up to date with the very latest fashions in curricula or classroom organisation.

It is interesting also, that the great semi-political battles over education have almost never been about what is actually taught. They have tended to focus on school structure, on the leaving age, on co-education, on the degree of choice of schools to be permitted and on the merits of separate schools for Catholics. While this last example does affect the content of teaching, separate schools for Catholics is also a broader issue. The bulk of educational conflicts have been about the effect of different kinds of education on the structure of society or at least about the relations between schools, schoolchildren and the community at large.

After an all too brief period (the recesses are short) talking to teachers, to those who specialise in education and reading some of the books being used, I have formed certain not very confident conclusions. The root of the problem seems to be a reaction against the old (very Scottish) assumption that children would rather play, that acquiring a mental discipline can only be by application, by repetition, by constant practice and that this must of necessity cause some discomfort. The teacher's task, according to this older view, is to exercise the necessary moral (or, a generation ago, physical) pressure to curb children's normal preference for light entertainment and to drill them in these mental disciplines. This attitude was particularly prevalent in the primary school where the basic techniques of reading, writing and arithmetic were being inculcated and where it was harder to explain the purpose of the work. It was enough that it had to be done.

Many pupils, some of whom later became teachers, reacted against this just because it did involve pressure so that children often did not like school. It was not always clear why these particular techniques were being taught and sometimes the teachers were not confident about this themselves. Looking back on their school days, the more sensitive teachers reflected that subjects had been killed for them by too much drilling and by the failure to let children proceed at the pace dictated by their own interest in the subject.

Some of this reaction became associated with objections first to segregation by academic ability between the old secondary and secondary-modern schools and then to streaming on similar grounds within schools, but there is no necessary connection. It is perfectly possible to apply the older methods in non-streamed classes while modern group teaching should mean that each pupil or at least each group goes at his or its own pace, which is a form of streaming.

Before commenting on these different basic approaches, some caution is necessary. There is an obvious danger that the middle-aged take alarm if their children are not following the same routines of learning as they themselves experienced. Also learning certain skills is not the only purpose or value of schooling, and it does seem to be undeniable that children are happier at school nowadays and that the schools are brighter, pleasanter places than they were 30 years ago. It is also clear that children will learn more readily and more rapidly if the work means something to them.

I recall a dissolute Highland cousin who turned out to be a brilliant teacher of maths to the less bright pupils. He used to hand out pools forms and the children worked out their perms and bankers, or he would put up a dartboard and throw the darts while the pupils each subtracted the scores from 301.

But when all this is said, there does seem to be more validity in the older assumptions and some real dangers in the view that there must be a painless way of acquiring all mental disciplines. It is curious that the objection to constant repetition of an exercise until it becomes automatic applies only to academic work.

No-one objects to the physical training instructor making the winger cross the ball again and again until he can drop it exactly outside the far goal post. No-one objects to the piano teacher's exercises being continued until the fingers automatically hit certain keys when certain signs are seen on the music sheet. But there seems to be a deep objection to a similar way of learning certain basic mathematical relationships.

Because some children find such things as memorising multiplication tables unpleasant or actually difficult, teachers have tried to devise methods of learning which make this information both evident and fun to acquire, but then there is a tendency to accept the idea that it is best for all children to acquire their information in the same way. In fact, for those who are adept with numbers, the easiest and most satisfying way of proceeding may well be simply to learn the numerical relationships; that is that x times y equals z. In front of me, I have 'Mathematics for Schools' by Fletcher and Howell, and its ingenuity in helping the non-numerate to visualise numerical relationships is impressive. But one has to witness the acute frustration of the numerate child (aged seven to 13 for this book) having to draw five blue cars and then three red cars to establish that 5–3 equals 2.

It is hard to see why there is anything wrong – and indeed there seems to be much right – in having different mathematics classes directly a clear gap appears between those who can deal with numbers in their minds and those who can only multiply when they can see the objects in the form of pictures or handle them as counters. If it is suggested that this introduces an invidious distinction, this does seem to imply some discrimination against academic aptitude.

No-one objects to the exclusion of the child who cannot hit a note from the school choir. It would be thought positively cruel if the uninterested or unadept were forced to play football with the skilled and able performers. So why insist that there should be a common pace and method in academic areas where aptitudes are equally diverse?

Two further dangers seem to follow from some of these newer approaches. The first is that if a pleasurable method, a learning-by-discovery method of acquiring a subject cannot be found, that subject should be left out of the curriculum. One cannot easily draw or model grammar and that seems to be why it has tended to be abandoned by some schools.

Secondly, though it need not happen, there is a tendency in this approach not to stretch pupils. Few people like being stretched, at least when they are young and unaware of their potentialities, yet this is surely an important part of education; to teach pupils to do the very best they can. And if it does not happen sometimes, then surely this can lead to as much boredom and rejection as the excesses of the older, didactic forms of instruction.

Perhaps all this article demonstrates is that I am 'an old square,' but I do feel some alarm over teaching methods in our schools, though I also sense that this alarm is being shared fairly widely and that there may be a swing back commencing – not leading to an abandonment of all the newer practices but a recognition of some merit in the more traditional forms of teaching in certain subjects and for certain kinds of pupils.

Part 8

Scotland's place in the EEC

8.1 'Scotland and Europe: regionalism and nationalism in the European community' (Unpublished lecture *Institut Royal des Relations Internationales of Belgium* on 22 October 1975)

John Mackintosh's part in the battle over British accession to the Treaty of Rome is covered in Professor Marquand's companion volume. Typically, however, he also turned his mind to the question of the effects on Scotland's constitutional position of joining the EEC.

The referendum was a tremendous victory for the Europeans in Britain. The outcome – a 68 per cent majority in favour of British membership – was higher than any of the Europeans had hoped for and a devastating defeat, both for the extreme Left and for the narrow Nationalists in Britain, both of whom had opposed British membership. The danger is that the completeness of the victory will lead to the European question being forgotten, or at least set aside, and that Britain will return to a passive interest in internal political problems and will forget about the whole problem of the Community now that the question of membership is settled. There is also the point that because senior politicians made commitments at a time when they thought that the result could be narrow, these commitments will lie around, affecting their conduct in the future, although the pro-European campaign has ceased, because of the victory. Thus Mr Callaghan gave commitments that Britain would look after its own energy problems and is adhering to those commitments, although British public opinion would be quite prepared to take a European approach to the energy problem.

What will happen now is that the further development of British politics will take up European questions in as much as they impinge on British political life and one area in which this will undoubtedly occur is the whole question of devolution and regional policy. One reason why the Scottish vote for membership of the European Community, though clearcut, was slightly lower than that in the UK on the whole, was a fear that membership of the Community would lead to an increased pull for Scottish talent and for all new activity, not merely to the South East of England, but into the heartland of the Community based between the Ruhr and the industrial North East of

France. As a result, the Scots are more interested in regional policy than other parts of the UK and would like to see this policy offset the pull, not merely to the South East of England, but into the heartland of the Community. At the same time, with a greater percentage of the Scots employed in fishing and in agriculture than in the rest of the UK, European policies on these matters also impinge more on Scottish affairs than they do on UK affairs.

Given this situation, the internal development of British politics links in with this connection with Europe. Within Britain there is disappointment at the overall economic record of the British Government and of British industry. At the same time, there is a greater desire for local control over environmental questions, services such as education, health and local government and the whole quality of life.

In the case of Scotland, this general tendency, which is evident throughout Europe, is intensified by the existence of certain characteristics of a separate nationality. These characteristics are a separate educational system, a separate local government system, a distinct Roman-based legal system and a Presbyterian church, all with their headquarters in Scotland and all helping to maintain a separate Scottish identity. Over the past 260 years since the Treaty of Union of 1707, the Scots have maintained a dual nationality, part based on these separate Scottish institutions and a separate history and tradition, but part ready and willing to be British because of the economic and international success of Britain and because of the special British features of parliamentary democracy and a respect for the rule of law – features which were not so true in Scotland before the Treaty of Union.

Now that Britain is less successful economically, is no longer a world power and has abandoned its colonial empire, the Scottish side of dual nationality has become more prominent and with Scottish membership of Europe as part of the UK membership, it is possible that in addition to the dual nationality they will develop a European conscience which may take the place of the British element in Scottish thinking. In this sense, the Scots may come to look to Brussels more than to London for those aspects of policy that are clearly outside the control of Scotland. For this reason, it is important that the Scots are about to obtain a separate Scottish Parliament and Executive which will deal with all those aspects of internal policy that are purely Scottish. All that will be left to London will be overall economic policy, defence policy and foreign policy. If these matters are increasingly dealt with from Brussels then the British aspect of the dual nationality may well be replaced by a European aspect and this will receive institutional recognition after there are direct elections of Scottish members to the European Parliament and some separate representation of Scotland in the European Commission in Brussels.

Here two important points arise. The first is the question of oil revenues and the Scots have been interested to see Mr Callaghan going as a British nationalist in this matter by reserving a special British position at the World Energy Conference; and if Mr Callaghan is going to insist on this line it encourages those Scots who believe that the oil deposits in the sea off Scotland are peculiarly Scottish and that Scottish interests are different from those of the UK. It is in Britain's interest in this case to play the European card and to argue that these deposits belong to the whole of Europe rather than particularly to Britain because too much emphasis on ownership only strengthens the hands of Scottish separatists. The second point is that the Scots are clearly more interested in a strong Europe than the English because the Scots wish for the kind of help out of the Community that goes particularly to weaker, or peripheral, areas and especially the Scots are interested in the agricultural, fishing and regional policies, as well as the energy policy, of the Community in a more real way than the South East of England which could conceivably get along without positive support from Brussels.

As a result, the problem is whether Scotland, which may well have its own subordinate Parliament and Executive from the latter half of 1977, should have separate representation in Brussels. At the moment this is done on an *ad hoc* basis, with one Commissioner who happens to be a Scotsman and with representatives in the UK permanent delegation who come from the Scottish Office and realise that area's special problems. There are Scottish politicians who think this is not enough and want separate Scottish representation at the Council of Ministers and in the Commission but to achieve this Scotland would have to be a separate country. I must not conceal that this is a political possibility, though I still believe a remote one. The most likely outcome is a devolved Scotland, with a separate representation in the UK delegation to the Community, and a special Scottish interest in European development, partly because Scotland needs this support and partly as a counter-balance to English domination from London so that if Europe tends over the next generation to develop a local or regional particularism, combined with a stronger centre in Brussels, this would suit the current development of Scottish politics. If this does not happen and if Europe remains a collection of national sovereign states, then the Scottish end of the UK connection will undoubtedly be one of the more positive factors pushing the UK into a definite and

Community-minded agricultural, fishing and regional policy. I regard any of these as welcome tendencies which will help to broaden the parochial character of Scottish politics and to reinstate Scotland as a small but lively section of the European Community.

Part 9

Back to fundamentals: the failure of institutional reform

The campaign for a Scottish Assembly engaged part of John Mackintosh's attention from 1958 until his death in 1978. Near the end it was all too clear that the job had been botched. John Mackintosh's disappointment with devolution was deep and his feeling was shared with the entire generation of political activists who had been drawn to politics by the early successes of the Attlee Government. Some reacted to these disappointments by giving up the fight, withdrawing from politics – or their instrument of reform, the Labour Party – and taking well paid jobs in some machine the Government – often a social democratic government – had created.

John Mackintosh continued the fight both on the party and the theoretical plane. Like the Scottish radical he was, he insisted that the root of the failure be sought: he turned back from institutional reform to political theory.

Towards the end of his life he was battling for a way beyond social democracy and the mere reform of the machinery of government. We print here, uninterrupted by comment, three pieces on this theme.

(*The Scotsman* of 15.8.1977 and 10.4.1978 and a typescript of the unpublished Earl Grey Memorial lecture, delivered in Newcastle University in 1977).

9.1 '"Overload" and compromises that conceal failure'

(*The Scotsman*, 15.8.1977.)

The position of Denis Healey, the Chancellor of the Exchequer, and of the other senior Ministers on wages is a peculiar one. They say the one thing that could ruin this country's economic recovery would be a series of wage settlements well above 10 per cent which would then push the inflation rate back up to its recent levels or even higher.

On this, they are absolutely right. For inflation to climb back above 20 per cent would ruin our export market and have terrible social consequences at home. This being true, one must wonder why the Government does not turn at once to the public sector (by far the biggest employer) and issue a simple instruction 'Pay no wage claims where the total is above 10 per cent.' Then the Government could turn to the private sector and say: 'It will be an offence for any employer to pay or for any worker to receive a rise of above 10 per cent and those that do will have to pay extra taxation to bring the amount down to 10 per cent.'

The answer in the case of a Labour Government could be that the unions are too integral a part of the party to permit any such tough line. Certainly some key Ministers would resign at once. But, in reality, the answer is that no Government of any party or combination of parties would do this for the simple reason that they would not believe they could enforce it.

Hence the paradoxical situation that the one crucial item in an economic policy, for whose success the Government will be held responsible, is something about which the Government can do nothing except make hopeful noises. The Conservatives, for their part, say they believe any incomes policy is worthless. What they would do is not yet clear but they will certainly blame the Government if the inflation rate turns up again (whereas their views would suggest an honourable admission that this is outside the control of all Governments).

This kind of situation, in which Governments set targets and accept responsibility for policies which they cannot achieve, has come to be known by students of politics by the jargon term 'overload.' Why have the public become more and more sceptical about parties and the whole machinery of government and why have politicians shown signs of a severe loss of confidence in themselves? The answer in economic terms (which matter most in modern consumer-conscious societies) is that over the last 15 years, parties have promised stable prices, full employment, steady growth and so on and have failed to produce the results.

The public are also to blame for this 'overload.' They expect the Government of the day to provide, to fix, to pay for, to settle everything. In the heyday of British democracy half a century or more ago, no-one thought the Government could do these things. It could pass laws on specific forms of conduct which the police and the courts enforced. But the Commons laughed at Keir Hardie when he asked 'What are you going to do about the unemployed?' not because they were callous but because it seemed ridiculous; Governments, they believed, could not create jobs. It was like saying: 'What will the Minister do about the weather?'

Now the public expect the Government to take everything on board. If the fishing fleet has a bad month of catches they are down in Westminster asking the Government what it will do to resolve the problem. If the livestock prices fall in the market for three weeks running, the farmers are on the phone to their MPs. When the public pay for holidays in the sun with a company, Court Line, which went bankrupt, the Government was expected to compensate the holidaymakers. Compare this with the failure of the City of Glasgow Bank in 1878 which ruined many families in the West of Scotland – yet no-one dreamt of asking the Government to step in, except to enact stiffer laws about banking conditions and limited liability which the law courts could enforce.

The problem of 'overload' does not just occur on economic matters. Sir Harold Wilson said (about 1966) that the Rhodesian rebellion would be over in days, not weeks. Now, British Ministers edge around hoping that with US and South African support they can have some marginal influence. No recent British Government has looked like settling the Northern Irish problem.

But these are foreign affairs. Surely, at least in matters of domestic institutional organisation there have been some successes? Perhaps, but overload or, to put it bluntly, failure, is also only too evident. Recently many of us (I plead guilty) argued that local government could be modernised in a way which would make it more efficient, more democratic and more independent of central Government. Yet the reformed system is unpopular, very costly and services are no better. The Health Service was reorganised in a way which is now admitted to be a failure and has created bad blood between doctors and the Government. After years of trying to reform the House of Commons to make it a more effective check on Government, the few MPs who were interested in this have had to admit defeat on general principles even if the present parliamentary situation has allowed a little scope for forcing amendments on this Government.

Apart from identifying 'overload,' what causes it? British Governments had far fewer resources of technique or of wealth before, say, the 1950s yet there was no such succession of failures. And how long can a political system fail to reach its targets and still hold the support of the people?

On the economic side, matters are worse in Britain than in other equivalent countries. One theory (still held by many in Westminster, Whitehall and the various think tanks) is that there is nothing seriously wrong. What happened was a series of misfortunes which 'blew the country off course.' The other theory is that there are special structural problems in Britain with far too few people of ability going into management, into engineering, into technology and into business.

It is certainly true that in fields where talent congregates, there is not the same sense of failure, an example being the top flights of medicine. Again, British TV and journalism are as good as anywhere in the world and there are few complaints about our services. The same can be said of British universities, of pop culture, music and of the arts in general. But these are all activities which attract the ablest people and where the resources, though tight, are available. There is no doubt that this does not apply to the whole area of making and selling goods. And the politicians are partly to blame, for neither party has worked out a sensible way of running a mixed economy which gives clear lines of guidance to the public sector and a sense of stability, of being wanted, appreciated and adequately rewarded to the private sector.

Looking beyond the economy, one cannot help wondering whether failures in this central and critical area have weakened the self-confidence of political leaders in all parties. Certainly the idea of pursuing a matter to a solution is unfashionable. The notion that everyone must be met, that consultations and compromises are of the essence of government, is deeply ingrained.

Take the Rhodesian case. Britain has endlessly consulted and negotiated but never taken action. It might have been better either to wash our hands of the whole thing, or, if a settlement really mattered to this country, to have put in an airborne division and thus have been in a position to lay down a settlement. To this, one gets endless questions such as 'Would the Army have gone?' or 'Could we spare the troops?' But Cuba, with the aid of Russian air transports, was able to alter completely what happened in Angola. Given the will, could Britain not have managed as much as the far, far poorer and smaller country of Cuba?

Or take the Northern Irish situation. The British Government could have announced that, on a certain date, the Army would be withdrawn and the two communities in Ulster left to sort out their differences. Or the Government could have said that if the two communities cannot live together, sections must be moved so that each gets what it wants. All Catholics could have been resettled west of the Bann and south of a certain line and those areas then transferred to the Republic while Protestant settlements were moved back to fill in the gaps. But of several – all cruel, drastic and unpleasant – solutions, successive Governments have preferred the cruel, drastic and unpleasant non-solution of letting the insurrection smoulder on.

In domestic matters, one sees the same deep-seated desire to avoid clearcut action. The present belief that the trade unions have a positive veto over certain policies and that wages guidelines cannot be enforced springs, in large part, from the miners' defeat of Mr Heath's Government in early 1974. Contrast this with the situation when the Baldwin Government knew it would face a challenge from the miners in 1925–6. Then the Government bought time, built up stocks, prepared emergency services, chose its moment and fought. It defeated a General Strike and then, after six months, the miners gave in.

In the case of Mr Heath, he could have decided that the miners were a special case and let them have their claim, or he could have prepared his ground. Had he used troops to ensure that coal supplies and oil reached the power stations and had no three-day week and no election, he might have won.

Now I must emphasise I am not necessarily recommending draconian policies – troops in Rhodesia or outside power stations or a repetition of Ulster. I am pointing out the consistent preference of Labour and Tory politicians for agreed or negotiated settlements rather than for attempts to cut through to a definite solution. There is a philosophy abroad that no-one must ever be hurt, no-one must ever lose. For example, when local government was reformed, everyone had to get a job at their former rate. The Health Service is reorganised so that no-one is ever sacked and no-one is clear how decisions are made.

Does the public want this kind of government? Most people think that the answer is 'Yes' and that modern Governments not only suffer from 'overload' but also from an incapacity to handle rough situations because they are dependent on so many groups. No solutions can be driven through because they hurt some people and the public would prefer problems to grumble on rather than be called on to support decisive but abrasive action.

I am not sure if this is true but I do think we are suffering too much from 'overload.' It would be far better, in my view, if Governments more often announced that they could do nothing about certain problems. But in cases where Governments can take action, I would also prefer a clear decision either to leave the problem alone or to go in and try to impose a solution. I do not think we can live with endless compromises which, in reality, conceal failure, for very much longer.

9.2 'Now is the time for all good men . . .'
(*The Scotsman*, 10.4.1978)

In a recent article, Mr Joe Rogaly of the *Financial Times*, said that the Labour Party did not deserve to win the coming General Election because it had run out of ideas; none of its leaders had thought through the major problems of our times. (He went on to add that the Conservatives did not deserve to win either as they were trying to conceal their lack of any policy by attacking the weaker element in society – immigrants, social misfits and the unemployed.)

As far as the first point is concerned, it is true that there has been a lack of cogent thinking and writing about the purposes of social democracy. When the Labour Party faced the 1945 General Election it had a coherent programme. There was an undercurrent of Marxist thinking in that production for profit was considered to be of dubious value and was regarded as the main cause of undesirable class divisions.

Hence the programme contained a list of industries to be nationalised. This, it was held, would cut down the numbers who lived on unearned incomes. Public ownership would make it possible to plan production according to social needs and would also help to create full employment and better labour relations in those industries.

But the objection to a class divided society owed as much to R. H. Tawney's ideas set out in 'Equality' and to a moral or even religious conviction that people were of equal value as it did to any Marxist analysis.

On top of this policy or supplementing it was the concept of a welfare state drawn from the Beveridge Report and J. M. Keynes' idea that demand could be managed in a way which would ensure full employment.

Thus the state was to take a series of concrete actions, pass certain laws, take over certain industries, set up certain welfare schemes and a National Health Service, and plan the economy so that living standards would improve, social gaps would diminish and people would be encouraged to think of each other's needs and to cooperate in meeting them.

By 1951 when the Conservatives came to power, this programme had not merely been enacted but had been accepted as part of the post-war consensus so that the incoming Government made no attempt to undo what had been done. The programme had achieved concrete results because it had consisted of certain far-reaching economic and social changes which the Labour Government had been able to carry through.

But, by doing all this, the Labour Party had, for practical purposes, worked itself out of a policy; its final objective of ending class divisions had not been achieved but all the steps it had devised to reach this end had been taken and they had many beneficial effects.

Nevertheless, the Labour Party needed a policy for forthcoming elections. The answer was provided, by Anthony Crosland, in his book, 'The Future of Socialism,' published in 1956. He began by rejecting the Marxist idea that class was based on the private ownership of industry; he did not accept that some got richer and the bulk of the community got poorer or that the capitalist system was bound to collapse.

Crosland argued that democracy meant that people could take over and modify their society as far as they wanted. As to the form of our society, ownership was no longer a key issue and he was clearly right that whatever nationalisation had done, it had not diminished class divisions.

Crosland, like those who put together the 1945 programme, saw these divisions as the major blemish in British life though he assumed this rather than explained why he came to this conclusion. But he put the blame for class divisions on what he called 'distance factors.'

The first and most important was in education. 'The school system in Britain remains the most divisive, unjust and wasteful of all the aspects of social inequality.' Then there was the unequal possession and inheritance of accumulations of property, the fact that some people are simply much better off than others, and finally the difference in the ways people are treated at work.

For Crosland, the key was economic growth. This would continue because managers had such a strong drive to achieve, to build up their concerns and the extra wealth they created could be used in two ways which would improve society.

First, it would go to the less well-off and since there is a limit to the number of houses, cars, food and clothes that people can use, when all have a reasonable amount of these goods, social gaps will have diminished.

Secondly, the extra wealth would be used by the state to build up social spending. For instance, a first-class, equally available education system would be used by everyone and would, like the Health Service, be acceptable to everyone thus ending educational advantages and disadvantages with all their unfortunate consequences.

Soon after he wrote, Professor Galbraith underpinned this attitude to public spending in his book, 'The Affluent Society,' which blamed private enterprise for taking all the advantage of growth and insisted that the state should improve its services as they particularly helped to raise the standards of the underprivileged.

This was the reformist or social democratic doctrine on which Labour fought the 1964 and 1966 elections. Harold Wilson added little in the form of ideas but he did create an atmosphere of modernity and of activity. His notion of harnessing technology to those Socialist policies was clever and exciting and suggested that growth could, under proper state planning, go even faster and further than Crosland had anticipated.

What then happened to the policies based on Crosland's ideas? The Labour Government which lasted from 1964 to 1970 did not leave a mark on British society as the 1945–51 Attlee Government had done. After 1970, the record of Wilson's Government was attacked from both Left and Right and these attacks have grown since Labour returned to office in 1974.

The Left has gone back to a Marxist critique and has argued that tampering with capitalism, indeed the whole concept of a mixed economy, is a failure. This system cannot now preserve full employment or maintain an adequate growth rate. The multi-national corporations are too much for democratic governments of the Left and the only answer is to return to wholesale nationalisation.

The Right have argued that Keynesian demand management cannot work when the unions monopolise the labour market. The result of trade union pressure is inflation, bad balance of payments figures, declining confidence and less investment. With low growth, the increased public spending advocated by social democrats has become an intolerable burden and has led to high, even penal, tax rates so that incentives, investment and output all decline even further.

Whatever is thought of these attacks, two points have to be conceded. The first is that the economic record since the mid-1960s has been dismal. With low growth, all the underpinning of Crosland's programme has gone. It has not been possible to provide both better living standards and the improved public services he had wanted.

But there is a deeper problem. What he was after was a change in the way people treated each other, in the way people regarded their fellows and this is far harder to achieve than the practical series of enactments listed in Labour's 1945 programme.

Of Crosland's proposals, some have been tried. For instance, comprehensive education has spread but it has not had the effect he wanted because schools take on the characteristics of the neighbourhood and parents can move to areas where the school is more desirable.

The capital transfer tax should cut deeply into inherited accumulations of wealth but one effect has been to give people an incentive to insure against such a reduction in what they want to pass on to their children.

In fact, the weaknesses of the social democratic philosophy go even deeper. One, which Crosland did not recognise, was that a mixed economy cannot be run successfully on the general view that the private sector is a reprehensible element which can be squeezed, reduced, hammered and appealed to as the Government's needs alter.

In reality, Crosland, like all the non-Marxists in the Labour Party (and many ostensible Marxists in Eastern Europe), believed that a mixed economy was essential to maintain the basic freedom of choice, the freedom to move from one employer to another and to bargain for wages.

But neither he nor his disciples ever produced an adequate rationale for the private sector which would have given its managers a reason for their existence, a justification of their work and a defence of the legitimate value of their efforts. If this plus heavy taxation meant that the private sector flagged, then growth was poor and down tumbled the whole edifice.

This problem also affected the public sector. Nationalisation by itself was not enough. There had to be methods of managing these industries which ensured that they contributed a reasonable amount to growth, yet these methods were never devised. It was a basic error to talk endlessly about distribution of wealth, its taxation and its use for this and that but very little about the creation of wealth.

Like Marxists and classical economists, social democrats assumed an unquenchable desire by industrialists, businessmen and traders in the public and private sectors alike to perform. What was to be done if all these people either preferred non-productive jobs or just slackened off was never contemplated.

A further serious difficulty that was ignored was that if the Government steadily extended its activities in planning, taxing, spending, and managing, a point is reached where there is a balance between gains for equality and losses for freedom.

To have similar schools for all enhances social equality, but may also penalise the bright child from a poor background. To build thousands of council houses gives people the enhanced freedom of having a home but if the only landlord is the council, it can impose very restrictive rules on its tenants.

In a sense, then, Rogaly is right. These weaknesses in social democratic theory have not been thought through. The Marxist critique is of no help as its solutions would destroy both growth and freedom. The Right wing attack is deficient as the result of following its advice would be to exacerbate class divisions. It would leave the poorest to carry the heaviest burdens and its concept of freedom is the freedom of minorities to buy special treatment.

But the central task of justifying and producing a thriving mixed economy remains. It is also necessary to have a much more careful analysis of the effects of action by the state and by large corporations on personal liberty, for one major objective in seeking a more just society is to enhance freedom. Finally, it is important to be clear just how far governmental changes can go in altering people's attitudes and social values.

In fact, all the major difficulties facing our society are contained in the dilemmas of social democracy and no other way forward has been found. It is too much to ask any individuals or any political party to produce clearcut answers between now and a General Election.

But it is to be hoped that the victors will be people who at least understand the nature of the problems and are prepared to grapple with them.

9.3 'How far is Britain a democracy?' (*Earl Grey Memorial Lecture* delivered at Newcastle University in 1977)

Anyone in political life is accustomed to the mixed attitude of the public towards our democratic system, towards politics and politicians. There is very little public enthusiasm for our machinery of government; indeed the way to win elections is to run on an anti-government ticket as Jimmy Carter showed. This battle takes place over devolution; demonstrate that it is anti-London government and the Scots support it. Demonstrate that it means more government, MPs, parties, taxes and bureaucrats and it is rejected. Further evidence comes from the fact that both main parties have lost members and, indeed, in some places barely exist. In Canada recently, I was told that the average Eskimo family was a husband, wife, two children and a social anthropologist. Here the average constituency Labour party is some old age pensioners, two Marxists trying to make a takeover and an American Ph.D. student. At the last election, I met a glum man and asked him what was wrong. 'It's this miserable election, Mr Mackintosh'. 'Well,' I said, 'I don't particularly like these occasions but what do you find so depressing about this one?' 'It's just that one of you two lots is going to win.'

As I say, one is used to this public attitude of doubt, mild derision and even distaste but what is less expected, as far as I was concerned, was that when I came back to teach politics, the situation was not very different in the academic world. I do not refer to academics' attitudes to politicians but to the actual academic theories of democracy. As far as I can see, there is no single, coherent view of the nature of British democracy or set of agreed criteria by which one can say how far Britain is a democracy or which way we should improve or develop our system of government.

This is curious for many reasons. So many people think and talk about it or at least about the converse. We spend so much time saying what we do not like about the Communist states of Eastern Europe, about Amin's Uganda, about Spain under Franco or about South Africa and about some Latin American dictatorships both of the right and of the left that it is surprising that we cannot, in contrast, say precisely what is good about our own system of government. For instance, most of us dislike Communist states because of their conviction that there is only one true view of history and politics, and while this may be a liberating force for those who believe in it, it is also a terrible restriction for those who want to take their own view and who believe that people cannot develop fully unless they can express themselves in this way. Equally most of us dislike a régime of the kind established in South Africa because it builds into its laws a lower valuation of the humanity of large sections of the population. We dislike right-wing dictatorships because they also consider their view of the structure of society, of its history and the forms of excellence permitted are the only ones allowed.

Now why is it not possible to invert these arguments and produce an account of the values of democracy which most of us could, by and large, accept and which could allow us to answer the question posed by the title of this lecture:— 'How far is Britain a democracy?' Before considering the problem it is worth dealing with a preliminary point. Some people will say, 'does it matter?' 'We may grumble about our system but there it is; we prefer it to others and it works after a fashion, so why worry?'

I would like to suggest two answers to this point. First, our society is always altering and this forces change in the machinery of government which has actually to deal with people and institutions. If the machinery of democratic control does not alter at the same time, it will not work. Monitoring machinery must alter in parallel with the things or processes it seeks to control. But if there is no democratic theory, then the changes may not take place or may even lead to an abandonment of control. A major reason for the failure of parliamentary reform in the 1960s was that there was no agreement about what Parliament's role in a democracy should be; was it to punch through lists of manifesto promises endorsed by the electorate at a general election or to subject all government proposals to a real and searching scrutiny. Because there was no agreed view on this, there was no change and as the administration spread and did more, Parliament was increasingly left behind.

Secondly, it is right to worry because the criticisms of Parliamentary government are swelling and while it is silly to be alarmist and there have always been criticisms, support for systems do weaken if there are trenchant criticisms and no positive convictions. So, there is Lord Hailsham on the right complaining of an 'elective dictatorship' and the left writing about 'the crisis of capitalism' – which includes a collapse of confidence in parliamentary institutions and no great retort from those who purport to believe in the system.

For both these reasons, then, it seems to be important to have an argument for valuing or defending the system of democracy in Britain. Looking at political theory, what could be said in defence of our institutions, what criteria could be applied to test their worth and show the direction in which they should be developing? One theory of democracy is that of consent or of a contract freely entered into which implies the existence of consent. This can be alleged to exist in several ways. First, individuals who do not consent to or agree with the current practice of democracy in Britain can vote for parties which resist it and, in some cases, vote to leave it. Most of them, at the coming general election, could vote for a National Front candidate and some could vote for left-wing candidates who reject parliamentary democracy but there is no evidence of an increasing number doing so. The National Front has not gathered any strength nor has the extreme left.

Then again, people can leave. Emigration to Canada, Australia or the United States is neither hopelessly crowded nor expensive yet the queues to leave, either among the skilled or in professions covered by the term 'the brain drain', have not got larger. In a sense, another way open to the Welsh and the Scots of indicating that if they no longer have any faith in the British system of government, they can vote for independence, that is to get out, yet the support for both Plaid Cymru and the SNP has apparently fallen off a little in the past year.

In this sense, there may be consent or acceptance of British democracy but is this enough? It is rather like the Churchillian remark that 'democracy is the worst system of government devised by man except for all the others'. The trouble with this approach is that it gives no positive reason for backing and no guide when it comes to choosing between alternative courses of action. For instance, do referenda strengthen British democracy because they give the people a chance to make their views known or do they undermine faith in Parliament's right and capacity to make decisions? Ought the leaders of British parties who are the actual or potential Prime Ministers to be chosen by MPs or by a poll of party activists or by the party conferences or by some kind of direct primary? Again, the fact that the British public are, by and large, willing to tolerate the present system gives no answer. This 'take it or leave it' approach is not a substitute for a belief that the system is positively valuable and some idea as to why this is so, a belief that can rally support and provide arguments for those who wish to rebut critics and refurbish aspects of the institutions that are showing signs of decay.

A second, more detailed or precise version of the consent argument is to say that British democracy does provide a means, through the ballot box, for a majority of voters to consent to the policies enacted by the government they elect. But this theory also poses many problems. Is it the majority that matters? No-one is very sure and critics of the present government point to the fact that it received only 39 per cent of the votes cast and 28 per cent of the votes that could have been cast. Some take this as an argument for proportional representation and say that the public's support would be far more positive if they knew that 50 per cent of voters had backed the combination of politicians who composed the government. But the Liberals had 18.3 per cent of those voting behind them in October, 1974, and when David Steel made his pact with the Government in March, 1977, this should have put up the total support level from 39 per cent to 57.3 per cent and have created the situation advocates of proportional representation find acceptable. Yet there was no evidence of new backing for the government or for its policies or for the two parties to the pact; indeed, the result has been disastrous for the Liberals.

What is not clear about this form of the consent theory is to what people are consenting. One reason for the view that MPs must vote for everything in the party manifesto is that this has been specifically endorsed by the public; by the voters. But this is obvious nonsense. The manifesto is drawn up by a committee or clique nominated by the leader of the party. Most MPs play no part in the process and most voters have no idea what is in it and, when asked most party adherents disagree with a fair number of items in the manifesto. Why then, does the manifesto have this special force? The answer is that there is a feeling that it has been endorsed or consented to by the voters and the whole notion shows that there is a deep confusion between the ideas of representative and of direct democracy. The idea of representative democracy is out of fashion, but it holds that voters choose people whose judgement they trust. They hold them responsible for what happens and if there is a failure, these representatives are sacked at the next election.

But for many, representative democracy is only a poor substitute for direct democracy. The ideal is all the citizens of Athens gathered together deciding what should be done. This is impossible in a modern state so one makes do with the poor substitute of representative democracy. If this is true, then the nearer the representatives conform to the views of the mass of voters, the better. The idea of the representative having a separate and independent judgement which he puts at the service of the voters has no place in this theory.

These two positions have been argued since the time of Burke but it is now possible to bring the argument to fundamentals. It is feasible with modern technology to recreate the Athenian democracy. Wedgwood Benn has talked about this. He has pointed out that it is not impossible to have a 'legislative half hour' on TV each night when issues are put to the 56 million in Britain. And when the case has been put, the audience can then press a red or a blue button on their sets and the electronic impulse can be picked up giving an immediate result – 22 million for a proposal and 17 million against. If this was feasible, would it be preferable to the system of representative democracy? We are in a primary confusion on this point which is why manifestoes have this special air of authenticity and why there is an increasing tendency to resort to referenda and to look over the heads of MPs at the reaction of the voters.

But there are objections to direct democracy which are not questions of its feasibility but which raise issues of principle, issues which indicate that representative democracy has a legitimacy of its own. The difficulty about direct democracy is that it would be easy to get majorities for a series of propositions – majorities in favour of stable prices, full employment, steady growth and so on when all of these things cannot be had simultaneously. To govern is to choose, it is to have a set of priorities and to show the capacity to carry these policies and priorities through. It is possible, after a reasonable period of time, to have a vote as to whether the result is acceptable but it is not possible to reduce sections of such policies to a set of 'Yes': 'No' propositions. The real problem is that running a nation is a highly complex operation involving more detailed policies than running a great university or a multi-national corporation. While democracy is in part, a theory of how consent is mobilised, it should also have a theory of leadership, the problem being how to keep leadership accountable and in touch and in tune with the people.

A third possible theoretical basis for any democracy is the old utilitarian arguments which have two elements. The first is that it is the sum total of well-being or happiness that matters and second that in assessing such happiness, each person is to count for one. Later on John Stuart Mill introduced problems of quality as to whether it was better to be Socrates unsatisfied than a pig satisfied but we are not dealing with pigs but with people. And it was and is one of the more appealing features of utilitarianism that it does not argue that one person knows better what constitutes another person's happiness than that person himself.

So democracy is the system of government that produces most contentment and if the government does not please people in this way, they can turn it out and in this respect, each person counts for one. Again the electoral system in Britain is a bit of a problem as given different sizes of seats and the first-past-the-post system, all votes do not count for the same. On the other hand, a small percentage deciding they would prefer another government (4 in 100 at the moment) could remove one government and install another. The electorate in Britain do know that governments can be sacked – this is a real power. But there is a question of the reality of the alternative open. I suspect that a major reason for public disenchantment and the questioning of traditional forms of government in Britain is simply a sense of disappointment among the electorate. In part, this may be because of Britain's decline from the position of a first class power but it is probably due more to economic disappointment. Since 1964, three successive administrations, the Wilson Government of 1964–70, the Heath Government of 1970–74 and now the Wilson-Callaghan administration have largely disappointed voters. There has been an average growth rate of 1.8 per cent compared with the 3 per cent of the 1950s, for two years, 1975 and 1976, real incomes actually fell and there is a great weariness over talk of economic crises, cut backs, the poor performance of British industry and so on. It is difficult to imagine that there would have been so much doubt about the electoral system, criticism of adversary politics, scepticism about parliament, attacks on local government and on the bureaucracy if the British growth rate had, like that of West Germany, averaged 4 per cent over these years and if there had been no serious inflation.

There is one response to this problem which is to say that politicians and governments have set their sights too high. In Lord Hailsham's words, they have failed to accept the actual limitations on their powers. They have raised expectations that cannot be met. In one sense I think this is wrong and in another, it has some substance. In terms of the targets set for this country, it is hard to blame Mr Butler when he said in 1954 that Britain's standard of life could double in 25 years – this would only have required a continuation of the level of growth achieved in the early 1950s and we were on target for almost a decade after he made this forecast. If one looks at the elections of 1959, 1964, 1966 and 1970, no leader ever promised growth rates of over 4 to 5 per cent (the 1965 National Plan was the most optimistic at 4¼ per cent) and there seems no reason why we should not have managed the growth rates of France, Germany and Italy; no reason why we should have slipped from a post-war position of being among the first rank of European powers to our present role of one of the poorest nations in the EEC. In this sense, then, I cannot blame the political system or its leaders for not accepting limitations which had not circumscribed this country in the 1950s and did not circumscribe other nations.

But there is a sense in which they may have themselves expected too much out of the political system. They may have failed to recognise structural problems in British society, in our attitude to industry and to wealth creation, in the relative prestige accorded to occupations outside industry, in our labour relations and qualities of management that were reducing Britain's competitive capacity and growth rate. The general assumption on both sides of the House of Commons has been that all is basically well with British industry so that Labour governments can control, tax, regulate it and steer it to the regions but it will go on producing – churning out the goods while the Conservatives feel that a few tax cuts, a few bankruptcies in lame duck firms and morale will soar and production go even better. There has been a refusal to recognise that there may be deep-seated social and structural problems and it is doubtful, even if such a diagnosis was made, whether governments are in a position to do the kind of social engineering, the kind of atmosphere changing necessary if these long-term trends are to be reversed.

This links in with another problem which would probably have arisen, as it has done in other democracies, whatever degree of economic success we might have enjoyed. The democratic conception that if those governing the country fail to please you, they can be thrown out implies that the real governors are the politicians or that they can control those other groups who were in power. But there is a widespread feeling that power now lies in the hands of the major pressure groups and of the civil service and that it makes relatively little difference who the electorate votes for. Michael Shanks has just written a book on 'What's Wrong with the Modern World?' and his conclusion is that government must proceed by a series of social contracts by which major issues normally settled by legislatures such as tax rates, pensions, industrial policy and so on should be traded with unions in return for wages policies and with employers for guarantees and investment. This has been happening. In 1976 and 1977 the Chancellor of the Exchequer proposed tax cuts dependent not on Parliament but on certain decisions by the TUC. We have had the curious spectacle of Mrs Thatcher actually asking a group of senior Conservatives whether, if there was a conflict between a Conservative Government and the major unions, the government could win and her advisers came up with the answer 'No'. When 54 per cent of respondents to a poll a year ago said that they thought Mr Jack Jones had more power than the Prime Minister, they were making the same point. For the left there are similar fears but they focus more on the civil service and on industry. Stuart Holland has argued that the multinationals can beat any democratically elected government and Brian Sedgmore MP produced a report from a sub-committee of the Select Committee on Expenditure which said that no Labour Government had or could overcome the built-in values of the senior civil service.

When there is a combination of disappointment about the overall performances of government with these views that little or nothing can be changed by the use of the ballot box, it is not surprising that the Benthamite case that democracy gives individuals the power to ensure the maximisation of their own happiness is not very effective.

It was customary, till recently, to say that there were no more modern political theories of democracy available. While Marxism continued to flourish as an intellectual exercise if not as a compelling political force among the people at large, there were no new or effective arguments in favour of democracy. In fact some ideas have emerged recently, mainly from Americans who seem to have been driven to think about these matters by the shocks of the Vietnamese War and the Watergate episode. Of these, one major defence of the western system is by John Rawls in his *A Theory of Justice*. He turns aside from traditional approaches to the control of political power and maintains that people ought to be content to live in and obey a just state. A just state is one which observes two principles. The first is that all citizens' rights to free speech, movement, belief and so on must be respected and these rights include the freedom to elect a government. This is political justice. Secondly there is economic justice or social justice and this principle requires that wealth should be so redistributed or shared so that no other arrangement of affairs would or could make the poorest sections of the community better off. His just society allows for differences of wealth and opportunity but only in as much as no change could improve the lot of the least privileged sections.

Is this, then, a better defence of British democracy? Are we, in this sense, a just society? In terms of the first principle, most people would accept that Britain remains one of the freest societies in the west. There have been examples of dubious acts – the refusal to let British passport holders exercise their right of entry unless they were 'patrials'; there were parts of the Prevention of Terrorism Act, and worries over the use of discretionary powers granted to governments for certain industrial purposes being used for different ends, for the unequal enforcement of incomes policies simply because a Bill explicitly granting such powers could not be got through Parliament.

But while the breaches of the first principle are few, the application of the second principle is less clear. After thirty years of the welfare state, it is still estimated that two million people are in some form of poverty. What seems so very unsatisfactory is not that there is a hierarchy in housing, some people being much better housed than others – this could be a matter of their priorities or preferences – but that the people who are at the bottom of the jobs hierarchy tend also to be at the bottom of the housing, education, pension and health hierarchies also. Could there be a redistribution of resources that would make these groups better off? There are two conflicting answers, one from the left and the other from the right but both agree that justice could be better served. On the right, Sir Keith Joseph holds that taxation has gone so far and welfare has reached such a level of complexity that further redistribution is impossible and the total wealth available is less than it should be and so welfare is more skimpy. At present the Department of Health and Social Security pay 21 million benefits each week to 13⅓ million people. Almost one in four of the population receive benefits and the figures for 1975–6 (the last available) show that these benefits amounted to £9.5 billion a year out of a national income of £94 billion or one tenth of all income. And yet there are considerable groups in relative poverty. The left would argue that further taxation of wealth was both possible and desirable and that this could be used to make our society more just.

But even if a situation could be reached where Rawls' second principle of justice was met, would this be a satisfactory defence of British democracy? I think that he could be setting up, in a perfectly just society, a form of paternalism because he does rate the 'do it yourself', 'power to the people' aspect of democracy as important only in as much as the right to vote is part of a just system. He says nothing about the self respect aspect of being in part at least in control of one's own destiny.

His thought is taken a stage further by another important American author, Ronald Dworkin in his book *Taking Rights Seriously*. He makes many points but his major argument is that democracy and the defence of basic rights are not incompatible in that the values of democracy, of respect for individual independence are damaged for all if they are damaged for one and that therefore defence of individual rights must, in his words, trump or take any trick even if the rest of the cards are in the hands of a popular majority. This is really a brilliant defence of entrenching individual rights so that even democratic majorities have to back down before violating them. But like Rawls, it is concerned with the quality and effect of government rather than with the control of government.

So what is to be done about the case for democracy and are we any further in deciding how far Britain is a democracy? One problem is what we are trying to do in a quest for a theory. Is this a wild goose chase? Burkean conservatives would say that it is wrong and impossible to construct theories which both explain situations and are guides to further action. This cannot but be damaging. If there are periods of history when our forms of government are confused, contradictory and unsatisfying, then there is nothing to be done but wait till matters resolve themselves. Those on the left would say that the economic substructure is altering and that the old institutions of an earlier more individualistic bourgeois society do not fit the state or corporate capitalism of the late twentieth century but again nothing can be done to restore harmony except to hasten the collapse or revolutionary change of capitalism.

I am in the old liberal tradition in that I believe that the first requirement of any theory is that it must be logically coherent and that it must explain current situations and provide a guide for action which will meet not only our practical problems but those intuitive feelings we have about the values underlying human life. Rawls, like the old theorists of natural rights and of various forms of contract and consent, is right to ask people to stand back from today's problems and ask themselves what is essential for people to live contentedly and fairly together. What he misses is that one must also consider the current form of society where special skills are needed, where production is so interdependent that concepts of justice must take account of the fact that power is lumpy. Some people will have more power than others and will have vested interests. This being so, justice, fairness and democracy as a form of government ensuring these qualities must incorporate a method of restraining those with power, of holding them accountable to the mass of the people, of making sure that the general well-being prevails over special interests.

To construct such a theory does not seem impossible to me. This is what our political philosophers ought to be doing. I am no political philosopher but without such a theory, mere students of political institutions and labourers in the field of practical politics such as myself are without guidelines, without criteria for action. All through the 1960s we in Britain tried to reform our institutions without such a philosophy and the results were confused, inadequate or just trivial. For instance, I served for seven years on the *Select Committee on Procedure* of the House of Commons and we produced report after report but got nowhere because there was no agreement about how far the House of Commons as an entity should be able to scrutinise, check or reject the work of the government. The reform of local government has been unfortunate for the same reasons; no-one was clear about the degree of local autonomy that was desirable. How far should local government have a free hand and over what subjects with what degree of financial independence. One could multiply these examples by looking at civil service reform, the reorganisation of the Health Service or the current debate on devolution.

This is why I think that the adoption of certain devices or reforms – for which there may be powerful arguments – such as direct primaries, fixed term parliaments, proportional representation, will only lead to further disappointment and frustration if the basic principles are not worked out first. Perhaps I can conclude by setting out a few possible pointers for such a theory. There must be two sides to it. One is the Rawls or utilitarian concentration on the outcome. We cannot consider our society to be democratic or fair to its members if basic freedoms are denied and if there are remediable social injustices. Happiness a fulfilment in this sense, together with respect for the dignity of each individual is essential. Dworkin is also right that special precautions must be taken so that, in the words of his title, rights are taken seriously and safe-guarded even against fits of anger or prejudice by the community at large.

Secondly, government must be controlled and checked and kept subject to review. But because it is a specialised and skilled activity it is a sheer hoax to pretend that democracy means government by the people. What the people need is alternative governments between which they can choose and which will act as a constant check on each other. This is needed at many levels. It is not enough at the centre to have a small counter-civil service. There is also a need for medical experts whose job it is to see that the Health Service gives a good service and so on. A few laymen taking a few hours a week to produce complaints is not an adequate countervailing force. The central most important countervailing force should be the legislature but it will always be ineffective so long as its main task is supporting and defending the executive. Also to act as an effective check on power, it is essential that authority should be clearly located and so if there is to be decentralised or local government then it should only exercise those functions that can be definitely allocated to these authorities so that responsibility is clear and an elected countervailing force knows what it is supposed to do.

Finally, there will always be disputes about the sharing out of incomes and resources in any just and democratic society. Those groups with power cannot easily be controlled by an unsupported set of elected individuals or even by a civil service machine. They can only be controlled properly by enlisting the other groups with power and so conflicts of this kind between regions, between unions, between industries and professions must be institutionalised and brought out into open debate; the case for a just distribution must be established, and defended in public. Democracy is not just a fair deal and full freedom for the individual. It is also a system in which the Scots get fair treatment among the regions, the state pensioners among the other retired groups, the miners and the nurses among wage earners, the railway users as opposed to car owners.

At the moment we have a partial confused and sometimes unsatisfactory democracy in Britain and as an old believer in the value of rational thought about problems, I only hope I have not made matters worse.

Appendix

J. P. Mackintosh: a Chronology

1929	24 August, born in Simla, India
1940	comes to UK to Melville College, Edinburgh
1946	to Edinburgh University
1948	joins Labour Party
1950	graduates 1st Class Honours in History from Edinburgh
1950–2	Oxford PPE, Second Class Honours
1952–3	Princeton MA in History
1953	Assistant Lecturer, Glasgow University
1954	Lecturer, Edinburgh
1956	adopted as Labour candidate for Edinburgh, Pentlands
1957	marries Janette Robinson
1961	Senior Lecturer, Ibadan, Nigeria
1962	*The British Cabinet* published
1963	divorced; marries Dr Una McLean
1963	Senior Lecturer, Glasgow
1963	adopted by Berwick & East Lothian as Labour candidate
1965	Professor of Politics, University of Strathclyde
1966	*Nigerian Government and Politics* published
1966	wins parliamentary seat and resigns from Strathclyde
1966–73	member, Select Committee on Procedure
1967–9	Vice-Chairman, Select Committee on Agriculture
1968–70	member, Select Committee on Scottish Affairs
1968	*The Devolution of Power* published
1970	*British Politics and Government* published
1974	February, loses seat
1974	October, regains seat
1975	Joint Editor, *Political Quarterly*
1977	Professor of Politics, Edinburgh University
1978	30 July, dies of cancer aged 48

Index